DISCOVERING THE AMERICAN PAST

A LOOK AT THE EVIDENCE

THIRD EDITION

❧ VOLUME I: TO 1877 ❧

William Bruce Wheeler
University of Tennessee

Susan D. Becker
University of Tennessee

HOUGHTON MIFFLIN COMPANY   Boston   Toronto

Geneva, Illinois   Palo Alto   Princeton, New Jersey

Sponsoring Editor: Sean Wakely
Senior Development Editor: Frances Gay
Editorial Assistant: Traci Beane
Managing Editor: Kathy Brown
Editorial Assistant: Stefanie Jacobs
Production/Design Coordinator: Jennifer Waddell
Senior Manufacturing Coordinator: Marie Barnes
Marketing Manager: Becky Dudley

Acknowledgments

Sources 3 (p. 61), 8–10 (p. 63), 14 (p. 64), 19 (p. 66): Excerpts from *The Minutemen and Their World* by Robert A. Gross. Copyright © 1976 by Robert A. Gross. Reprinted by permission of Hill and Wang, a division of Farrar, Straus & Giroux, Inc.

Source 25 (p. 187): Excerpts from *Incidents in the Life of a Slave Girl* by Linda Brent and edited by Walter Magnes Teller. Introduction and notes copyright © 1973 by Walter Magnes Teller. Reprinted by permission of Harcourt Brace & Company.

CHAPTER ONE

Source 2: German Woodcut, 1509. The British Library.

Source 3: Portuguese oil on panel, 1550. Museo National de Arte Antiga, Lisbon.

Source 4: German engraving, 1590. Library of Congress/Rare Book Division.

Source 5: German engraving, 1591. Library of Congress/Rare Book Division.

Source 6: German engraving, 1591 (Vespucci discovering America). Metropolitan Museum of Art.

Acknowledgments are continued on pp. 291–292, which constitute an extension of the copyright page.

Cover: *Cincinnati in 1880*, after a painting by A. J. Swing, Strobridge Lithograph Company. From the collection of The Cincinnati Historical Society.

Printed in the U.S.A.
Library of Congress Catalog Card Number: 93-78664
ISBN: 0-395-66865-4

4   5   6   7   8   9-DH-97   96   95

CONTENTS

∽ CHAPTER SIX ∾

Vested Interests and Economic Democracy:
The Taney Court and
the *Charles River Bridge* Decision 1837 121

∽ CHAPTER SEVEN ∾

Away from Home:
The Working Girls of Lowell 134

PREFACE

This book is based on the premise that students have a strong desire to learn about United States history and will put forth considerable effort to do so, provided the nation's history is presented in a challenging and stimulating way. Students tell us they enjoy "doing history" rather than simply being told about it and welcome the opportunity to become "active learners" rather than passive notetakers.

The third edition of *Discovering the American Past: A Look at the Evidence* follows, both in spirit and in format, the effective approach established by its predecessors. The unique structure of this book clusters primary sources around a set of historical questions that students are asked to "solve." Unlike a source reader, this book prompts students to actually *analyze* a wide variety of authentic primary source material, to make inferences, and to draw conclusions in much the same way that historians do.

As in previous editions, we expose students to the broad scope of the American experience by providing a mixture of types of historical problems and a balance among political, social, diplomatic, economic, intellectual, and cultural history. This wide variety of historical topics and events engages students' interest and rounds out their view of American history.

∽ FORMAT OF THE BOOK ∽

Historians are fully aware that everything that is preserved from the past can be used as evidence to solve historical problems. In that spirit, we have included as many different *types* of historical evidence as we could. Almost every chapter gives students the opportunity to work with a different type of evidence: works of art, first-person accounts, trial transcripts, statistics, maps, letters, charts, biographical sketches, court decisions, music lyrics, prescriptive literature, newspaper accounts, congressional debates, speeches, diaries, proclamations and laws, political cartoons, photographs, architectural plans, advertisements, posters, film reviews, fiction, memoirs, oral interviews, and interpretations by past historians. In this book, then, we have created a kind of historical sampler that we believe will help students learn the methods and skills historians use, as well as help them learn historical content.

Each type of historical evidence is combined with an introduction to the appropriate methodology in an effort to teach students a wide variety of research skills. As much as possible, we have tried to let the evidence speak for itself and have avoided leading students to one particular interpretation or another. This approach is effective in many different classroom situations, including seminars, small classes, discussion sections, and large lecture classes. Indeed, we have found that the first and second editions of *Discovering the American Past* have proven themselves equally stimulating and effective in very large classes as well as very small ones. An Instructor's Resource Manual that accompanies the book offers numerous suggestions on how *Discovering the American Past* can be used effectively in large classroom situations.

Each chapter is divided into six parts: The Problem, Background, The Method, The Evidence, Questions to Consider, and Epilogue. Each of the parts relates to or builds upon the others, creating a uniquely integrated chapter structure that helps guide the reader through the analytical process. "The Problem" section begins with a brief discussion of the central issues of the chapter and then states the questions students will explore. A "Background" section follows, designed to help students understand the historical context of the problem. The section called "The Method" gives students suggestions for studying and analyzing the evidence. "The Evidence" section is the heart of the chapter, providing a variety of primary source material on the particular historical event or issue described in the chapter's "Problem" section. The section called "Questions to Consider" focuses students' attention on specific evidence and on linkages among different evidence material. The "Epilogue" section gives the aftermath or the historical outcome of the evidence—what happened to the people involved, who won the election, the results of a debate, and so on.

⤜ CHANGES IN THE THIRD EDITION ⤜

In response to student and faculty reactions, we have made significant alterations in the content of this edition. Six new chapters have been written, three for Volume I and three for Volume II. As with all other chapters, the six new chapters have been tested extensively in the classroom.

Volume I begins with a completely revised chapter on Europeans' first encounters with Native Americans. The first chapter now includes Native American as well as European accounts of the same event: the encounter between the Aztecs and Hernando Cortés and his troops. Chapter 6 is entirely new, an examination of Chief Justice Taney's decision in the *Charles River Bridge* v. *Warren Bridge* Supreme Court case (1837). The chapter focuses on the issue of the proper role of government in the private economic sector, a continuing controversy in America's past and present. Chapter 9 is also new. This chapter examines the difficult problem of the responsibilities of Americans during wartime, in this case the Mexican War. Henry David Thoreau's "Civil Disobedience" is juxtaposed against President James Knox Polk's Second Annual Message and Stephen A. Douglas's speech on that subject in the House of Representatives.

New chapters in Volume II include Chapter 6, which uses popular fiction and memoirs to examine the "new" woman of the 1920s. Fictional portrayals of women are presented side-by-

side with selected women's own memories of the "roaring" decade. Chapter 7, a new treatment of the Great Depression of the 1930s, uses photographic evidence from the archives of the Farm Security Administration to discuss the problems of work, unemployment, and poverty during that difficult era. Finally, Chapter 11, on cultural diversity and American history, is entirely new. In this chapter, students will read five distinctly different accounts of the same event written by six historians (George Bancroft, Charles and Mary Beard. John A. Garraty, Howard Zinn, and their own textbook) to see how historical treatments have changed during the past century.

In addition to these six new chapters, all the chapters from the second edition have been rethought, discussed, revised, and tested in classrooms.

∽ INSTRUCTOR'S RESOURCE MANUAL ∾

An Instructor's Resource Manual suggests ways that might be useful in guiding students through the evidence, provides answers to questions students often ask, and explains a variety of ways in which the students' learning may be evaluated. Many of

those ideas have come from instructors who have used the first and second editions. For this edition, we have added a new section explaining how this book can be used with large classes, based on the authors' own experience with the text.

∽ ACKNOWLEDGMENTS ∾

We would like to thank the many students and instructors who have helped

us in our effort. In addition to our colleagues across the United States, we would like to thank especially our colleagues at the University of Tennessee, who offered suggestions, read chapter drafts, and tested the new problems in their own classes. John R. Finger, Michael J. McDonald, Charles W. Johnson, and Jonathan G. Utley were especially helpful. Mary Ann Bright and Lisa Medlin were helpful in preparing the manuscript. Finally, colleagues at other institutions who reviewed chapter drafts made significant contributions to this edition, and we would like to thank them for their generosity, both in time and in helpful ideas and suggestions. These reviewers were:

Sherri Broder
  Boston College
Kenneth Bruce
  DeAnza College
Margaret Caffrey
  Memphis State University

Catherine Caraher
  University of Detroit—Mercy
Wilton Fowler
  University of Washington
Theresa McGinley
  North Harris College
Burton Peretti
  University of California—Berkeley
Ingrid Scobie
  Texas Women's University
Stan Underdal
  San Jose State University
Sue Zschoche
  Kansas State University

As with our first and second editions, we dedicate this effort to our colleagues who seek to offer a challenging and stimulating academic experience to their students and to those students themselves, who make all our efforts so worthwhile.

CHAPTER 1

FIRST ENCOUNTERS:
THE CONFRONTATION BETWEEN
CORTÉS AND MONTEZUMA
(1519–1521)

∞ THE PROBLEM ∞

In 1492, Christopher Columbus became the first European to meet Indians[1] and record his observations. In the next few years, Europeans became increasingly fascinated with the New World and its inhabitants. Explorers' accounts were published and widely circulated, as were artistic renderings of the Indians by European artists, many of whom had never traveled to the New World or met a single Indian.

In turn, Native Americans doubtless recorded their own impressions of Europeans. Since most Indian cultures had not developed forms of writing, these impressions were preserved orally, largely through stories and songs. In central Mexico, however, the Aztecs and other peoples did record their observations of Europeans in writing and art. And although the Spanish *conquistadores* (conquerors) attempted to destroy all such records, a few of the written and artistic renderings did survive to tell the Indians' side of the story of the first encounters.[2]

---

1. Although Europeans quickly realized that the name Columbus conferred on Native Americans was inaccurate, the word "Indian" continued to be used. Alternative names have never replaced it.

2. The major repositories for these written and artistic works are museums in Paris, Florence, and Mexico City.

CHAPTER 1

FIRST
ENCOUNTERS:
THE
CONFRONTATION
BETWEEN
CORTÉS AND
MONTEZUMA
(1519–1521)

There is little doubt that the impressions created by these written and artistic works fostered perceptions that made Indian–white relations confusing, difficult, and ultimately tragic. The European hunger for land and treasure may have made the tragedies that followed almost inevitable, and yet Europeans' early perceptions of Indians were an important factor in how explorers and early colonists dealt with Native American peoples and, in the end, subdued them. At the same time, the early impressions that Indians gained of Europeans (whether passed down orally or by other means) offered to many Native Americans a clear message concerning how they should respond to white encroachment.

In this chapter, you will be concentrating on the conquest of Mexico by Hernando Cortés, which took place between 1519 and 1521. In many ways, that confrontation was typical of the "first encounters" between Europeans and Native Americans. You will be examining and analyzing two separate sets of evidence: (1) selections written by Cortés to King Charles V of Spain, together with some artistic representations of Native Americans by European artists, and (2) selected written and artistic impressions of Cortés and his *conquistadores* by Aztecs and other Native Americans of central Mexico created within a few years of the events they described. Your task is twofold. First, you must use written and artistic accounts to determine the impressions that each side created of the other. Second, you must reach some conclusions about how those impressions (whether totally accurate or inaccurate) might have influenced how Europeans and early colonists dealt with Native Americans and how Native Americans dealt with them.

Before you begin, we would like to issue a note of caution. When dealing with the evidence provided by European conquerors such as Cortés or by European artists, you will *not* be trying to determine what the Native Americans the Europeans encountered were really like, but only what Cortés and selected European artists perceived them to be like. To find out what the diverse peoples collectively known as Indians were really like, you would have to consult the works of archaeologists, cultural anthropologists, and cultural geographers. And yet, if we want to determine how Europeans perceived Indians, Cortés's letters and selected European works of art can provide excellent clues.

❧ BACKGROUND ❧

By the time Europeans first encountered the various peoples they collectively called Indians, Native Americans had inhabited the Western Hemisphere for approximately 20,000 to 40,000 years.[3] Although there is considerable disagreement about when these people first appeared in the Americas, it is reasonable to assume that they first migrated to the Western Hemisphere sometime in the middle of the Pleistocene Age. During that period (roughly from 75,000 to 8000 B.C.), huge glaciers covered a large portion of North America, the ice cap extending southward to the approximate present border of the United States and Canada. These glaciers, which in some places were more than 9,000 feet thick, interrupted the water cycle because moisture falling as rain or snow was caught by the glaciers and frozen and was thus prevented from draining back into the seas or evaporating into the atmosphere.

This process lowered ocean levels 250 to 300 feet, exposing a natural land bridge spanning the Bering Strait (between present-day Alaska and the former Soviet Union)[4] across which people from Asia could easily migrate, probably in search of game. It is almost certain that various peoples from Asia did exactly that and then followed an ice-free corridor along the base of the Rocky Mountains southward into the more temperate areas of the American Southwest (which, because of the glaciers, were wetter, cooler, and contained large lakes and forests) and then either eastward into other areas of North America or even farther southward into Central and South America. These migrations took thousands of years, and some Indian peoples were still moving when Europeans first encountered them.

About 8000 B.C., the glacial cap began to retreat fairly rapidly, raising ocean levels to approximately their present-day levels and cutting off further migration from Asia, thus isolating America's first human inhabitants from other peoples for thousands of years. This isolation was almost surely the cause of the inhabitants' extraordinarily high susceptibility to the diseases that Europeans later brought with them, such as measles, tuberculosis, and smallpox, to which the peoples of other continents had built up natural resistance. The glacial retreat also caused large portions of the American Southwest to become hot and arid, thus scattering Indian peoples in almost all directions. Nevertheless, for thousands of years a strong oral tradition enabled Indians to preserve stories of their origins and subsequent isolation. Almost all Indian peoples retained accounts of a long migration from the west and a flood.

3. Other estimates run as high as 70,000 years. Whatever the case, it is almost certain that Indians were not native to the Western Hemisphere because no subhuman remains have ever been found.
4. Today the Bering Strait is only 180 feet deep. Thus a lowering of ocean levels 250 to 300 feet would have exposed a considerable land bridge between Asia and North America.

[3]

CHAPTER 1

FIRST
ENCOUNTERS:
THE
CONFRONTATION
BETWEEN
CORTÉS AND
MONTEZUMA
(1519–1521)

The original inhabitants of the Western Hemisphere obtained their food principally by hunting and gathering, killing mammoths, huge bison, deer, elk, antelope, camels, horses, and other game with stone weapons and picking wild fruits and grasses. Beginning about 5000 B.C., however, Indians in present-day Mexico began practicing agriculture. By the time Europeans arrived, most Indians were domesticating plants and raising crops, although their levels of agricultural sophistication were extremely diverse.

The development of agriculture (which occurred about the same time in Europe and the Americas) profoundly affected Indian life. Those peoples who adopted agriculture abandoned their nomadic ways and lived in settled villages (some of the Central American ones became magnificent cities). This more sedentary life permitted them to erect permanent housing, create and preserve pottery and art, and establish more complex political and social institutions. Agriculture also led to a sexual division of labor, with women planting, raising, and harvesting crops and men hunting to supplement their villages' diets with game. With more and better food, most likely Indian populations grew more rapidly, thus furthering the need for more complex political and social structures. The development of agriculture also affected these peoples' religious beliefs and ceremonies, increasing the homage to sun and rain gods who could bring forth good harvests. Contact with other Indian peoples led to trading, a practice with which Indians were quite familiar by the time of European intrusion.

Those Indian cultures that made the transition from food gathering to food producing often attained an impressive degree of economic, political, social, and technological sophistication. In Central America, the Mayas of present-day Mexico and Guatemala built great cities, fashioned elaborate gold and silver jewelry, devised a form of writing, were proficient in mathematics and astronomy, and constructed a calendar that could predict solar eclipses and was more accurate than any system in use in Europe at the time. The conquerors of the Mayas, the Aztecs, built on the achievements of their predecessors, extending their political and economic power chiefly by subjugating other Indian peoples. By the time Cortés and his army of 400 men, 16 horses, and a few cannon landed at Vera Cruz in 1519, the Aztecs had constructed the magnificent city of Tenochtitlán (the site of present-day Mexico City), which rivaled European cities in both size (approximately 300,000 people) and splendor.

Tenochtitlán contained magnificent pyramids and public buildings, a fresh water supply brought to the city by complex engineering, causeways that connected the island city to other islands and the mainland, numerous skilled craftsmen, and even a compulsory education system for all male children (no state in the United States would have such a system for more than 300 years). Raw materials and treasure flowed into Tenochtitlán from all over the Aztec empire, which stretched from the Pacific Ocean to the Gulf of Mexico and from central Mexico to present-day Guatemala. Little wonder that the *conquistadores* with Hernando Cortés were awed and enchanted when they saw it.

In many ways, Cortés was the typical Spanish *conquistador*. Born in 1485 to a respected but poor family (his father had been a career military officer but never rose above the rank of captain), Cortés spent two unsuccessful years studying for the law. Abandoning that goal, he became a soldier and was determined to gain fame and fortune through a military career. In 1504 (when he was but nineteen years old), he boarded a ship bound for the Spanish possessions in the New World. After fourteen years of military service, Cortés finally got his big break in 1518, when he was chosen to command a new armada whose purpose was to conquer Mexico. Earlier, unsuccessful expeditions had given some indications of gold in Mexico, and Cortés was sent to find it (as well as to try to locate members of the earlier expeditions who might still be alive). Since Cortés himself financed a good portion of the new armada (he had to borrow money to do so), he had the opportunity to realize his dreams of wealth if his men found treasure. When Cortés landed at Vera Cruz, he was thirty-four years old.

❧ THE METHOD ❧

In this chapter, you will be working with two distinct types of evidence: (1) written accounts and (2) artistic representations. In addition, the evidence has been divided into two sets: (1) Hernando Cortés's and European artists' perceptions of Indians and (2) Indians' written and artistic accounts of Cortés's invasion of the Aztec capital, Tenochtitlán (1519–1521). As noted previously, Cortés's account comes from letters he wrote to the Spanish king soon after the events he described took place. As for the European artists, some of them undoubtedly used their active imaginations to construct their images of Indians, whereas others relied on explorers' accounts or word-of-mouth reports from those who had seen Native Americans the explorers had brought to Europe.

The Indians' accounts of Europeans pose something of a problem. We cannot be sure that all (or any) of the written or artistic representations were done by eyewitnesses to the events they describe. We do know, however, that most of the written selections were completed by 1528 (only seven years after Cortés's conquest of Tenochtitlán) and that all the written and artistic representations were created within the normal lifetimes of eyewitnesses. Therefore, if the writers and artists themselves were not eyewitnesses, they doubtless knew of eyewitnesses who could have reported to them what they saw. Thanks to Ro-

[5]

CHAPTER 1

FIRST
ENCOUNTERS:
THE
CONFRONTATION
BETWEEN
CORTÉS AND
MONTEZUMA
(1519–1521)

man Catholic missionaries who saved these accounts from the *conquistadores,* we have what we can assume are firsthand reactions by Native Americans to European intruders.

The two types of evidence in this chapter (written accounts and artistic representations) must be dealt with differently. As you read the written accounts (whether by Cortés or by Native Americans), think of some adjectives that, after reading these accounts, Europeans who read Cortés's letters (some of which were published and widely distributed) might have used to describe Indians. For the Native American written accounts, imagine what adjectives Native Americans who shared the accounts might have used to describe Europeans. How do those adjectives present a collective image of Indians? Of Europeans? How do the stories each author tells reinforce that image? As you read each written account, make a list of adjectives for each set of evidence, then combine them to form a collective image. Be willing to read between the lines. Sometimes, for example, Cortés may simply have been trying to explain a specific incident or practice of the Indians. Yet, intentionally or un-

intentionally, he was creating an image in the minds of readers. Be equally cautious and sensitive when reading the Indians' written accounts.

The second type of evidence, artistic representations, is quite different from the written accounts. If you think of art as words made into pictures, you will see that you can approach this type of evidence as you approached the written accounts. Study each picture carefully, looking especially for how Native Americans or Europeans are portrayed. How are they portrayed physically? How is their supposed nature or character portrayed in their behavior in the works of art? Again, as with the written accounts, create a list of adjectives and deduce the images Europeans would have had of Indians and the images Indians would have had of Europeans. As you analyze the evidence in this chapter, keep two central questions in mind: (1) What images do the written and artistic accounts create of Native Americans and of Europeans? (2) How might those images (or impressions) have influenced how European explorers and early colonists dealt with Native Americans and how Native Americans dealt with them?

∽ THE EVIDENCE ∽

EUROPEAN ACCOUNTS

Source 1 from Francis Augustus MacNutt, *Fernando Cortés: His Five Letters of Relation to the Emperor Charles V* (Cleveland: Arthur H. Clark Co., 1908), Vol. I, pp. 161–166, 211–216.

1. Selections from Cortés's Letters.

. . . According to our judgment, it is credible that there is everything in this country which existed in that from whence Solomon is said to have brought the gold for the Temple, but, as we have been here so short a time, we have not been able to see more than the distance of five leagues inland, and about ten or twelve leagues of the coast length on each side, which we have explored since we landed; although from the sea it must be more, and we saw much more while sailing.

The people who inhabit this country, from the Island of Cozumel, and the Cape of Yucatan to the place where we now are, are a people of middle size, with bodies and features well proportioned, except that in each province their customs differ, some piercing the ears, and putting large and ugly objects in them, and others piercing the nostrils down to the mouth, and putting in large round stones like mirrors, and others piercing their under lips down as far as their gums, and hanging from them large round stones, or pieces of gold, so weighty that they pull down the nether lip, and make it appear very deformed. The clothing which they wear is like long veils, very curiously worked. The men wear breech-cloths about their bodies, and large mantles, very thin, and painted in the style of Moorish draperies. The women of the ordinary people wear, from their waists to their feet, clothes also very much painted, some covering their breasts and leaving the rest of the body uncovered. The superior women, however, wear very thin shirts of cotton, worked and made in the style of *rochets*. Their food is maize and grain, as in the other Islands, and *potuyuca,* as they eat it in the Island of Cuba, and they eat it broiled, since they do not make bread of it; and they have their fishing, and hunting, and they roast many chickens, like those of the Tierra Firma, which are as large as peacocks.[5]

There are some large towns well laid out, the houses being of stone, and mortar when they have it. The apartments are small, low, and in the Moorish style, and, when they cannot find stone, they make them of adobes, whitewashing them, and the roof is of straw. Some of the houses of the principal people are very cool, and have many apartments, for we have seen more than five courts in one house, and the apartments very well distributed, each principal department of service being separate. Within them they have their wells and reservoirs for water, and rooms for the slaves and dependents, of whom they have many. Each of these chiefs has at the entrance of his house, but outside of it, a large court-yard, and in

---

5. These were turkeys, which were unknown in Europe.

CHAPTER 1

FIRST
ENCOUNTERS:
THE
CONFRONTATION
BETWEEN
CORTÉS AND
MONTEZUMA
(1519–1521)

some there are two and three and four very high buildings, with steps leading up to them, and they are very well built; and in them they have their mosques and prayer places, and very broad galleries on all sides, and there they keep the idols which they worship, some being of stone, some of gold, and some of wood, and they honour and serve them in such wise, and with so many ceremonies, that much paper would be required to give Your Royal Highnesses an entire and exact description of all of them. These houses and mosques,[6] wherever they exist, are the largest and best built in the town, and they keep them very well adorned, decorated with feather-work and well-woven stuffs, and with all manner of ornaments. Every day, before they undertake any work, they burn incense in the said mosques, and sometimes they sacrifice their own persons, some cutting their tongues and others their ears, and some hacking the body with knives; and they offer up to their idols all the blood which flows, sprinkling it on all sides of those mosques, at other times throwing it up towards the heavens, and practising many other kinds of ceremonies, so that they undertake nothing without first offering sacrifice there.

They have another custom, horrible, and abominable, and deserving punishment, and which we have never before seen in any other place, and it is this, that, as often as they have anything to ask of their idols, in order that their petition may be more acceptable, they take many boys or girls, and even grown men and women, and in the presence of those idols they open their breasts, while they are alive, and take out the hearts and entrails, and burn the said entrails and hearts before the idols, offering that smoke in sacrifice to them. Some of us who have seen this say that it is the most terrible and frightful thing to behold that has ever been seen. So frequently, and so often do these Indians do this, according to our information, and partly by what we have seen in the short time we are in this country, that no year passes in which they do not kill and sacrifice fifty souls in each mosque; and this is practised, and held as customary, from the Isle of Cozumel to the country in which we are now settled. Your Majesties may rest assured that, according to the size of the land, which to us seems very considerable, and the many mosques which they have, there is no year, as far as we have until now discovered and seen, when they do not kill and sacrifice in this manner some three or four thousand souls. Now let Your Royal Highnesses consider if they ought not to prevent so great an evil and crime, and certainly God, Our Lord, will be well pleased, if, through the command of Your Royal Highnesses, these peoples should

6. Temples.

be initiated and instructed in our Very Holy Catholic Faith, and the devotion, faith, and hope, which they have in their idols, be transferred to the Divine Omnipotence of God; because it is certain, that, if they served God with the same faith, and fervour, and diligence, they would surely work miracles.

It should be believed, that it is not without cause that God, Our Lord, has permitted that these parts should be discovered in the name of Your Royal Highnesses, so that this fruit and merit before God should be enjoyed by Your Majesties, of having instructed these barbarian people, and brought them through your commands to the True Faith. As far as we are able to know them, we believe that, if there were interpreters and persons who could make them understand the truth of the Faith, and their error, many, and perhaps all, would shortly quit the errors which they hold, and come to the true knowledge; because they live civilly and reasonably, better than any of the other peoples found in these parts.

To endeavour to give to Your Majesties all the particulars about this country and its people, might occasion some errors in the account, because much of it we have not seen, and only know it through information given us by the natives; therefore we do not undertake to give more than what may be accepted by Your Highnesses as true. Your Majesties may, if you deem proper, give this account as true to Our Very Holy Father, in order that diligence and good system may be used in effecting the conversion of these people, because it is hoped that great fruit and much good may be obtained; also that His Holiness may approve and allow that the wicked and rebellious, being first admonished, may be punished and chastised as enemies of Our Holy Catholic Faith, which will be an occasion of punishment and fear to those who may be reluctant in receiving knowledge of the Truth; thereby, that the great evils and injuries they practise in the service of the Devil, will be forsaken. Because, besides what we have just related to Your Majesties about the men, and women, and children, whom they kill and offer in their sacrifices, we have learned, and been positively informed, that they are all sodomites,[7] and given to that abominable sin. In all this, we beseech Your Majesties to order such measures taken as are most profitable to the service of God, and to that of Your Royal Highnesses, and so that we who are here in your service may also be favoured and recompensed. . . .

. . . Along the road we encountered many signs, such as the natives of this province had foretold us, for we found the high road blocked up, and

7. People who practice anal or oral copulation with members of the opposite (or same) gender or who have sex with animals.

[9]

CHAPTER 1

FIRST
ENCOUNTERS:
THE
CONFRONTATION
BETWEEN
CORTÉS AND
MONTEZUMA
(1519–1521)

another opened, and some pits, although not many, and some of the city streets were closed, and many stones were piled on the house tops. They thus obliged us to be cautious, and on our guard.

I found there certain messengers from Montezuma, who came to speak with those others who were with me, but to me they said nothing, because, in order to inform their master, they had come to learn what those who were with me had done and agreed with me. These latter messengers departed, therefore, as soon as they had spoken with the first, and even the chief of those who had formerly been with me also left.

During the three days which I remained there I was ill provided for, and every day was worse, and the lords and chiefs of the city came rarely to see and speak to me. I was somewhat perplexed by this, but the interpreter whom I have, an Indian woman of this country whom I obtained in Putun-chan, the great river I have already mentioned in the first letter to Your Majesty, was told by another woman native of this city, that many of Montezuma's people had gathered close by, and that those of the city had sent away their wives, and children, and all their goods, intending to fall upon us and kill us all; and that, if she wished to escape, she should go with her, as she would hide her. The female interpreter told it to that Geronimo de Aguilar, the interpreter whom I obtained in Yucatan, and of whom I have written to Your Highness, who reported it to me. I captured one of the natives of the said city, who was walking about there, and took him secretly apart so that no one saw it, and questioned him; and he confirmed all that the Indian woman and the natives of Tascaltecal had told me. As well on account of this information as from the signs I had observed, I determined to anticipate them, rather than be surprised, so I had some of the lords of the city called, saying that I wished to speak with them, and I shut them in a chamber by themselves. In the meantime I had our people prepared, so that, at the firing of a musket, they should fall on a crowd of Indians who were near to our quarters, and many others who were inside them. It was done in this wise, that, after I had taken these lords, and left them bound in the chamber, I mounted a horse, and ordered the musket to be fired, and we did such execution that, in two hours, more than three thousand persons had perished.

In order that Your Majesty may see how well prepared they were, before I went out of our quarters, they had occupied all the streets, and stationed all their men, but, as we took them by surprise, they were easily overcome, especially as the chiefs were wanting, for I had already taken them prisoners. I ordered fire to be set to some towers and strong houses, where they defended themselves, and assaulted us; and thus I scoured the city fighting during five hours, leaving our dwelling place which was very strong, well guarded, until I had forced all the people out of the city at various points, in which those five thousand natives of Tascaltecal and the four hundred of Cempoal gave me good assistance. . . .

CHAPTER 1

FIRST
ENCOUNTERS:
THE
CONFRONTATION
BETWEEN
CORTÉS AND
MONTEZUMA
(1519–1521)

Sources 2 through 5 from Hugh Honor, *The European Vision of America* (Cleveland: Cleveland Museum of Art, 1975), plates 3, 8, 64, 65.

2. German Woodcut, 1509.

3. Portuguese Oil on Panel, 1550.

4. German Engraving, 1590.

CHAPTER 1

FIRST
ENCOUNTERS:
THE
CONFRONTATION
BETWEEN
CORTÉS AND
MONTEZUMA
(1519–1521)

5. German Engraving, 1591.

Sources 6 and 7 from Stefan Lorant, ed., *The New World: The First Pictures of America* (New York: Duell, Sloan & Pearce, 1946), pp. 51, 119.

6. German Engraving, 1591.

7. German Engraving, 1591.

CHAPTER 1

FIRST
ENCOUNTERS:
THE
CONFRONTATION
BETWEEN
CORTÉS AND
MONTEZUMA
(1519–1521)

Sources 8 and 9 from Honor, *The European Vision of America,* plates 85, 91.

8. French Engraving, 1575.

9. French Engraving, 1579–1600.

AMERICA.

CHAPTER 1

FIRST
ENCOUNTERS:
THE
CONFRONTATION
BETWEEN
CORTÉS AND
MONTEZUMA
(1519–1521)

NATIVE AMERICAN ACCOUNTS

Source 10 from Miguel Leon-Portilla, ed., *The Broken Spears: The Aztec Account of the Conquest of Mexico,* trans. Lysander Kemp (Boston: Beacon Press, 1962), pp. viii–ix, 30, 92–93, 128–144.

10. Cortés's Conquest of Tenochtitlán.

Year 1-Canestalk. The Spaniards came to the palace at Tlayacac. When the Captain[8] arrived at the palace, Motecuhzoma[9] sent the Cuetlaxteca[10] to greet him and to bring him two suns as gifts. One of these suns was made of the yellow metal, the other of the white.[11] The Cuetlaxteca also brought him a mirror to be hung on his person, a gold collar, a great gold pitcher, fans and ornaments of quetzal feathers and a shield inlaid with mother-of-pearl.

The envoys made sacrifices in front of the Captain. At this, he grew very angry. When they offered him blood in an "eagle dish," he shouted at the man who offered it and struck him with his sword. The envoys departed at once. . . .

When the sacrifice was finished, the messengers reported to the king. They told him how they had made the journey, and what they had seen, and what food the strangers ate. Motecuhzoma was astonished and terrified by their report, and the description of the strangers' food astonished him above all else.

He was also terrified to learn how the cannon roared, how its noise resounded, how it caused one to faint and grow deaf. The messengers told him: "A thing like a ball of stone comes out of its entrails: it comes out shooting sparks and raining fire. The smoke that comes out with it has a pestilent odor, like that of rotten mud. This odor penetrates even to the brain and causes the greatest discomfort. If the cannon is aimed against a mountain, the mountain splits and cracks open. If it is aimed against a tree, it shatters the tree into splinters. This is a most unnatural sight, as if the tree had exploded from within."

The messengers also said: "Their trappings and arms are all made of iron. They dress in iron and wear iron casques on their heads. Their swords are iron; their bows are iron; their shields are iron; their spears are iron.

---

8. Cortés.
9. Montezuma.
10. The Cuetlaxteca were an Indian people allied with the Aztecs.
11. Gold and silver.

Their deer[12] carry them on their backs wherever they wish to go. These deer, our lord, are as tall as the roof of a house.

"The strangers' bodies are completely covered, so that only their faces can be seen. Their skin is white, as if it were made of lime. They have yellow hair, though some of them have black. Their beards are long and yellow, and their moustaches are also yellow. Their hair is curly, with very fine strands.

"As for their food, it is like human food. It is large and white, and not heavy.[13] It is something like straw, but with the taste of a cornstalk, of the pith of a cornstalk. It is a little sweet, as if it were flavored with honey; it tastes of honey, it is sweet-tasting food.

"Their dogs are enormous, with flat ears and long, dangling tongues. The color of their eyes is a burning yellow; their eyes flash fire and shoot off sparks. Their bellies are hollow, their flanks long and narrow. They are tireless and very powerful. They bound here and there, panting, with their tongues hanging out. And they are spotted like an ocelot."

When Motecuhzoma heard this report, he was filled with terror. It was as if his heart had fainted, as if it had shriveled. It was as if he were conquered by despair. . . .

Then the Captain marched to Tenochtitlan. He arrived here during the month called Bird, under the sign of the day 8-Wind. When he entered the city, we gave him chickens, eggs, corn, tortillas and drink. We also gave him firewood, and fodder for his deer. Some of these gifts were sent by the lord of Tenochtitlan, the rest by the lord of Tlatelolco.

Later the Captain marched back to the coast, leaving Don Pedro de Alvarado—The Sun—in command.

During this time, the people asked Motecuhzoma how they should celebrate their god's fiesta. He said: "Dress him in all his finery, in all his sacred ornaments."

During this same time, The Sun commanded that Motecuhzoma and Itzcohuatzin, the military chief of Tlatelolco, be made prisoners. The Spaniards hanged a chief from Acolhuacan named Nezahualquentzin. They also murdered the king of Nauhtla, Cohualpopocatzin, by wounding him with arrows and then burning him alive.

For this reason, our warriors were on guard at the Eagle Gate. The sentries from Tenochtitlan stood at one side of the gate, and the sentries from Tlatelolco at the other. But messengers came to tell them to dress the

12. Horses.
13. Probably pasta.

[19]

CHAPTER 1

FIRST
ENCOUNTERS:
THE
CONFRONTATION
BETWEEN
CORTÉS AND
MONTEZUMA
(1519–1521)

figure of Huitzilopochtli. They left their posts and went to dress him in his sacred finery: his ornaments and his paper clothing.

When this had been done, the celebrants began to sing their songs. That is how they celebrated the first day of the fiesta. On the second day they began to sing again, but without warning they were all put to death. . . . They ran in among the dancers, forcing their way to the place where the drums were played. They attacked the man who was drumming and cut off his arms. Then they cut off his head, and it rolled across the floor.

They attacked the celebrants, stabbing them, spearing them, striking them with their swords. They attacked some of them from behind, and these fell instantly to the ground with their entrails hanging out. Others they beheaded: they cut off their heads, or split their heads to pieces.

They struck others in the shoulders, and their arms were torn from their bodies. They wounded some in the thigh and some in the calf. They slashed others in the abdomen, and their entrails all spilled to the ground. Some attempted to run away, but their intestines dragged as they ran; they seemed to tangle their feet in their own entrails. No matter how they tried to save themselves, they could find no escape. . . .

The Sun treacherously murdered our people on the twentieth day after the Captain left for the coast. We allowed the Captain to return to the city in peace. But on the following day we attacked him with all our might, and that was the beginning of the war.

The Spaniards attempted to slip out of the city at night, but we attacked furiously at the Canal of the Toltecs, and many of them died. This took place during the fiesta of Tecuilhuitl. The survivors gathered first at Mazatzintamalco and waited for the stragglers to come up.

Year 2-Flint. This was the year in which Motecuhzoma died. Itzcohuatzin of Tlatelolco died at the same time.

The Spaniards took refuge in Acueco, but they were driven out by our warriors. They fled to Teuhcalhueyacan and from there to Zoltepec. Then they marched through Citlaltepec and camped in Temazcalapan, where the people gave them hens, eggs and corn. They rested for a short while and marched on to Tlaxcala.

Soon after, an epidemic broke out in Tenochtitlan. . . . It began to spread during the thirteenth month and lasted for seventy days, striking everywhere in the city and killing a vast number of our people. Sores erupted on our faces, our breasts, our bellies; we were covered with agonizing sores from head to foot.

The illness was so dreadful that no one could walk or move. The sick were so utterly helpless that they could only lie on their beds like corpses, unable to move their limbs or even their heads. They could not lie face down or roll from one side to the other. If they did move their bodies, they screamed with pain.

A great many died from this plague, and many others died of hunger. They could not get up to search for food, and everyone else was too sick to care for them, so they starved to death in their beds.

Some people came down with a milder form of the disease; they suffered less than the others and made a good recovery. But they could not escape entirely. Their looks were ravaged, for wherever a sore broke out, it gouged an ugly pockmark in the skin. And a few of the survivors were left completely blind. . . .

[*Here the account describes Cortés's siege of Tenochtitlán, a siege that was successful due in part to bickering among the Aztecs themselves (in which several leaders were put to death), in part to the panic caused by Cortés's cannon, and in part to a number of nearby Indian peoples whom the Aztecs had dominated turning on their former masters and supporting the Spanish. Of course, the devastating smallpox epidemic and general starvation due to the siege also played important roles.*]

Broken spears lie in the roads;
we have torn our hair in our grief.
The houses are roofless now, and their walls
are red with blood.

Worms are swarming in the streets and plazas,
and the walls are splattered with gore.
The water has turned red, as if it were dyed,
and when we drink it,
it has the taste of brine.

We have pounded our hands in despair
against the adobe walls,
for our inheritance, our city, is lost and dead.
The shields of our warriors were its defense,
but they could not save it.

We have chewed dry twigs and salt grasses;
we have filled our mouths with dust and bits of adobe;
we have eaten lizards, rats and worms. . . .

Cuauhtemoc was taken to Cortes along with three other princes. The Captain was accompanied by Pedro de Alvarado and La Malinche.

[21]

CHAPTER 1

FIRST
ENCOUNTERS:
THE
CONFRONTATION
BETWEEN
CORTÉS AND
MONTEZUMA
(1519–1521)

When the princes were made captives, the people began to leave, searching for a place to stay. Everyone was in tatters, and the women's thighs were almost naked. The Christians searched all the refugees. They even opened the women's skirts and blouses and felt everywhere: their ears, their breasts, their hair. Our people scattered in all directions. They went to neighboring villages and huddled in corners in the houses of strangers.

The city was conquered in the year 3-House. The date on which we departed was the day 1-Serpent in the ninth month. . . .

[*The account next describes Cortés's torture of the remaining Aztec leaders in an attempt to find where the Aztecs' treasures were hidden.*]

When the envoys from Tlatelolco had departed, the leaders of Tenochtitlan were brought before the Captain, who wished to make them talk. This was when Cuauhtemoc's feet were burned. They brought him in at daybreak and tied him to a stake.

They found the gold in Cuitlahuactonco, in the house of a chief named Itzpotonqui. As soon as they had seized it, they brought our princes—all of them bound—to Coyoacan.

About this same time, the priest in charge of the temple of Huitzilopochtli was put to death. The Spaniards had tried to learn from him where the god's finery and that of the high priests was kept. Later they were informed that it was being guarded by certain chiefs in Cuauhchichilco and Xaltocan. They seized it and then hanged two of the chiefs in the middle of the Mazatlan road. . . .

They hanged Macuilxochitl, the king of Huitzilopochco, in Coyoacan. They also hanged Pizotzin, the king of Culhuacan. And they fed the Keeper of the Black House, along with several others, to their dogs.

And three wise men of Ehecatl, from Tezcoco, were devoured by the dogs. They had come only to surrender; no one brought them or sent them there. They arrived bearing their painted sheets of paper. There were four of them, and only one escaped; the other three were overtaken, there in Coyoacan. . . .

Sources 11–14 are present-day adaptations of Aztec artistic works that were created not long after the events they depict took place. The modern adaptations can be found in Leon-Portilla, *The Broken Spears*, pp. 21, 82, 75, 143.

11. Native Americans Greet Cortés and His Men.

12. Spanish Response to Native American Greeting.

CHAPTER 1

FIRST
ENCOUNTERS:
THE
CONFRONTATION
BETWEEN
CORTÉS AND
MONTEZUMA
(1519–1521)

13. The Massacre at the Fiesta.

14. Fate of the Wise Men of Ehecatl.

CHAPTER 1

FIRST
ENCOUNTERS:
THE
CONFRONTATION
BETWEEN
CORTÉS AND
MONTEZUMA
(1519–1521)

 QUESTIONS TO CONSIDER

As you read Cortés's account (Source 1), it helps to look for five factors:

1. Physical appearance (bodies, hair, clothing, jewelry, and so on). This description can provide important clues about Cortés's attitude toward the Indians he confronted.
2. Nature or character (childlike, bellicose, cunning, honest, intellectual, lazy, and so on). Be sure to note the examples Cortés used to provide his analysis of the Indians' nature or character.
3. Political, social, and religious practices (behavior of women, ceremonies, eating habits, government, and so on). Descriptions of these practices can provide excellent insight into the explorer's general perception of the Indians he encountered. Be especially sensitive to Cortés's use of descriptive adjectives.
4. Overall impression of the Indians. What was Cortés's collective image or impression?
5. What did Cortés think should be done with the Indians?

Once you have analyzed Cortés's account using points 1 through 4, you should be able to explain how, based on his overall impression of the Indians, he thought the Indians should be dealt with (point 5). Sometimes Cortés comes right out and tells you, but in other cases you will have to use a little imagination. Ask yourself the following question: If I had been living in Spain in 1522 and read Cortés's account, what would my perception of

Native Americans have been? Based on that perception, how would I have thought those peoples should be dealt with?

You can handle the artistic representations (Sources 2 through 9) in the same way. Each artist tried to convey his notion of the Indians' nature or character. Some of these impressions are obvious, but others are less so. Think of the art as words made into pictures. How are the Indians portrayed? What are they doing? How are they dealing with Europeans? On the basis of these artistic representations, decide how the various artists believed Indians should be dealt with. For example, the Indian woman with child in Source 4 depicts Native Americans in a particular way. What is it? On the basis of this depiction, what would you say was the artist's perception of Indians? Moreover, how would that perception have affected the artist's—and viewer's—opinion of how Indians should be treated? Follow these steps for all the artistic representations.

Finally, put together the two types of evidence. Is there more than one "image" of Native Americans? How might each perception have affected the ways Europeans and early colonists dealt with Indians?

On the surface, the Native Americans' perception of Europeans was one-dimensional and is easily discovered: the Aztec writers and artists portrayed Cortés and his men as brutal and sadistic murderers who were driven mad by their lust for gold. Closer examination of the early section of the written account (Source 10) and one of the artistic representations (Source 11), however, reveals other perceptions as well. In the written account, when Montezuma's envoys reported back to him, how did they describe the Europeans (you may use points 1 through 4 above)? What was Montezuma's reaction to the report? The remainder of the written and artistic accounts are quite direct, and you should have no difficulty discovering the Indians' overall perception of Europeans. You will, however, have to infer from the accounts how Indians believed Europeans should be dealt with in the future, since none of the written or artistic accounts deals with that question.

⤷ EPILOGUE ⤶

In many respects, the encounter between Cortés and the native peoples of Mexico was typical of many first encounters between Europeans and Native Americans. For one thing, the Indian peoples were terribly vulnerable to the numerous diseases that Europeans unwittingly brought with them. Whether warlike or peaceful, millions of Native Americans fell victim to smallpox, measles, and other diseases against which they had no resistance. Whole villages were wiped out and whole nations decimated as (in the words of one Roman Catholic priest who traveled with Cortés) "they died in heaps."

In addition, Indians were no match for European military technology and modes of warfare. Although many Indian peoples were skillful and courageous warriors, their weaponry was no equal to the European broadsword, pike, musket, or cannon. Moreover, battles between Indian peoples could best be described as skirmishes, in which few lives were lost and several prisoners taken. The Indians could not imagine wholesale slaughtering of their enemies, a practice some Europeans found acceptable as a means of acquiring gold and land. By no means passive peoples in what ultimately would become a contest for a hemisphere, Indians nevertheless had not developed the military technology and tactics to hold Europeans permanently at bay.

Nor were the Indians themselves united against their European intruders. All the explorers and early settlers were able to pit one Indian people against another, thus dividing the opposition and in the end conquering them all. In this practice Cortés was particulary adept; he found a number of villages ready to revolt against Montezuma and used those schisms to his advantage. Brief attempts at Indian unity against European intruders generally proved temporary and therefore unsuccessful.

Sometimes the Native Americans' initial misperceptions of Europeans worked to their own disadvantage. As we have seen, some Central American

CHAPTER 1

FIRST
ENCOUNTERS:
THE
CONFRONTATION
BETWEEN
CORTÉS AND
MONTEZUMA
(1519–1521)

Indians, including the mighty Aztecs, thought Cortés's men were the "white gods" from the east who prophets predicted would appear. Cortés's actions quickly disabused them of this notion, but by then much damage had been done. In a somewhat similar vein, Indians of the Powhatan Confederacy in Virginia at first thought the Europeans were indolent because they could not grow their own food. Like the Aztecs' misperception, this mistaken image was soon shattered. In sum, Native Americans' perceptions of Europeans often worked against any notions that they were a threat—until it was too late.

Finally, once Europeans had established footholds in the New World, the Indians often undercut their own positions. For one thing, they rarely were able to unite against the Europeans, fractured as they so often were by intertribal conflicts and jealousies. Therefore, Europeans often were able to enlist Indian allies to fight against those Native Americans who opposed them. Also, after the Indians came to recognize the value of European manufactured goods, they increasingly engaged in wholesale hunting and trapping of animals with the skins and furs Europeans wanted in exchange for those goods. Before the arrival of Europeans, Native Americans saw themselves as part of a complete ecosystem that could sustain all life so long as it was kept in balance. In contrast, Europeans saw the environment as a series of commodities to be expoited, a perception that Indians who desired European goods were quickly forced to adopt. Thus not only did the Indians lose their economic and cul-

tural independence, but they also nearly eliminated certain animal species that had sustained them for so long. An ecological disaster was in the making, driven by the European view of the environment as something to conquer and exploit.

For a number of reasons, Native Americans were extremely vulnerable to the European "invasion" of America. At the same time, however, a major biological "event" was in process that would change life in both the Old World and the New. Called by historians the Columbian exchange, the process involved the transplantation to the New World (sometimes accidentally) of various plants (cabbages, radishes, bananas, wheat, onions, sugar cane), animals (horses, pigs, cattle, sheep, cats), and diseases. At the same time, Europeans returned home with maize, peanuts, squash, sweet potatoes, pumpkins, pineapples, tomatoes, and cocoa. Less beneficial was the possible transportation from the New World to the Old of venereal syphilis. Indeed, some five hundred years later, the Columbian exchange is still going on. In the Great Smoky Mountains of North Carolina and Tennessee, wild boars (imported from Germany in the nineteenth century for sportsmen) threaten the plants, grasses, and small animals of the region. The zebra mussel, released by accident into the Great Lakes in ballast water from Eastern Europe, has spread into the Illinois, Mississippi, Ohio, and Tennessee rivers. An Asian variety of the gypsy moth is chewing its way through the forests of the Pacific Northwest. A recent survey in Olympic National Park has identified 169 species of plants and animals not indigenous to the Western Hemisphere. In the South, the kudzu vine (imported from Japan to combat erosion) was dubbed by the *Los Angeles Times* (July 21, 1992) "the national plant of Dixie." Whether purposeful or by accident, whether beneficial or detrimental, the Columbian exchange continues.

Because Europeans ultimately were victorious in their "invasion" of the Western Hemisphere, it is their images of Native Americans that for the most part have survived. Christopher Columbus, who recorded the Europeans' first encounter, depicted Native Americans as innocent, naive children. But he also wrote, "I could conquer the whole of them with fifty men, and govern them as I pleased." For his part, Amerigo Vespucci was less kind, depicting Native Americans as barbarous because "they have no regular time for their meals . . . [and] in making water they are dirty and without shame, for while talking with us they do such things. . . ." By placing this badge of inferiority on Indian peoples, most Europeans could justify a number of ways Indians could be dealt with (avoidance, conquest, "civilizing," trading, removal, extermina-

tion). Ultimately for the Indian peoples, all methods proved disastrous. Although different European peoples (Spanish, French, English) often treated Indians differently, in the end the results were the same.

Hernando Cortés returned to Spain in 1528 a fabulously wealthy man. But the ultimate *conquistador* lost most of his fortune in ill-fated expeditions and died in modest circumstances in 1547. In his will, he recognized the four children he had fathered by Native American women while in Mexico (Cortés was married at the time) and worried about the morality of what he had done. In 1562, his body was taken to Mexico to be reburied, but for Hernando Cortés's remains, there would be no rest. In 1794, they were moved again, this time to the chapel of a Mexican hospital that he had endowed. In 1823, Cortés's remains disappeared for good, perhaps as the result of an effort to protect them from politically oriented grave robbers after Mexico declared its independence from Spain. (Rumors abound that they were secretly carried back across the Atlantic, this time to Italy.) The ultimate *conquistador* has vanished, but his legacy lives on.

CHAPTER 2

THE THREAT OF ANNE HUTCHINSON

∽ THE PROBLEM ∽

In the cold, early spring of 1638, Anne Hutchinson and her children left Massachusetts to join her husband and their many friends who had moved to an island in Narragansett Bay. Just a year before, in 1637, Hutchinson and her family had been highly respected, prominent members of a Puritan church in Boston. But then she was put on trial and sentenced to banishment from the Massachusetts Bay col-ony and excommunication from her church—next to death, the two worst punishments that could befall a Puri-tan in the New World.

What had Anne Hutchinson done? Why was she such a threat to the Mas-sachusetts Bay colony? You will be reading the transcript of her trial in 1637 to find the answers to these questions.

∽ BACKGROUND ∽

The English men and women who came to the New World in the seven-teenth and early eighteenth centuries did so for a variety of reasons. Many who arrived at Jamestown colony were motivated by the promise of wealth; at one point, Virginians grew tobacco in the streets and even threat-ened their own existence by favoring tobacco (a crop they could sell) over food crops. In contrast, the majority of the early settlers of Pennsylvania were Friends (Quakers) in search of religious freedom. In short, the Ameri-can colonies represented for thousands of English men and women a chance to make significant changes in their lives.

Such was the case with the Puritans who settled and dominated the colony of Massachusetts Bay, founded in 1630. Although technically still members of the Church of England, the Puritans were convinced that many of that church's beliefs and practices were wrong and that the Church of England needed to be thoroughly purified (hence their name). Puritans were convinced that the Church of England, which had broken away from the Roman Catholic church and the pope during the reign of Henry VIII, was still encumbered with unnecessary ceremony, rituals, and hierarchy—things they called "popery." Popery, the Puritans believed, actually obstructed the ties between God and human beings, and therefore should be eliminated.

The Puritans were more Calvinist than many of their English contemporaries, and they did not believe that human salvation could be earned by individual effort (such as going to church, leading a good life, or helping one's neighbors). The Puritans called this type of salvation a "covenant of works," a notion they believed was simply wrong. Instead, they insisted that salvation came only as a free gift from God (a "covenant of grace"), and those few who received it were the true "saints." Of course, God expected everyone to lead a good life—those who were not yet saved would be preparing for the possibility of God's grace, while those who were already saints would naturally live according to God's laws. Some ministers, like John Cotton, de-emphasized the idea

of preparation and believed that God's grace could be granted instantaneously to anyone. All Puritans, however, agreed that only saints should be full members of the church.

Believing it impossible to effect their reforms in England, many Puritans sought "voluntary banishment," as one of them called it, to the New World. Fired by the sense that God was using them to revolutionize human history, more than one thousand men, women, and children arrived during the first decades of the founding of New England to form their model community based on the laws of God and following His commandments. "We shall be as a city upon a hill," exulted Puritan leader and colonial governor John Winthrop, "the eyes of all people are upon us."

Probably the best protection the Puritans had against the harsh New England environment was their sense of community and mission. Seeing themselves as the modern version of the ancient Israelites, Puritans believed that God had made a covenant (contract) with the Puritans of New England. As Winthrop explained, "Thus stands the cause between God and us: we are entered into covenant with Him. . . . The God of Israel is among us." Puritans believed the covenant stipulated that the entire community must follow God's laws as interpreted by Puritan leaders. If they did, God would reward them; if not, the community would be punished. Therefore, community solidarity was essential, and individual desires and thoughts had to be subjugated to those of the community.

Thus, although Puritans sought religious freedom for themselves, they were not really willing to grant it to others. Dissent and discord, they reasoned, would lead to the breakdown of community cohesion, the inevitable violation of the covenant, and the punishment of the community in the same way God had punished the ancient Israelites when they had broken their covenant. Non-Puritans who migrated to the Massachusetts Bay colony were required to attend the Puritan church, although they could not become members and hence could not vote in either church or civil elections. Those who refused to abide by these rules were banished from the colony. Moreover, those Puritans who were not saints also had to obey these regulations and similarly could not be church members and could not vote. Thus there was a hierarchy of authority in Massachusetts that controlled both the colony's church and the government. To become a saint, one had to be examined by a committee and demonstrate to that committee's satisfaction that he or she had experienced a personal revelation from God and that the Holy Spirit resided in him or her. There was no agreement among the ministers about the exact nature of this revelation. For most, it simply meant that individuals would recognize the Holy Spirit moving within them. Other ministers urged their congregations to seek out (and not fear) more direct revelations. This was far more controversial, as you will see in Anne Hutchinson's trial.

In fact, there was a good deal of dissension in Massachusetts Bay colony. Religious squabbles were common, often arising between saints over biblical interpretation, the theological correctness of one minister or another, or the behavior of certain fellow colonists. Indeed, to a limited extent, Puritans actually welcomed these disputes because they seemed to demonstrate that religion was still a vital part of the colonists' lives. As John Winthrop said, "The business of religion is the business of the Puritans." Participants of weeknight gatherings at various church members' homes often engaged in these religious debates, and they were tolerated by both the ministers and the colony's civil leaders as long as the squabbles did not get out of control.

By the mid-1630s, however, one of the disputes had grown to such an extent that it threatened the religious and secular unity of the colony. Some Puritans in both England and Massachusetts Bay had begun to espouse an extreme version of the covenant of grace: they believed that, having been assured of salvation, an individual was virtually freed from the man-made laws of both church and state, taking his or her commands only from God, who communicated His wishes to the saints. Called Antinomians (from *anti,* "against," and *nomos,* "law"), these Puritan extremists attacked what one of them called the "deadness" of religious services and charged that several ministers were preaching the covenant of works. This charge was extremely offensive to these ministers, who did not at all believe they were teaching salvation through good behavior but rather preparation for the possibility of God's grace. Carried to its logical extension, of course, Antinomianism threatened to overthrow the authority of the ministers and even the power of the colonial government itself. Growing in number and intensity, the Antinomians in 1636 were able to elect one of their followers to replace Winthrop as colonial governor, although Winthrop managed to return to office the next year.

Into this highly charged atmosphere stepped Anne Hutchinson, age forty-three, who had arrived in Massachusetts Bay in 1634 and soon became embroiled in the Antinomian controversy, or, as other Puritans called it, the "Antinomian heresy." The daughter of a clergyman who had been imprisoned twice for his religious unorthodoxy, Anne had married prosperous businessman William Hutchinson in 1612, when she was twenty-one years old. Before arriving in Massachusetts Bay, she had given birth to fourteen children, eleven of whom were alive in 1634.

In a society that emphasized the greater good of the community rather than the concept of individual happiness, relationships between men and women were complementary and complex. New England "goodwives," as married women were called, performed a variety of tasks essential to their families and communities. Spiritually, they were equal to their husbands in the eyes of God, but economically and politically, wives were expected to help with and supplement their husbands' public activities. In other words, both men and women had rights and responsibilities with respect to each other, their children, their neighbors, their communities, and their church. In carrying out these responsibilities, male and female roles sometimes overlapped, but more often they were divided into public (male) and private (female) spheres.

As in any society, there were some unhappy marriages, cases of domestic violence and desertion, and even what we would call divorce. But the shared ideals and sense of mission of so many of the immigrants ensured that such dysfunctional relationships were relatively uncommon. Although building a new society in a wilderness was a difficult and dangerous undertaking, most women fulfilled their roles willingly and competently.

Anne Hutchinson's many duties at home did not prevent her from remaining very active in the church. Extremely interested in religion and theological questions, she was particularly influenced by John Cotton, a Puritan minister who had been forced to flee from England to Massachusetts Bay in 1633 because of his religious ideas. Upon arrival in the colony, Cotton said he was shocked by the extent to which colonists had been "lulled into security" by their growing belief that they could earn salvation through good works. Attacking this in sermons and in letters to other clergymen, Cotton helped fuel the Antinomian cause as well as Anne Hutchinson's religious ardor.

At first the Hutchinsons were seen as welcome additions to the community, largely because of William's prosperity and Anne's expertise in herbal medicines, nursing the sick, and midwifery. Soon, however, Anne Hutchinson began to drift into religious issues. She began to hold weeknight meetings in her home, at first to expand upon the previous Sunday's sermons and later to expound her own religious notions—ideas very close to those of the Antinomians. In November 1637, Anne's brother-in-law (John Wheelwright, another Puritan minister) was banished from the colony because of his radical sermons, and Anne was brought to trial before the General Court of Massachusetts Bay. With Governor Winthrop presiding, the court met to decide the fate of Anne Hutchinson. Privately, Winthrop called Hutchinson a person of "nimble wit and active spirit and a very voluble [fluent] tongue." Winthrop himself, however, believed that women should be submissive and supportive like his wife and sister, and there was ample support for his position in the Bible.[1] No matter what he thought of

Hutchinson's abilities, publicly the governor was determined to be rid of her.

Why were Winthrop and other orthodox Puritans so opposed to Hutchinson? What crime had she committed? Some of Wheelwright's followers had been punished for having signed a petition supporting him, but Hutchinson had not signed the petition. Many other Puritans had held religious discussions in their homes, and more than a few had opposed the views of their ministers. Technically, Hutchinson had broken no law. Why, then, was she considered such a threat that she was brought to trial and ultimately banished from the colony?

⌘ THE METHOD ⌘

For two days, Anne Hutchinson stood before the General Court, presided over by the unsympathetic Governor John Winthrop. Fortunately, a fairly complete transcript of the proceedings has been preserved. In that transcript are the clues that you as the historian-detective will need to answer the questions previously posed. Although spelling and punctuation have been modernized in most cases, the portions of the transcript you are about to read are reproduced verbatim. At first, some of the seventeenth-century phraseology might seem a bit strange. As

are most spoken languages, English is constantly changing—think of how much English has changed since Chaucer's day. Yet if you read slowly and carefully, the transcript should give you no problem.

Before you begin studying the transcript, keep in mind two additional instructions:

1. Be careful not to lose sight of the central question: why was Anne Hutchinson such a threat to Massachusetts Bay colony? The transcript raises several other questions, some of them so interesting that they might pull you off the main track. As you read through the transcript, make a list of the various ways you think Hutchinson

---

1. Genesis 1:28–3:24; the First Letter of Paul to the Corinthians 11:1–16; the Letter of Paul to the Ephesians, Chapters 5 and 6, all verses.

might have threatened Massachusetts Bay.

2. Be willing to read between the lines. As you read each statement, ask yourself what is being said. Then try to deduce what is actually meant by what is being said. Sometimes people say exactly what they mean, but often they do not. They might intentionally or unintentionally disguise the real meaning of what they are saying, but the real meaning can usually be found. In conversation with a person face to face, voice inflection, body language, and other visual clues often provide the real meaning to what is being said. In this case, where personal observation is impossible, you must use both logic and imagination to read between the lines.

∽ THE EVIDENCE ∾

Source 1 from an excerpt of the examination from Thomas Hutchinson (Anne's great-grandson), *The History of the Colony and Province of Massachusetts-Bay*, Vol. II, ed. Lawrence Shaw Mayo (Cambridge, Mass.: Harvard University Press, 1936), pp. 366–391.

1. The Examination of Mrs. Anne Hutchinson at the Court of Newton, November 1637.[2]

CHARACTERS

Mrs. Anne Hutchinson, the accused

General Court, consisting of the governor, deputy governor, assistants, and deputies

Governor, John Winthrop, chair of the court

Deputy Governor, Thomas Dudley

Assistants, Mr. Bradstreet, Mr. Nowel, Mr. Endicott, Mr. Harlakenden, Mr. Stoughton

Deputies, Mr. Coggeshall, Mr. Bartholomew, Mr. Jennison, Mr. Coddington, Mr. Colborn

Clergymen and Ruling Elders:

　Mr. Peters, minister in Salem

　Mr. Leveret, a ruling elder in a Boston church

　Mr. Cotton, minister in Boston

---

2. Normally the trial would have been held in Boston, but Anne Hutchinson had numerous supporters in that city, so the proceedings were moved to the small town of New Town, where she had few allies.

Mr. Wilson, minister in Boston, who supposedly made notes of a
previous meeting between Anne Hutchinson, Cotton, and the other
ministers
Mr. Sims, minister in Charlestown

MR. WINTHROP, GOVERNOR. Mrs. Hutchinson, you are called here as one of
those that have troubled the peace of the commonwealth and the
churches here; you are known to be a woman that hath had a great
share in the promoting and divulging of those opinions that are causes
of this trouble, and to be nearly joined not only in affinity and affection
with some of those the court had taken notice of and passed censure
upon, but you have spoken divers things as we have been informed
very prejudicial to the honour of the churches and ministers thereof,
and you have maintained a meeting and an assembly in your house
that hath been condemned by the general assembly as a thing not
tolerable nor comely in the sight of God nor fitting for your sex, and
notwithstanding that was cried down you have continued the same.
Therefore we have thought good to send for you to understand how
things are, that if you be in an erroneous way we may reduce you that
so you may become a profitable member here among us. Otherwise if
you be obstinate in your course that then the court may take such
course that you may trouble us no further. Therefore I would intreat
you to express whether you do assent and hold in practice to those
opinions and factions that have been handled in court already, that is
to say, whether you do not justify Mr. Wheelwright's sermon and the
petition.

MRS. HUTCHINSON. I am called here to answer before you but I hear no
things laid to my charge.

GOV. I have told you some already and more I can tell you.

MRS. H. Name one, Sir.

GOV. Have I not named some already?

MRS. H. What have I said or done?

[*Here, in a portion of the transcript not reproduced, Winthrop accused Hutchinson
of harboring and giving comfort to a faction that was dangerous to the colony.*]

MRS. H. Must not I then entertain the saints because I must keep my
conscience?

GOV. Say that one brother should commit felony or treason and come to his
brother's house. If he knows him guilty and conceals him he is guilty

[36]

of the same. It is his conscience to entertain him, but if his conscience comes into act in giving countenance and entertainment to him that hath broken the law he is guilty too. So if you do countenance those that are transgressors of the law you are in the same fact.

MRS. H. What law do they transgress?

GOV. The law of God and of the state.

MRS. H. In what particular?

GOV. Why in this among the rest, whereas the Lord doth say honour thy father and thy mother.[3]

MRS. H. Ey, Sir, in the Lord.

GOV. This honour you have broke in giving countenance to them.

MRS. H. In entertaining those did I entertain them against any act (for there is the thing) or what God hath appointed?

GOV. You knew that Mr. Wheelwright did preach this sermon and those that countenance him in this do break a law?

MRS. H. What law have I broken?

GOV. Why the fifth commandment.[4]

MRS. H. I deny that for he [Wheelwright] saith in the Lord.

GOV. You have joined with them in the faction.

MRS. H. In what faction have I joined with them?

GOV. In presenting the petition.

MRS. H. Suppose I had set my hand to the petition. What then?

GOV. You saw that case tried before.

MRS. H. But I had not my hand to the petition.

GOV. You have councelled them.

MRS. H. Wherein?

GOV. Why in entertaining them.

MRS. H. What breach of law is that, Sir?

GOV. Why dishonouring of parents.

MRS. H. But put the case, Sir, that I do fear the Lord and my parents. May not I entertain them that fear the Lord because my parents will not give me leave?

GOV. If they be the fathers of the commonwealth, and they of another religion, if you entertain them then you dishonour your parents and are justly punishable.

---

3. Exodus 20:12. Anne Hutchinson's natural father was in England and her natural mother was dead. To what, then, was Winthrop referring?
4. "Honour thy father and thy mother: that thy days may be long upon the land which the Lord thy God giveth thee." Exodus 20:12.

MRS. H. If I entertain them, as they have dishonoured their parents I do.

GOV. No but you by countenancing them above others put honour upon them.

MRS. H. I may put honour upon them as the children of God and as they do honour the Lord.

GOV. We do not mean to discourse with those of your sex but only this: you do adhere unto them and do endeavour to set forward this faction and so you do dishonour us.

MRS. H. I do acknowledge no such thing. Neither do I think that I ever put any dishonour upon you.

GOV. Why do you keep such a meeting at your house as you do every week upon a set day? . . .

MRS. H. It is lawful for me so to do, as it is all your practices, and can you find a warrant for yourself and condemn me for the same thing? The ground of my taking it up was, when I first came to this land because I did not go to such meetings as those were, it was presently reported that I did not allow of such meetings but held them unlawful and therefore in that regard they said I was proud and did despise all ordinances. Upon that a friend came unto me and told me of it and I to prevent such aspersions took it up, but it was in practice before I came. Therefore I was not the first.

GOV. For this, that you appeal to our practice you need no confutation. If your meeting had answered to the former it had not been offensive, but I will say that there was no meeting of women alone, but your meeting is of another sort for there are sometimes men among you.

MRS. H. There was never any man with us.

GOV. Well, admit there was no man at your meeting and that you was sorry for it, there is no warrant for your doings, and by what warrant do you continue such a course?

MRS. H. I conceive there lies a clear rule in Titus that the elder women should instruct the younger and then I must have a time wherein I must do it.

GOV. All this I grant you, I grant you a time for it, but what is this to the purpose that you Mrs. Hutchinson must call a company together from their callings to come to be taught of you?

MRS. H. Will it please you to answer me this and to give me a rule for then I will willingly submit to any truth. If any come to my house to be instructed in the ways of God what rule have I to put them away?

GOV. But suppose that a hundred men come unto you to be instructed. Will you forbear to instruct them?

MRS. H. As far as I conceive I cross a rule in it.

GOV. Very well and do you not so here?

MRS. H. No, Sir, for my ground is they are men.

GOV. Men and women all is one for that, but suppose that a man should come and say, "Mrs. Hutchinson, I hear that you are a woman that God hath given his grace unto and you have knowledge in the word of God. I pray instruct me a little." Ought you not to instruct this man?

MRS. H. I think I may. Do you think it is not lawful for me to teach women and why do you call me to teach the court?

GOV. We do not call you to teach the court but to lay open yourself.

[In this portion of the transcript not reproduced, Hutchinson and Winthrop continued to wrangle over specifically what law she had broken.]

GOV. Your course is not to be suffered for. Besides that we find such a course as this to be greatly prejudicial to the state. Besides the occasion that it is to seduce many honest persons that are called to those meetings and your opinions being known to be different from the word of God may seduce many simple souls that resort unto you. Besides that the occasion which hath come of late hath come from none but such as have frequented your meetings, so that now they are flown off from magistrates and ministers and since they have come to you. And besides that it will not well stand with the commonwealth that families should be neglected for so many neighbours and dames and so much time spent. We see no rule of God for this. We see not that any should have authority to set up any other exercises besides what authority hath already set up and so what hurt comes of this you will be guilty of and we for suffering you.

MRS. H. Sir, I do not believe that to be so.

GOV. Well, we see how it is. We must therefore put it away from you or restrain you from maintaining this course.

MRS. H. If you have a rule for it from God's word you may.

GOV. We are judges, and not you ours and we must compel you to it.

[Here followed a discussion of whether or not men as well as women attended Hutchinson's meetings. In response to one question, Hutchinson denied that women ever taught at men's meetings.]

DEPUTY GOVERNOR. I would go a little higher with Mrs. Hutchinson. About three years ago we were all in peace. Mrs. Hutchinson from that time she came hath made a disturbance, and some that came over with her in the ship did inform me what she was as soon as she was landed. I being then in place dealt with the pastor and teacher of Boston and desired them to enquire of her, and then I was satisfied that she held nothing different from us. But within half a year after, she had vented divers of her strange opinions and had made parties in the country, and at length it comes that Mr. Cotton and Mr. Vane[5] were of her judgment, but Mr. Cotton had cleared himself that he was not of that mind. But now it appears by this woman's meeting that Mrs. Hutchinson hath so forestalled the minds of many by their resort to her meeting that now she hath a potent party in the country. Now if all these things have endangered us as from that foundation and if she in particular hath disparaged all our ministers in the land that they have preached a covenant of works,[6] and only Mr. Cotton a covenant of grace,[7] why this is not to be suffered, and therefore being driven to the foundation and it being found that Mrs. Hutchinson is she that hath depraved all the ministers and hath been the cause of what is falled out, why we must take away the foundation and the building will fall.

MRS. H. I pray, Sir, prove it that I said they preached nothing but a covenant of works.

DEP. GOV. Nothing but a covenant of works. Why a Jesuit[8] may preach truth sometimes.

MRS. H. Did I ever say they preached a covenant of works then?

DEP. GOV. If they do not preach a covenant of grace clearly, then they preach a covenant of works.

MRS. H. No, Sir. One may preach a covenant of grace more clearly than another, so I said.

DEP. GOV. We are not upon that now but upon position.

MRS. H. Prove this then Sir that you say I said.

DEP. GOV. When they do preach a covenant of works do they preach truth?

MRS. H. Yes, Sir. But when they preach a covenant of works for salvation, that is not truth.

DEP. GOV. I do but ask you this: when the ministers do preach a covenant of works do they preach a way of salvation?

MRS. H. I did not come hither to answer to questions of that sort.

DEP. GOV. Because you will deny the thing.

---

5. Henry Vane, an ally of the Antinomians, was elected governor of Massachusetts Bay colony in 1636 and lost that office to Winthrop in 1637.
6. For an explanation of the covenant of works, see the "Background" section.
7. For an explanation of the covenant of grace, see the "Background" section.
8. The Society of Jesus (Jesuits) was a Roman Catholic order that placed special emphasis on missionary work and combating Protestantism. The Jesuits were particularly detested by many Protestants, including the Puritans.

MRS. H. Ey, but that is to be proved first.

DEP. GOV. I will make it plain that you did say that the ministers did preach a covenant of works.

MRS. H. I deny that.

DEP. GOV. And that you said they were not able ministers of the New Testament, but Mr. Cotton only.

MRS. H. If ever I spake that I proved it by God's word.

COURT. Very well, very well.

MRS. H. If one shall come unto me in private, and desire me seriously to tell then what I thought of such an one, I must either speak false or true in my answer.

[*In this lengthy section, Hutchinson was accused of having gone to a meeting of ministers and accusing them all—except John Cotton—of preaching a covenant of works rather than a covenant of grace. The accusation, if proven, would have been an extremely serious one. Several of the ministers testified that Hutchinson had made this accusation.*]

DEP. GOV. I called these witnesses and you deny them. You see they have proved this and you deny this, but it is clear. You said they preached a covenant of works and that they were not able ministers of the New Testament; now there are two other things that you did affirm which were that the scriptures in the letter of them held forth nothing but a covenant of works and likewise that those that were under a covenant of works cannot be saved.

MRS. H. Prove that I said so.

GOV. Did you say so?

MRS. H No, Sir. It is your conclusion.

DEP. GOV. What do I do charging of you if you deny what is so fully proved?

GOV. Here are six undeniable ministers who say it is true and yet you deny that you did say that they did preach a covenant of works and that they were not able ministers of the gospel, and it appears plainly that you have spoken it, and whereas you say that it was drawn from you in a way of friendship, you did profess then that it was out of conscience that you spake and said, "The fear of man is a snare. Wherefore shall I be afraid, I will speak plainly and freely."

MRS. H. That I absolutely deny, for the first question was thus answered by me to them: They thought that I did conceive there was a difference between them and Mr. Cotton. At the first I was somewhat reserved. Then said Mr. Peters, "I pray answer the question directly as fully and as plainly as you desire we should tell you our minds. Mrs. Hutchinson we come for plain dealing and telling you our hearts." Then I said I would deal as plainly as I could, and whereas they say I said they were under a covenant of works and in the state of the apostles why these two speeches cross one another. I might say they might preach a covenant of works as did the apostles, but to preach a covenant of works and to be under a covenant of works is another business.

DEP. GOV. There have been six witnesses to prove this and yet you deny it.

MRS. H. I deny that these were the first words that were spoken.

GOV. You make the case worse, for you clearly shew that the ground of your opening your mind was not to satisfy them but to satisfy your own conscience.

[*There was a brief argument here about what Hutchinson actually said at the gathering of ministers, after which the court adjourned for the day.*]

The next morning

GOV. We proceeded the last night as far as we could in hearing of this cause of Mrs. Hutchinson. There were divers things laid to her charge: her ordinary meetings about religious exercises, her speeches in derogation of the ministers among us, and the weakening of the hands and hearts of the people towards them. Here was sufficient proof made of that which she was accused of in that point concerning the ministers and their ministry, as that they did preach a covenant of works when others did preach a covenant of grace, and that they were not able ministers of the New Testament, and that they had not the seal of the spirit, and this was spoken not as was pretended out of private conference, but out of conscience and warrant from scripture alleged the fear of man is a snare and seeing God had given her a calling to it she would freely speak. Some other speeches she used, as that the letter of the scripture held forth a covenant of works, and this is offered to be proved by probable grounds. If there be any thing else that the court hath to say they may speak.

[*At this point, a lengthy argument erupted when Hutchinson demanded that the ministers who testified against her be recalled as witnesses, put under oath, and repeat their accusations. One member of the court said that "the ministers are so well known unto us, that we need not take an oath of them."*]

GOV. I see no necessity of an oath in this thing seeing it is true and the substance of the matter confirmed by divers. Yet that all may be satisfied, if the elders will take an oath they shall have it given them. . . .

MRS. H. I will prove by what Mr. Wilson hath written[9] that they [the ministers] never heard me say such a thing.

MR. SIMS. We desire to have the paper and have it read.

MR. HARLAKENDEN. I am persuaded that is the truth that the elders do say and therefore I do not see it necessary how to call them to oath.

GOV. We cannot charge any thing of untruth upon them.

MR. HARLAKENDEN. Besides, Mrs. Hutchinson doth say that they are not able ministers of the New Testament.

MRS. H. They need not swear to that.

DEP. GOV. Will you confess it then?

MRS. H. I will not deny it or say it.

DEP. GOV. You must do one.

[*More on the oath followed.*]

DEP. GOV. Let her witnesses be called.

GOV. Who be they?

MRS. H. Mr. Leveret and our teacher and Mr. Coggeshall.

GOV. Mr. Coggeshall was not present.

MR. COGGESHALL. Yes, but I was. Only I desired to be silent till I should be called.

GOV. Will you, Mr. Coggeshall, say that she did not say so?

MR. COGGESHALL. Yes, I dare say that she did not say all that which they lay against her.

MR. PETERS. How dare you look into the court to say such a word?

MR. COGGESHALL. Mr. Peters takes upon him to forbid me. I shall be silent.

MR. STOUGHTON. Ey, but she intended this that they say.

GOV. Well, Mr. Leveret, what were the words? I pray, speak.

MR. LEVERET. To my best remembrance when the elders did send for her, Mr. Peters did with much vehemency and intreaty urge her to tell what difference there was between Mr. Cotton and them, and upon his urging of her she said, "The fear of man is a snare, but they that trust upon the Lord shall be safe." And being asked wherein the difference was, she answered that they did not preach a covenant of grace so clearly as Mr. Cotton did, and she gave this reason of it: because that as the apostles were for a time without the spirit so until they had received

9. Wilson had taken notes at the meeting between Hutchinson and the ministers. Hutchinson claimed that these notes would exonerate her. They were never produced and are now lost.

the witness of the spirit they could not preach a covenant of grace so clearly.

[*Here Hutchinson admitted that she might have said privately that the ministers were not able ministers of the New Testament.*]

GOV. Mr. Cotton, the court desires that you declare what you do remember of the conference which was at the time and is now in question.

MR. COTTON. I did not think I should be called to bear witness in this cause and therefore did not labour to call to remembrance what was done; but the greatest passage that took impression upon me was to this purpose. The elders spake that they had heard that she had spoken some condemning words of their ministry, and among other things they did first pray her to answer wherein she thought their ministry did differ from mine. How the comparison sprang I am ignorant, but sorry I was that any comparison should be between me and my brethren and uncomfortable it was. She told them to this purpose that they did not hold forth a covenant of grace as I did. . . . I told her I was very sorry that she put comparisons between my ministry and theirs, for she had said more than I could myself, and rather I had that she had put us in fellowship with them and not have made the discrepancy. She said she found the difference. . . . And I must say that I did not find her saying they were under a covenant of works, not that she said they did preach a covenant of works.

[*Here John Cotton tried to defend Hutchinson, mostly by saying he did not remember most of the events in question.*]

MRS. H. If you please to give me leave I shall give you the ground of what I know to be true. Being much troubled to see the falseness of the constitution of the Church of England, I had like to have turned Separatist. Whereupon I kept a day of solemn humiliation and pondering of the thing, the scripture was brought unto me—he that denies Jesus Christ to be come in the flesh is antichrist. This I considered of and in considering found that the papists[10] did not deny him to come in the flesh, nor we did not deny him. Who then was antichrist? Was the Turk antichrist only? The Lord knows that I could not open scripture; he must by his prophetical office open it unto me. So after that being

---

10. "Papists" is a Protestant term for Roman Catholics, referring to the papacy.

unsatisfied in the thing, the Lord was pleased to bring this scripture out of the Hebrews. He that denies the testament denies the testator, and in this did open unto me and give me to see that those which did not teach the new covenant had the spirit of antichrist, and upon this he did discover the ministry unto me, and ever since, I bless the Lord. He hath let me see which was the clear ministry and which the wrong. Since that time I confess I have been more choice and he hath left me to distinguish between the voice of my beloved and the voice of Moses, the voice of John Baptist and the voice of antichrist, for all those voices are spoken of in scripture. Now if you do condemn me for speaking what in my conscience I know to be truth I must commit myself unto the Lord.

MR. NOWEL. How do you know that that was the spirit?

MRS. H. How did Abraham know that it was God that bid him offer his son, being a breach of the sixth commandment?

DEP. GOV. By an immediate voice.

MRS. H. So to me by an immediate revelation.

DEP. GOV. How! an immediate revelation.

MRS. H. By the voice of his spirit to my soul. . . .

[*In spite of the general shock that greeted her claim that she had experienced an immediate revelation from God, Hutchinson went on to state that God had compelled her to take the course she had taken and that God had said to her, as He had to Daniel of the Old Testament, that "though I should meet with affliction, yet I am the same God that delivered Daniel out of the lion's den, I will also deliver thee."*]

MRS. H. You have power over my body but the Lord Jesus hath power over my body and soul, and assure yourselves thus much: you go on in this course you begin you will bring a curse upon you and your posterity, and the mouth of the Lord hath spoken it.

DEP. GOV. What is the scripture she brings?

MR. STOUGHTON. Behold I turn away from you.

MRS. H. But now having seen him which is invisible I fear not what man can do unto me.

GOV. Daniel was delivered by miracle. Do you think to be deliver'd so too?

MRS. H. I do here speak it before the court. I took that the Lord should deliver me by his providence.

MR. HARLAKENDEN. I may read scripture and the most glorious hypocrite may read them and yet go down to hell.

MRS. H. It may be so.

[Hutchinson's "revelations" were discussed among the stunned court.]

MR. BARTHOLOMEW. I speak as a member of the court. I fear that her revelations will deceive.

[More on Hutchinson's revelations followed.]

DEP. GOV. I desire Mr. Cotton to tell us whether you do approve of Mrs. Hutchinson's revelations as she hath laid them down.

MR. COTTON. I know not whether I do understand her, but this I say: If she doth expect a deliverance in a way of providence, then I cannot deny it.

DEP. GOV. No, sir. We did not speak of that.

MR. COTTON. If it be by way of miracle then I would suspect it.

DEP. GOV. Do you believe that her revelations are true?

MR. COTTON. That she may have some special providence of God to help her is a thing that I cannot bear witness against.

DEP. GOV. Good Sir, I do ask whether this revelation be of God or no?

MR. COTTON. I should desire to know whether the sentence of the court will bring her to any calamity, and then I would know of her whether she expects to be delivered from that calamity by a miracle or a providence of God.

MRS. H. By a providence of God I say I expect to be delivered from some calamity that shall come to me.

[Hutchinson's revelations were further discussed.]

DEP. GOV. These disturbances that have come among the Germans[11] have been all grounded upon revelations, and so they that have vented them have stirred up their hearers to take up arms against their prince and to cut the throats of one another, and these have been the fruits of them, and whether the devil may inspire the same into their hearts here I know not, for I am fully persuaded that Mrs. Hutchinson is deluded by the devil, because the spirit of God speaks truth in all his servants.

GOV. I am persuaded that the revelation she brings forth is delusion.

[All the court but some two or three ministers cried out, "We all believe—we all believe it." Hutchinson was found guilty. Coddington made a lame attempt to defend Hutchinson but was silenced by Governor Winthrop.]

11. This reference is to the bloody and violent fighting that took place between orthodox Protestants and the followers of the radical Anabaptist John of Leiden in 1534 and 1535.

GOV. The court hath already declared themselves satisfied concerning the things you hear, and concerning the troublesomeness of her spirit and the danger of her course amongst us, which is not to be suffered. Therefore if it be the mind of the court that Mrs. Hutchinson for these things that appear before us is unfit for our society, and if it be the mind of the court that she shall be banished out of our liberties and imprisoned till she be sent away, let them hold up their hands.

[*All but three did so.*]

GOV. Those that are contrary minded hold up yours.

[*Only Mr. Coddington and Mr. Colborn did so.*]

MR. JENNISON. I cannot hold up my hand one way or the other, and I shall give my reason if the court require it.

GOV. Mrs. Hutchinson, the sentence of the court you hear is that you are banished from out of our jurisdiction as being a woman not fit for our society, and are to be imprisoned till the court shall send you away.

MRS. H. I desire to know wherefore I am banished?

GOV. Say no more. The court knows wherefore and is satisfied.

❧ QUESTIONS TO CONSIDER ❧

Now that you have examined the evidence, at least one point is very clear: the political and religious authorities of Massachusetts Bay were determined to get rid of Anne Hutchinson, whether or not she actually had broken any law. They tried to bait her, force admissions of guilt from her, confuse her, browbeat her. Essentially, they had already decided on the verdict before the trial began. So we know that Anne Hutchinson was a threat—and a serious one—to the colony.

And yet the colony had dealt quite differently with Roger Williams, a Puritan minister banished in 1635 because of his extreme religious beliefs.

Williams was given every chance to mend his ways, Governor Winthrop remained his friend throughout Williams's appearances before the General Court, and it was only with great reluctance that the court finally decided to send him out into the "wilderness."

Why, then, was Anne Hutchinson such a threat, and why was her trial such an ordeal? Obviously, she did pose a religious threat. As you look back through the evidence, try to clarify the exact points of difficulty between Hutchinson and the ministers. What was the basis of the argument over covenants of grace and works?

[47]

What was Hutchinson supposed to have said? Under what circumstances had she allegedly said this? To whom? What was the role of her own minister, John Cotton, in the trial?

One must remember that Hutchinson's trial took place in the midst of the divisive Antinomian controversy. What threat did the Antinomians pose to Massachusetts Bay and Puritanism? Did Hutchinson say anything in her testimony that would indicate she was an Antinomian? How would you prove whether or not she was?

Hutchinson's place or role in the community also seems to have come into question during the trial. What do the questions about the meetings she held in her home reveal? Look beyond what the governor and members of the court are actually saying. Try to imagine what they might have been thinking. How might Hutchinson's meetings have eventually posed a threat to the larger community?

Finally, look through the transcript one more time. It provides some clues, often subtle ones, about the relationships between men and women in colonial Massachusetts. Puritan law and customs gave women approximately equal status with men, and of course women could join the church, just as men could. But in every society, there are unspoken assumptions about how men and women should behave. Can you find any evidence that Hutchinson violated these assumptions? If so, what did she do? Again, why would this be dangerous?

In conclusion, try to put together all you know from the evidence to answer the central question: why was Anne Hutchinson such a threat to Massachusetts Bay colony?

☙ EPILOGUE ☙

Even after their banishment, misfortune continued to plague the Hutchinson family. After moving to Narragansett Bay, Hutchinson once again became pregnant. By then she was more than forty-five years old and had begun menopause. The fetus did not develop naturally and was aborted into a hydatidiform mole (resembling a cluster of grapes), which was expelled with considerable pain and difficulty. Many believed that the "birth" of this "monster baby" was proof of Hutchinson's religious heresy.

In 1642, Hutchinson's husband died, and she moved with her six youngest children to the Dutch colony of New Netherland in what is now the Bronx borough of New York City. The next year, she and all but one of her children were killed by Indians.

Ten years after Hutchinson was banished from Massachusetts Bay, John Winthrop died. Winthrop believed to the end of his life that he had had no choice other than to expel Hutchinson and her family. However, even Winthrop's most sympathetic biographer, historian Edmund S. Morgan, describes the Hutchinson trial and its aftermath as "the least attractive episode" in Winthrop's long public career.

Massachusetts Bay continued to try to maintain community cohesion for years after Anne Hutchinson and her family were expelled. But as the colony grew and prospered, change ultimately did come. New generations seemed unable to embrace the original zeal of the colony's founders. New towns increased the colony's size and made uniformity more difficult. Growth and prosperity also seemed to bring an increased interest in individual wealth and a corresponding decline in religious fervor. Reports of sleeping during sermons, fewer conversions of young people, blasphemous language, and growing attention to physical pleasures were numerous, as were reports of election disputes, intrachurch squabbling, and community bickering.

To those who remembered the old ways of Massachusetts Bay, such straying from the true path was more than unfortunate. The Puritans believed that as the ancient Israelites had been punished by God when they broke their covenant, so they would have to pay for their indiscretions. As one Puritan minister said, "In the time of their prosperity, see how the Jews turn their backs and shake off the authority of the Lord." The comparison was lost on almost no one.

Jeremiads—stories that predicted disasters because of the decline in religious zeal and public morality—were especially popular in the 1660s. The minister and physician Michael Wigglesworth's poem "The Day of Doom" (specifically written for the general public) was "read to pieces," according to historian Perry Miller. Wigglesworth's more sophisticated but heartfelt poem "God's Controversy with New England" was equally popular among more educated readers. Hence it is not surprising that by the late 1680s (more than forty years after Anne Hutchinson's death), a wave of religious hysteria swept across Massachusetts Bay colony. Convinced that they had broken their covenant with God, many Puritans grimly awaited their punishment, spending long hours in churches listening to sermons. When in 1692 a few young girls in Salem Village began accusing some of their neighbors of being possessed by Satan, many were convinced that the day of punishment had arrived. Before that incident had run its course, twenty people had been killed, nineteen of them by hanging, and many more had been temporarily imprisoned. Although the Puritans' congregational church remained the official established church of Massachusetts until 1822, the original community cohesion had been altered long before that.

CHAPTER 3

RHYTHMS OF COLONIAL LIFE:
THE STATISTICS OF
COLONIAL MASSACHUSETTS BAY

⤬ THE PROBLEM ⤬

An important benefit of studying history is the ability to measure both change over time and people's reactions or adjustments to those changes. Today's world is changing with incredible speed. Recently you probably drove a fuel-injected automobile along an interstate highway while listening to an FM stereo radio station or a cassette tape, exited from the highway for a fast-food snack, continued home and prepared a full meal in a microwave oven, and then watched a film or a previously taped television program on your videocassette recorder or worked with your personal computer. These are all activities that no American could have engaged in thirty years ago. Indeed, we live in a society that expects change, generally welcomes it, and tries to plan for it.

Centuries ago, change took place at a considerably slower pace. Yet change did occur in colonial America, sometimes with what for the colonists must have seemed like startling speed. Colonial Massachusetts Bay was such a society. A child born in that colony in 1650, whether male or female, experienced a profoundly different life from that of a child born in 1750. In some ways, the differences in those two children's lives were dramatic and unwelcome.

What were the differences in the lives of the people of Massachusetts Bay between 1650 and 1750? How can we account for those differences? How might those differences have affected those people's thoughts, attitudes, feelings, and behavior? In this chapter, you will be using statistics to measure change over time in colonial Massachusetts Bay and how men, women, and children reacted to and attempted to adapt to those changes. Then, using your historical imagination, you will explain how those changes and adaptations might have affected the emotions and actions of those colonists. More specifically, by the 1760s and early 1770s, an increasing number of Massachusetts Bay colonists were willing to protest and ultimately take up arms against Great Britain. Do the changes in the lives of the people of Massachusetts Bay help explain why these colonists made those momentous decisions?

BACKGROUND

The years between the settlement of the colonies and the American Revolution are critical ones in American history. In those years, which in some colonies stretched to more than a century,[1] stability was gradually achieved, economic bases were laid, political institutions were established, social structures and institutions evolved, and intellectual and cultural life eventually thrived. As the population increased and as older settlements matured, new towns and settlements were founded on the edge of the receding wilderness, thus repeating the process of settlement, stability, growth, and maturation. And, although most colonists were still tied to England by bonds of language, economics, government, and affection, over the years those bonds gradually loosened until the colonists, many without fully realizing it, had become something distinctly different than simply English men and women who happened to reside in another land. In some ways, then, the American Revolution was the political realization of earlier economic, social, cultural, and political trends and events in colonial life.

These trends and events occurred, with some variations, in all the colonies, especially the Massachusetts Bay colony. Founded in 1630 by Puritans from England, Massachusetts Bay grew rapidly, aided in its first decade by 15,000 to 20,000 immigrants from England, and after that by natural increase.[2] By 1700, Massachusetts Bay's population had risen to almost 56,000 and by 1750, to

1. The following colonies had been in existence for a century or more when the American Revolution broke out in 1775: Virginia, Massachusetts Bay, Rhode Island, Connecticut, Maryland, New York, and New Jersey. Settlements of Europeans also existed in New Hampshire and Delaware areas more than a century before the Revolution, although they did not formally become colonies until later.

2. The outbreak of the English civil war in 1642 drastically reduced emigration from England to Massachusetts Bay, largely because Puritans in England believed it was important to stay and fight against Charles I. In 1649, when Charles I was deposed and beheaded, a Puritan commonwealth was established in England, which lasted until 1660.

CHAPTER 3

RHYTHMS OF
COLONIAL LIFE:
THE STATISTICS
OF COLONIAL
MASSACHUSETTS
BAY

approximately 188,000, making it one of Great Britain's most populous North American possessions.

This rapid population growth forced the government of Massachusetts Bay (called the General Court, which included the governor, the deputy governor, the executive council of assistants, and the representatives, all elected annually by the freemen[3]) to organize new towns. Within the first year of settlement, the six original towns of Massachusetts Bay were laid out—Dorchester, Roxbury, Watertown, Newtown (now Cambridge), Charlestown, and Boston, all on the Charles River. By the time Middlesex County (west of Boston) was organized in 1643, there were eight towns in that county alone, and by 1700, there were twenty-two.

The organization of towns was an important way for Puritan leaders to keep control of the rapidly growing population. Unlike settlers in the middle and southern colonies, colonists in Massachusetts Bay could not simply travel to an uninhabited area, select a parcel of land, and receive individual title to the land from the colonial governor. Instead, a group of men who wanted to establish a town had to apply to the General Court for a land grant for the entire town. Leaders of the prospective new town were then selected, and the single church was organized. Having received the grant from the General Court, the new town's leaders apportioned the available land among the male heads of households who were church members, holding in common some land for grazing and other uses (hence the "town common"). In this way, the Puritan leadership retained control of the fast-growing population, ensured Puritan economic and religious domination, and guaranteed that large numbers of dissenters—men and women who might divert the colony from its "holy mission" in the wilderness—would not be attracted to Massachusetts Bay.

Economically, Massachusetts Bay prospered from the very beginning, witnessing no "starving time" as did Virginia. Yet of all the major colonies, Massachusetts Bay fit the least well into England's mercantile system, whereby colonies supplied raw materials to the mother country and in turn purchased the mother country's manufactured products. Because comparatively rocky soil and a short growing season kept crop yields low and agricultural surpluses meager, many people in Massachusetts Bay had to seek other ways of making a living. Many men petitioned the General Court to organize new towns on the frontier; others turned to either the sea as fishermen, traders, shippers, and seamen or native manufacturing enterprises such as iron product manufacturing, rum distilling, shipbuilding, and ropemaking. Except for fishing, none of these activities fit into England's mercantile plans for her empire, and some undertakings were prohibited outright by the Navigation Acts (1660, 1663, and later, which set up the mercantile system), which most citizens of Massachusetts Bay ignored.

3. A freeman was an adult male who was accepted by his town (hence a landowner) and was a member of the Puritan congregational church.

The restoration of the English monarchy in 1660 in the person of Charles II greatly concerned the Massachusetts Bay colonists. It was no secret that Charles II loathed Puritanism. The new monarch also made it clear that the Navigation Acts would be enforced. After more than twenty years of wrangling among the colony, the king, and the Lords of Trade, in 1684 the Massachusetts Bay charter was revoked; in 1685, the colony was included in a grand scheme to reorganize the northern colonies into the Dominion of New England, with one royal governor and no elected assembly.[4] The dominion's governor, the undiplomatic Sir Edmund Andros, further alienated Massachusetts Bay colonists by levying taxes on them without consultation or consent, enforcing the Navigation Acts, favoring religious toleration in Massachusetts Bay, and calling their land titles into question. As a result, Massachusetts Bay colonists were only too glad to use the confusion and instability accompanying England's Glorious Revolution of 1688 to stage a bloodless coup that deposed Andros and returned the colony to its original form of government, an act that the mother country ultimately approved. Thus from almost the very beginning, the colonists of Massachusetts Bay were politically aware and jealously guarded their representative government.

Not only were the Massachusetts Bay colonists' political ideas sharp-

4. The Dominion of New England included the colonies of New Jersey, New York, Connecticut, Rhode Island, Plymouth, and Massachusetts Bay, which included lands that later became New Hampshire and Maine.

ened and refined decades before the American Revolution, their other ways of thinking also were greatly affected. Two important intellectual movements in Europe, the Enlightenment and the Great Awakening, had an enormous impact in America. The Enlightenment was grounded in the belief that human reason could discover the natural laws that governed the universe, nature, and human affairs; human reason and scientific observation would reveal those natural laws to human beings. Although the Enlightenment's greatest impact was on the well-educated and therefore the wealthier citizens, even the "common" people were affected by it. The Great Awakening was a religious revival that swept through the colonies in the 1740s and 1750s. Touched off by English preacher George Whitefield, the Great Awakening emphasized humanity's utter sinfulness and need for salvation. In hundreds of emotional revival meetings, complete with shouting, moaning, and physical gyrations, thousands were converted. Because the Great Awakening undermined the traditional churches and their leaders, most clergymen (called "Old Lights") opposed the movement, but to little avail.

On the surface, the Enlightenment and the Great Awakening seemed to have nothing in common. The Enlightenment emphasized human reason, whereas the Great Awakening appealed more to emotion than to reason. Both movements, however, contained a strong streak of individualism: the Enlightenment emphasized the potential of the human mind, and the Great Awakening concentrated on the indi-

CHAPTER 3

RHYTHMS OF
COLONIAL LIFE:
THE STATISTICS
OF COLONIAL
MASSACHUSETTS
BAY

vidual soul. Each movement in its own way increased the colonists' sense of themselves as individuals who possessed both individual rights and individual futures. The colonists who once huddled together for protection and mutual assistance in tiny settlements had, by the mid-eighteenth century, grown, changed, and matured, as had the settlements they had built. They harbored new attitudes about themselves, their society, their individual futures, and, almost inevitably, their government. Hence the life and thought of a Massachusetts Bay colonist (or, indeed, any colonist) born in 1750 was profoundly different from that of one born in 1650.

When most people think of the colonial period in America, they invariably think of the colonial leaders, men and women who held the economic, social, and political reins of the society. But these leaders—the John Winthrops and Anne Hutchinsons, the Jonathan Edwardses and Benjamin Franklins, the William Penns and Nathaniel Bacons—represent only a tiny fraction of the men and women who lived in the colonies between 1607 and 1775. And yet to understand the processes of growth, change, and maturation fully, it is necessary for us to study the lives of the "ordinary" men, women, and children as well as those of their economic, social, and political "betters." How did the processes of growth, change, and maturation affect small farmers and artisans and their spouses, sons, and daughters? How did the situations of these people change over time? How did they react to those changes? Indeed, if we can learn more about the lives of all Americans, not just those of the prominent colonists, we will be able to better understand the extent to which growth, change, and maturation helped effect the American Revolution.

It is considerably easier to collect information about the leading colonial figures than the "average" men and women. Few of the farmers, artisans, or laborers left diaries or letters to provide clues to their thoughts and behavior; fewer made speeches or participated in decision making; fewer still talked with leaders like Washington and Jefferson, so their thoughts and actions were much less likely to be recorded for us by others. In some ways, then, a curtain has been drawn across a large part of American colonial history, obscuring the lives, thoughts, and feelings of the vast majority of the colonists. Sometimes even their names have been lost.

∞ THE METHOD ∞

How can we hope to reconstruct the lives, thoughts, and feelings of people who left no letters, diaries, sermons, speeches, or votes for us to analyze? Recently, historians have become more imaginative in using the relatively limited records at their disposal to examine the lives of ordinary men, women, and children who lived during the colonial period. Almost every per-

Table 1

Type of Record	Questions
Census	Is the population growing, shrinking, or stationary? Is the ratio of males to females roughly equal?[5] Does that ratio change over time?
Marriage	At what age are women marrying? Is that age changing over time?
Wills, probate	How are estates divided? Is that method changing over time? Based on real estate and personal property listed, is the collective standard of living rising, falling, or stationary? Based on dates of death, is the population living longer?
Land, tax	What percentage of the adult male population owns land? Is that percentage changing over time? Is the land evenly distributed among the adult male population?

son, even the poorest, left some record that she or he existed. That person's name may appear in any of a number of records, including church records stating when she or he was baptized, marriage records, property-holding records, civil- or criminal-court records, military records, tax records, and death or cemetery records. It is in these records that the lives of the ordinary men, women, and children of colonial America can be examined. An increasing number of historians have been carefully scrutinizing those records to re-create the lives and attitudes of those who left no other evidence.

How is this done? Most historians interested in the lives of the ordinary colonists rely heavily on statistics. Instead of trying to uncover all the records relating to one person or family (which might not be representative of the whole population), these historians use statistics to create *collective biographies*—that is, biographies of population groups (farmers in Andover, Massachusetts, for example) rather than biographies of certain individuals. The historians collect all (or a sample of all) the birth, death, and marriage records of a community and look at all (or a sample of all) the wills, probate records,[6] tax and landholding records, and census data. These historians are forming an aggregate or collective picture of a community and how that community has changed over time. Are women marrying later? What percentage of women remain unmarried? Are women having fewer children than they were in another time? Are inheritance patterns (the methods of dividing estates among heirs) changing over time? Are farms

5. Because males and females are born in roughly equal numbers, an unequal ratio of males to females (called a sex ratio) must be explained by events such as wars, out-migration, in-migration, or differing mortality rates for males and females.

6. Probate records are public records of processed wills.

CHAPTER 3

RHYTHMS OF
COLONIAL LIFE:
THE STATISTICS
OF COLONIAL
MASSACHUSETTS
BAY

increasing or decreasing in size? To the historian, each statistical summary of records (each set of statistics or *aggregate* picture) contains information that increases understanding of the community being studied.

After the statistics are compiled, what does the historian do next? Each set of statistics is examined separately to see what changes are occurring over time. Table 1 shows the types of questions historians ask of several different types of records.

Having examined each set of statistics, the historian places the sets in some logical order, which may vary depending on the available evidence, the central questions the historian is attempting to answer, and the historian's own preferences. Some historians prefer a "birth-to-death" ordering, actually beginning with age-at-marriage statistics for females and moving chronologically through the collective life of the community's population. Others prefer to isolate the demographic statistical sets (birth, marriage, migration, and death) from the economic sets (such as landholding and division of estates).

Up to this point, the historian has (1) collected the statistics and arranged them into sets, (2) examined each set and measured tendencies or changes over time, and (3) arranged the sets in some logical order. Now the historian must begin asking "why" for each set. For example:

1. Why does the method of dividing estates change over time?
2. Why are women marrying later?
3. Why are premarital pregnancies increasing?

In many cases, the answer to each question (and other "why" questions) is in one of the other statistical sets. That may cause the historian to alter his or her ordering of the sets to make the story clearer.

The historian is actually linking the sets to one another to form a chain. When two sets have been linked (because one set answers the "why" question of another set), the historian repeats the process until all the sets have been linked to form one chain of evidence. At that point, the historian can summarize the tendencies that have been discovered and, if desired, can connect those trends or tendencies with other events occurring in the period, such as the American Revolution.

One example of how historians link statistical sets together to answer the question "why" is sufficient. Source 1 in the Evidence section shows that the white population growth in Massachusetts Bay was extremely rapid between 1660 and 1770 (the growth rate actually approximates those of many non-Western developing nations today). How can we account for this rapid growth? Look at Source 4, which deals with the survival rate of children born in the town of Andover between 1640 and 1759. Note that between 1640 and 1699, the survival rate was very high (in Sweden between 1751 and 1799, 50 percent of the children born did not reach the age of fifteen). Also examine Source 16, the average number of births per marriage in Andover. Note that between 1655 and 1704, the average number of births per marriage was very high, between 5.3 and 7.6. Thus we can conclude that the population grew so rapidly in Massachusetts Bay between 1660 and 1700 because women gave birth to large numbers of children *and* a high percentage of those children survived. By following this process, you will be able to link together all the statistical sets.

Occasionally, however, you will need more information than statistics (some of which are unavailable) can provide. For example, notice in Sources 1 and 2 that the average annual growth rates were generally declining but there was a sharp *increase* in the population growth rates in the 1720s. This increase cannot be explained by the statistics in Sources 4 and 16, so another reason must be found. In fact, beginning in 1713, the number of religious dissenters who immigrated to Massachusetts Bay from Great Britain increased significantly, due to the end of intermittent warfare and to crop failures in northern Ireland. That swelling of immigration lasted for only about twenty years, after which it once again subsided. The town of Andover was host (albeit unwillingly) to some of those immigrants. Thus you can see that population increases in Massachusetts Bay and in Andover between 1713 and 1740 were the results of natural increase *plus* a temporary jump in immigration. If you have similar problems with other statistical sets, consult your instructor for assistance.

Remember that we are dealing with a society that was not as statistically oriented as ours. Several of the statistics you would like to have simply are not obtainable. The statistics we do have, however, provide a fascinating window for us to observe the lives of "ordinary" men, women, and children who lived centuries ago.

In this chapter, you will be using the statistics provided to identify important trends affecting the men, women, and children of Massachusetts Bay in the century preceding the American Revolution. Use the process described below:

1. Examine each statistical set, especially for a change over time.
2. Ask why that change took place.
3. Find the answer in another set, thereby establishing a linkage.
4. Repeat the process until all the sets have been linked together.
5. Then ask the central questions: What important trends affected the men, women, and children of colonial Massachusetts Bay in the century preceding the American Revolution? How were people likely to think and feel about those trends? Finally, how might those trends have contributed to the decision of Massachusetts Bay colonists to revolt against Great Britain?

As you will see, most of the statistical sets deal with Concord and Andover, two older towns in the Massachusetts Bay colony (see the following map). These two towns were chosen because historians Robert Gross and Philip Greven collected much statistical information about Concord and Andover, respectively; we have arranged the data in tabular form. Evidence suggests that these two towns are fairly representative of other towns in the eastern part of the colony. Concord, a farm town founded in 1635, was the first town in Massachusetts Bay established away from the

[57]

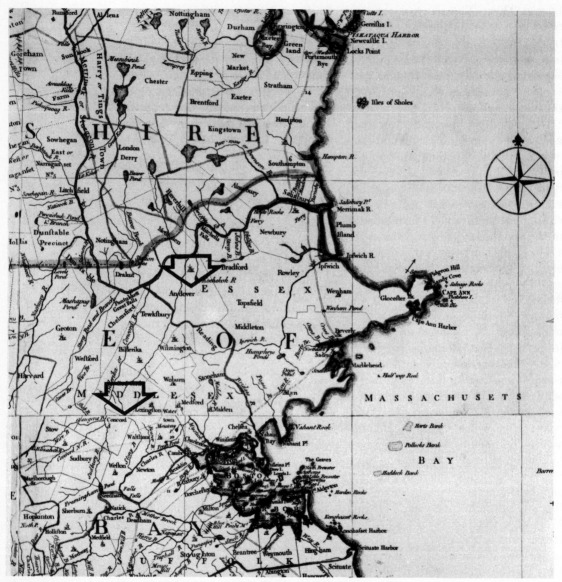

The eastern part of Massachusetts Bay colony, 1755. Reproduced from Thomas Jefferys's "A Map of the Most Inhabited Part of New England, Containing the Provinces of Massachusetts Bay, and New Hampshire, with the Colonies of Connecticut and Rhode Island. November 29, 1755"; in Jefferys's *A General Topography of North America and the West Indies* (London, 1768); courtesy of the Map Division, The New York Public Library, Astor, Lenox and Tilden Foundations.

Charles River. The area was rich in furs, and settlers initially were able to trap the furs (especially beaver) for income. Andover was organized in 1646, the original settlers mainly from other towns in the colony. In Andover, the people lived in the village and walked out to farm their land, which was organized in the open-field system (landowners owned several strips of land in large open fields and worked the fields in common). In Concord, many settlers lived outside the village and near the fields, building clusters of houses along the Concord River (which was spanned by the soon-to-be-famous Concord Bridge).

As you examine the statistical sets from these two towns, note that the dates for the sets do not always match. Understand both *what* you are examining and *when* that particular factor is being measured. For example, the statistical set on premarital conceptions in Andover records that phenom-enon from 1655 to 1739, whereas the same phenomenon in Concord is measured from 1740 to 1774 (see Source 17). Assuming that this trend is similar in both towns, how would you use those two sets of statistics?

At first the statistics appear cold and impersonal and seem to tell us little that is worth knowing. But we cannot just skip this problem and get on to the political events leading up to the American Revolution (such as the Boston Massacre) and the important battles of the Revolution. It is crucial to remember that some of the men and boys who were on the streets of Boston on the evening of March 5, 1770, are counted in these statistics. And some of the men who participated in the Battles of Lexington and Concord also appear in these statistics. Are there any links between what the statistics represent and the subsequent behaviors of these people?

CHAPTER 3

RHYTHMS OF
COLONIAL LIFE:
THE STATISTICS
OF COLONIAL
MASSACHUSETTS
BAY

⮰ THE EVIDENCE ⮰

Source 1 reprinted from U.S. Bureau of the Census, *Historical Statistics of the United States, Colonial Times to 1957* (Washington, D.C.: U.S. Government Printing Office, 1960), p. 756.

1. Growth of White Population, Massachusetts Bay, 1660–1770.

Year	Total Population	Average Annual Growth Rate (%)
1660	20,082	—
1670	30,000	4.9
1680	39,752	3.3
1690	49,504	2.5
1700	55,941	1.3
1710	62,390	1.2
1720	91,008	4.6
1730	114,116	2.6
1740	151,613	3.3
1750	188,000	2.4
1760	222,600	1.8
1770	235,308	.57

Source 2 data from Philip J. Greven, Jr., *Four Generations: Population, Land, and Family in Colonial Andover, Massachusetts* (Ithaca, N.Y.: Cornell University Press, 1970), p. 179.

2. Growth of White Population, Town of Andover, 1680–1776.

Year	Population	Average Annual Growth Rate (%)
1680	435	—
1685	600	7.6
1695	710	1.8
1705	945	3.3
1715	1,050	1.1
1725	1,305	2.4
1735	1,630	2.5
1745	1,845	1.3
1755	2,135	1.6
1764	2,442	1.6
1776	2,953	1.8

Source 3 data from Robert A. Gross, *The Minutemen and Their World* (New York: Hill and Wang, 1976), p. 15.

3. Growth of Population, Town of Concord, 1679–1750.

Year	Population	Average Annual Growth Rate (%)
1679	480	—
1706	920	3.3
1710	c. 1,000	2.2
1725	c. 1,500	3.3
1750	c. 2,000	1.3

Sources 4 through 6 data from Greven, *Four Generations: Population, Land, and Family in Colonial Andover, Massachusetts,* pp. 191, 189, 177. Source 6 data also from Gross, *The Minutemen and Their World,* p. 209.

4. Children Born Between 1640 and 1759 Who Lived to at Least Age 10, Andover.

Years	Rate
1640–1669	917 per 1,000
1670–1699	855 per 1,000
1700–1729	805 per 1,000
1730–1759	695 per 1,000

5. Children Who Died Before Reaching Age 20, Andover, 1670–1759.

Years	Number	Mortality Rate[7]
1670–1699	87	225 per 1,000
1700–1729	206	381 per 1,000
1730–1759	142	534 per 1,000

7. The mortality rate is the ratio of the number of deaths per thousand people. It is used to compare the deaths in two or more populations of unequal size, such as those of Andover and Boston.

CHAPTER 3

RHYTHMS OF
COLONIAL LIFE:
THE STATISTICS
OF COLONIAL
MASSACHUSETTS
BAY

6. Population Density (persons per square mile), Concord and Andover.

Year	Concord	Andover
1705		16.0
1706	14.7	
1754	44.2[8]	
1755		36.2
1764		41.0
1765	48.0	
1776	62.7	50.0

8. In 1729, the town of Bedford was formed from lands originally in Concord. Then, in 1735, the town of Acton was created from lands that had been part of Concord. Finally, in 1754, the town of Lincoln was set off from Concord. These losses of lands were taken into account when computing population density for 1754, 1765, and 1776.

Source 7 data from James A. Henretta, *The Evolution of American Society, 1700–1815: An Interdisciplinary Approach*, 1st ed. (Lexington, Mass.: D. C. Heath, 1973), p. 15.

7. Average New England Farm Size.

1650s: 200–300 acres (3–6% cultivated)
1750s: under 100 acres (10–15% cultivated)

Sources 8 through 10 data from Gross, *The Minutemen and Their World*, pp. 210, 215, 214.

8. Average Landholding, Concord.

Year	Amount of Land
1663	259 acres
1749	56 acres

9. Crop Yields per Acre, Concord.

Year	Grain	Hay
1749	13.2 bushels	0.82 ton
1771	12.2 bushels	0.71 ton

10. Amount of Land Necessary to Pasture One Cow, Concord.

Year	Average
1749	1.4
1771	2.2

CHAPTER 3

RHYTHMS OF
COLONIAL LIFE:
THE STATISTICS
OF COLONIAL
MASSACHUSETTS
BAY

Source 11 data from Henretta, *The Evolution of American Society*, p. 19.

11. Average Period of Fallow,[9] New England Farms.

1650: field left fallow between 7 and 15 years
1770: field left fallow between 1 and 2 years

Source 12 data from Greven, *Four Generations: Population, Land, and Family in Colonial Andover, Massachusetts*, p. 216.

12. Abbot Family, Andover, Massachusetts.

1650: George Abbot was only adult male Abbot
1750: 25 adult male Abbots in Andover

Source 13 data from Henretta, *The Evolution of American Society*, pp. 29–30.

13. Division of Estates, Andover, Massachusetts.[10]

First generation: 95% of all estates divided among all male heirs
Second generation: 75% of all estates divided among all male heirs
Third generation: 58% of all estates divided among all male heirs
Fourth generation (came to maturity after 1750): under 50% of all estates
    divided among all male heirs

Source 14 from Gross, *The Minutemen and Their World*, p. 216.

14. Insolvent Estates, Concord.

Years	Total Estates	Number of Insolvent Estates
1740–1760	19	1
1760–1774	30	11

9. Fallow land is plowed and tilled but left unseeded during a growing season. Land is left fallow to replenish the soil's nutrients. Colonial farmers as a rule did not use fertilizer.
10. A widow inherited her late husband's estate only if the couple had no male heirs (sons). Otherwise, the land was passed down to the sons. Daughters received personal property (money, silverware, livestock, etc.).

Sources 15 through 17 data from Greven, *Four Generations: Population, Land, and Family in Colonial Andover, Massachusetts*, pp. 33, 23, 105, 183, 113. Source 17 data also from Gross, *The Minutemen and Their World*, p. 217.

15. Average Age at Marriage for Females, Andover, 1650–1724.

Year	Age
1650–1654	18.0
1660–1664	18.8
1670–1674	20.4
1680–1684	21.6
1690–1694	21.6
1700–1704	21.0
1710–1714	24.0
1720–1724	23.9

16. Average Births per Marriage, Andover, 1655–1764.

Year	Births
1655–1664	5.8
1665–1674	5.3
1675–1684	5.7
1685–1694	6.0
1695–1704	7.6
1705–1714	7.5
1715–1724	5.7
1725–1734	4.8
1735–1744	4.1
1745–1754	4.0
1755–1764	3.9

CHAPTER 3

RHYTHMS OF
COLONIAL LIFE:
THE STATISTICS
OF COLONIAL
MASSACHUSETTS
BAY

17. Percentage of Premarital Conceptions,[11] Andover and Concord.

Years	Andover	Concord
1655–1674	0.0	
1675–1699	7.0	
1770–1739	11.3	
1740–1749		19
1750–1759		26
1760–1774		41

Source 18 data from Gary B. Nash, "Urban Wealth and Poverty in Pre-Revolutionary America," *Journal of Interdisciplinary History*, 6 (Spring 1976), pp. 545–584.

18. Percentage of Group Migration[12] into Boston, 1747, 1759, and 1771.

Group	1747	1759	1771
Single men	3.0	8.5	23.4
Single women	4.0	16.8	20.0
Widows and widowers	7.9	8.9	4.4
Married couples	33.6	27.4	27.5
Children	51.5	38.4	24.7
	100.0%	100.0%	100.0%

Source 19 data from Gross, *The Minutemen and Their World*, p. 218.

19. Sex Ratio, Concord, 1765.

88 males to 100 females

11. *Premarital conceptions* refers to first-born children who were born less than nine months from the date of marriage.
12. *Migration* refers to internal migration, not immigration from Europe.

Sources 20 through 22 data from Nash, "Urban Wealth and Poverty in Pre-Revolutionary America," pp. 545–584.

20. Distribution of Wealth by Percentage[13] in Boston, 1687 and 1771.

Wealth Distribution	1687	1771
Wealth possessed by the richest 5% of the people	30.2	48.7
Wealth possessed by the next wealthiest 5% of the people	16.1	14.7
Wealth possessed by the next wealthiest 30% of the people	39.8	27.4
Wealth possessed by the next wealthiest 30% of the people	11.3	9.1
Wealth possessed by the poorest 30% of the people	2.6	0.1

21. Taxables[14] in Boston, 1728–1771.

Year	Population	Taxables
1728	12,650	c. 3,000
1733	15,100	c. 3,500
1735	16,000	3,637
1738	16,700	3,395
1740	16,800	3,043
1741	16,750	2,972
1745	16,250	2,660
1750	15,800	c. 2,400
1752	15,700	2,789
1756	15,650	c. 2,500
1771	15,500	2,588

22. Poor Relief in Boston, 1700–1775.

Years	Population	Average Annual Expenditure in Pounds	Expenditure in Pounds per 1,000 Population
1700–1710	7,500	173	23
1711–1720	9,830	181	18
1721–1730	11,840	273	23
1731–1740	15,850	498	31
1741–1750	16,240	806	50
1751–1760	15,660	1,204	77
1761–1770	15,520	1,909	123
1771–1775	15,500	2,478	156

13. See Questions to Consider for assistance in reading this source.
14. *Taxables* refers to the number of people who owned a sufficient amount of property (real estate and buildings) to be taxed.

CHAPTER 3

RHYTHMS OF
COLONIAL LIFE:
THE STATISTICS
OF COLONIAL
MASSACHUSETTS
BAY

 QUESTIONS TO CONSIDER

When using statistics, one must first look at each set individually. For each set, ask the following questions:

1. What does this set of statistics measure?
2. How does what is being measured change over time?
3. Why does that change take place? As noted, the answer to this question can be found in another set or sets. When you connect one set to another, statisticians say that you have made a "linkage."

A helpful way of examining the statistical sets is to think of three children born in Massachusetts Bay—one in 1650, a second in 1700, and the third in 1750. As you look at the statistical evidence, ask yourself how the lives of these three children (male or female) were different. What factors accounted for those differences?

Begin by examining Sources 1 through 3, which deal with population increase in Massachusetts Bay as a whole, in Andover, and in Concord. How did population growth change over time? How can Sources 4, 5, 15, and 16 help you answer the "why" question for population growth?

Because immigration to Massachusetts Bay from Europe declined drastically in the 1640s and did not resume significantly until the early 1700s, population increases in the period in between can be explained only by migration from other colonies (which was negligible) or by natural increase. How did natural increase change over time (Sources 4, 5, and 16)? How

would you explain this change? To answer that question, you will have to use your historical imagination as well as *all* the rest of the sources. For example, how might you explain the dramatic increase in child mortality, as seen in Sources 4 and 5? Look again at Sources 6 through 12 and Source 14, this time with that specific question in mind. As you now see, the same statistics can be used to answer different questions.

We can see that one result of population growth in Andover and Concord was a rise in population density. What were the *results* of that increase in population density? Begin by examining Sources 6 through 11. How did farming change over time? Why was this so (see earlier sources plus Source 12, on the Abbot family)? How did those changes affect the division of estates (Source 13) and the number of insolvent estates (Source 14), and why? Did economic changes have any effect on the female life cycle? Consider the following demographic changes: the average age at marriage for Andover females (Source 15), the number of births per marriage (Source 16), and the significant increase in premarital conceptions (Source 17).

At this point, it helps to pause and take stock of what you have learned. What was the relationship between population growth and farming? Between changes in farming and social conditions? Would you say that the lifestyle of Massachusetts Bay colonists was improving, declining, or stationary during the first century of the colony's history? How would you prove your answer?

As noted at the beginning of this chapter, one important factor that historians study is the ability of people to adapt to changes in their environment or circumstances. In your view, how were Massachusetts Bay colonists attempting to adapt to these changes? Would you say they were or were not successful?

Many of the people we have been examining chose to adapt by leaving their towns and migrating to the frontier to set up new communities where they could make fresh starts. Many others, however, adapted by migrating to Boston (Source 18). How could you prove this? How did migration to Boston change in character between 1747 and 1771? How did migration affect the towns from which these people migrated (see Source 19)? What were the likely results of that migration?

Our attention now should follow those migrants to Boston. Were these migrants able to improve their collective situation in that large seaport? How could you prove your answer to that question?

At this point, we are at Source 20, wealth distribution in Boston. Note that Boston was not a farming village like Andover and Concord. Read the set this way: the richest 5 percent of those living in Boston in 1687 owned 30.2 percent of the town's taxable wealth (essentially real estate and buildings), but by 1771 the richest 5 percent owned 48.7 percent of the town's taxable wealth; the poorest 30 percent of those living in Boston in 1687 owned 2.6 percent of the town's taxable wealth, but by 1771 the poorest 30 percent owned 0.1 percent of the town's taxable wealth. Read the chart the same way for the groups in between. As you examine the chart, note which groups were gaining in wealth and which groups were losing in wealth.

Sources 21 and 22 are different ways of looking at the same problem. How are those sources related to one another? How can you link them back to the chain you have made?

At this point, you should be able to answer these central questions:

1. What important trends regarding growth, change, and maturation affected the people of colonial Massachusetts Bay?
2. How were people likely to think and feel about those trends?
3. How might those trends have contributed to the decision of Massachusetts Bay colonists to revolt against Great Britain?

✂ EPILOGUE ✂

Many of the men who fought on the Patriot side in either Continental Line (the troops under the central government) or the Massachusetts Bay militia came from the towns, farms, and seaports of Massachusetts Bay. If asked why they would endure such hardships to fight against the mother

CHAPTER 3

RHYTHMS OF
COLONIAL LIFE:
THE STATISTICS
OF COLONIAL
MASSACHUSETTS
BAY

country, most probably would have said that they were fighting for liberty and independence—and undoubtedly they were. But we now realize that a number of other factors were present that may very well have provided strong reasons for these men to contest the British. Whether they fully understood these forces can never be known with certainty because very few left any written record that might help us comprehend their thoughts or behavior.

The American Revolution was a momentous event not just for Americans but ultimately for many other people as well. As Ralph Waldo Emerson wrote years later, it was a "shot heard 'round the world." The American Revolution was the first anticolonial rebellion that was successful on the first try, and as such it provided a model for others in Latin America and elsewhere. As a revolt against authority, the American Revolution made many European rulers tremble because if the ideas contained in the Declaration of Independence (especially that of the right of revolution against unjust rulers) ever became widespread, their own tenures might well be doomed. And, beginning with the French Revolution, this is precisely what happened; gradually, crowns began to topple all across the Continent. Indeed, many would have agreed with the Frenchman Turgot, who, writing of America in the 1780s, noted the following:

This people is the hope of the human race. It may become the model. It ought to show the world, by facts, that men can be free and yet peaceful, and

may dispense with the chains in which tyrants and knaves . . . have presumed to bind them. . . . The Americans should be an example of political, religious, commercial and industrial liberty. The asylum they offer to the oppressed of every nation, the avenue of escape they open, will compel governments to be just and enlightened.[15]

The Revolution obviously brought independence and in the long run became one of the significant events in world history. But did it alter or reverse the economic and social trends that, as we have seen, were affecting the men, women, and children of colonial New England? In 1818, the United States Congress passed an act providing pensions for impoverished veterans of the War of Independence and their widows. Congressmen believed that there were approximately 1,400 poor veterans and widows who were still alive. Yet an astounding 30,000 applied for pensions, 20,000 of whom were ultimately approved to receive these benefits. Clearly, the American Revolution, although an event that had worldwide significance, did not necessarily change the lives of all the men and women who participated in it. Or did it?

15. Richard Price, *Observations on the Importance of the American Revolution, and the Means of Making It a Benefit to the World* (London: printed for T. Cadell, 1785), pp. 102, 123.

CHAPTER 4

WHAT REALLY HAPPENED IN THE BOSTON MASSACRE? THE TRIAL OF CAPTAIN THOMAS PRESTON

❧ THE PROBLEM ❧

On the chilly evening of March 5, 1770, a small group of boys began taunting a British sentry (called a "Centinel" or "Sentinel") in front of the Boston Custom House. Pushed to the breaking point by this goading, the soldier struck one of his tormentors with his musket. Soon a crowd of fifty or sixty gathered around the frightened soldier, prompting him to call for help. The officer of the day, Captain Thomas Preston, and seven British soldiers hurried to the Custom House to protect the sentry.

Upon arriving at the Custom House, Captain Preston must have sensed how precarious his position was. The crowd had swelled to more than one hundred, some anxious for a fight, oth-

ers simply curiosity seekers, and still others called from their homes by the town's church bells, a traditional signal that a fire had broken out. Efforts by Preston and others to calm the crowd proved useless. And because the crowd had enveloped Preston and his men as it had the lone sentry, escape was nearly impossible.

What happened next is a subject of considerable controversy. One of the soldiers fired his musket into the crowd, and the others followed suit, one by one. The colonists scattered, leaving five dead[1] and six wounded,

1. Those killed were Crispus Attucks (a black seaman in his forties, who also went by the name of Michael Johnson), James Caldwell

CHAPTER 4

WHAT REALLY
HAPPENED IN
THE BOSTON
MASSACRE?
THE TRIAL OF
CAPTAIN
THOMAS
PRESTON

some of whom were probably innocent bystanders. Preston and his men quickly returned to their barracks, where they were placed under house arrest. They were later taken to jail and charged with murder.

Preston's trial began on October 24, 1770, delayed by the authorities in an attempt to cool the emotions of the townspeople. Soon after the March 5 event, however, a grand jury had taken sworn depositions from Preston, the soldiers, and more than ninety Bostonians. The depositions leaked out (in a pamphlet, probably published by anti-British extremists), helping to keep emotions at a fever pitch.

John Adams, Josiah Quincy, and Robert Auchmuty had agreed to defend Preston,[2] even though the first two were staunch Patriots. They believed that the captain was entitled to a fair trial and did their best to defend

him. After a difficult jury selection, the trial began, witnesses for the prosecution and the defense being called mostly from those who had given depositions to the grand jury. The trial lasted for four days, an unusually long trial for the times. The case went to the jury at 5.00 P.M. on October 29. Although it took the jury only three hours to reach a verdict, the decision was not announced until the following day.

In this chapter, you will be using portions of the evidence given at the murder trial of Captain Thomas Preston to reconstruct what actually happened on that March 5, 1770, evening in Boston, Massachusetts. Was Preston guilty as charged? Or was he innocent? Only by reconstructing the event that we call the Boston Massacre will you be able to answer these questions.

BACKGROUND

The town of Boston[3] had been uneasy throughout the first weeks of 1770. Tension had been building since the early 1760s because the town was in-

creasingly affected by the forces of migration, change, and maturation. The protests against the Stamp Act had been particularly bitter there, and men such as Samuel Adams were encouraging their fellow Bostonians to be even bolder in their remonstrances. In response, in 1768 the British government ordered two regiments of soldiers to Boston to restore order and enforce the laws of Parliament. "They

(a sailor), Patrick Carr (an immigrant from Ireland who worked as a leather-breeches maker), Samuel Gray (a rope-maker), and Samuel Maverick (a seventeen-year-old apprentice).
2. Adams, Quincy, and Auchmuty (pronounced Aŭk′mŭty) also were engaged to defend the soldiers, a practice that would not be allowed today because of the conflict of interest (defending more than one person charged with the same crime).
3. Although Boston was one of the largest urban centers in the colonies, the town was

not incorporated as a city. Several attempts were made, but residents opposed them, fearing they would lose the institution of the town meeting.

will not *find* a rebellion," quipped Benjamin Franklin of the soldiers, "they may indeed *make* one" (italics added).

Instead of bringing calm to Boston, the presence of soldiers only increased tensions. Incidents between Bostonians and redcoats were common on the streets, in taverns, and at the places of employment of British soldiers who sought part-time jobs to supplement their meager salaries. Known British sympathizers and informers were harassed, and Crown officials were openly insulted. Indeed, the town of Boston seemed to be a powder keg just waiting for a spark to set off an explosion.

On February 22, 1770, British sympathizer and informer Ebenezer Richardson tried to tear down an anti-British sign. He was followed to his house by an angry crowd that proceeded to taunt him and break his windows with stones. One of the stones struck Richardson's wife. Enraged, he grabbed a musket and fired almost blindly into the crowd. Eleven-year-old Christopher Seider[4] fell to the ground with eleven pellets of shot in his chest. The boy died eight hours later. The crowd, by now numbering about one thousand, dragged Richardson from his house and through the streets, finally delivering him to the Boston jail. Four days later, the town conducted a huge funeral for Christopher Seider, probably arranged and organized by Samuel Adams. Seider's casket was carried through the streets by children, and approximately two thousand mourners (one-seventh of Boston's total population) took part.

All through the next week Boston was an angry town. Gangs of men and boys roamed the streets at night looking for British soldiers foolish enough to venture out alone. Similarly, off-duty soldiers prowled the same streets looking for someone to challenge them. A fight broke out at a ropewalk between some soldiers who worked there part-time and some unemployed colonists.

With large portions of both the Boston citizenry and the British soldiers inflamed, an incident on March 5 touched off an ugly confrontation that took place in front of the Custom House, a symbol of British authority over the colonies. Both sides sought to use the event to support their respective causes. But Samuel Adams, a struggling attorney with a flair for politics and propaganda, clearly had the upper hand. The burial of the five "martyrs" was attended by almost every resident of Boston, and Adams used the event to push his demands for British troop withdrawal and to heap abuse on the mother country. Therefore, when the murder trial of Captain Thomas Preston finally opened in late October, emotions had hardly diminished.

Crowd disturbances had been an almost regular feature of life, in both England and America. Historian John Bohstedt has estimated that England was the scene of at least one thousand crowd disturbances and riots between 1790 and 1810.[5] Colonial American towns were no more placid; demon-

---

4. Christopher Seider is sometimes referred to as Christopher Snider.

5. John Bohstedt, *Riots and Community Politics in England and Wales, 1790–1810* (Cambridge, Mass.: Harvard University Press, 1983), p. 5.

CHAPTER 4

WHAT REALLY
HAPPENED IN
THE BOSTON
MASSACRE?
THE TRIAL OF
CAPTAIN
THOMAS
PRESTON

strations and riots were almost regular features of the colonists' lives. Destruction of property and burning of effigies were common in these disturbances. In August 1765 in Boston, for example, crowds protesting against the Stamp Act burned effigies and destroyed the homes of stamp distributor Andrew Oliver and Massachusetts Lieutenant Governor Thomas Hutchinson. Indeed, it was almost as if the entire community was willing to countenance demonstrations and riots as long as they were confined to parades, loud gatherings, and limited destruction of property. In almost no cases were there any deaths, and the authorities seldom fired on the crowds. Yet on March 5, 1770, both the crowd and the soldiers acted uncharacteristically. The result was the tragedy that colonists dubbed the "Boston Massacre." Why did the crowd and the soldiers behave as they did?

To repeat, your task is to reconstruct the so-called Boston Massacre so as to understand what really happened on that fateful evening. Spelling and punctuation in the evidence have been modernized only to clarify the meaning.

⟳ THE METHOD ⟳

Many students (and some historians) like to think that facts speak for themselves. This is especially tempting when analyzing a single incident like the Boston Massacre, many eyewitnesses of which testified at the trial. However, discovering what really happened, even when there are eyewitnesses, is never quite that easy. Witnesses may be confused at the time, they may see only part of the incident, or they may unconsciously "see" only what they expect to see. Obviously, witnesses also may have some reasons to lie. Thus the testimony of witnesses must be carefully scrutinized, for both what the witnesses *mean* to tell us and other relevant information as well. Therefore, historians approach such testimony with considerable skepticism and are concerned not only with the testimony itself but also with the possible motives of the witnesses.

Neither Preston nor the soldiers testified at the captain's trial because English legal custom prohibited defendants in criminal cases from testifying in their own behalf (the expectation was that they would perjure themselves). One week after the massacre, however, in a sworn deposition, Captain Preston gave his side of the story. Although the deposition was not introduced at the trial and therefore the jury was not aware of what Preston himself had said, we have reproduced a portion of Preston's deposition for you to examine. How does Preston's deposition agree or disagree with other eyewitnesses' accounts?

No transcript of Preston's trial survives, if indeed one was ever made.

Trial testimony comes from an anonymous person's summary of what each person said, the notes of Robert Treat Paine (one of the lawyers for the prosecution), and one witness's (Richard Palmes's) reconstruction of what his testimony and the cross-examination had been. Although historians would prefer to use the original trial transcript and would do so if one were available, the anonymous summary, Paine's notes, and one witness's recollections are acceptable substitutes because probably all three people were present in the courtroom (Paine and Palmes certainly were) and the accounts tend to corroborate one another.

Almost all the witnesses were at the scene, yet not all their testimony is of equal merit. First try to reconstruct the scene itself—the actual order in which the events occurred and where the various participants were standing. Whenever possible, look for corroborating testimony—two or more reliable witnesses who heard or saw the same things.

Be careful to use all the evidence. You should be able to develop some reasonable explanation for the conflicting testimony and those things that do not fit into your reconstruction very well.

Almost immediately you will discover that some important pieces of evidence are missing. For example, it would be useful to know the individual backgrounds and political views of the witnesses. Unfortunately, we know very little about the witnesses themselves, and we can reconstruct the political ideas of only about one-third of them. Therefore, you will have to rely on the testimonies given, deducing which witnesses were telling the truth, which were lying, and which were simply mistaken.

The fact that significant portions of the evidence are missing is not disastrous. Historians seldom have all the evidence they need when they attempt to tackle a historical problem. Instead, they must be able to do as much as they can with the evidence that is available, using it as completely and imaginatively as they can. They do so by asking questions of the available evidence. Where were the witnesses standing? Which one(s) seem more likely to be telling the truth? Which witnesses were probably lying? When dealing with the testimony of the witnesses, be sure to determine what is factual from what is a witness's opinion. A rough sketch of the scene has been provided. How can it help you?

Also included in the evidence is Paul Revere's famous engraving of the incident, probably plagiarized from a drawing by artist Henry Pelham. It is unlikely that either Pelham or Revere was an eyewitness to the Boston Massacre, yet Revere's engraving gained widespread distribution, and most people—in 1770 and today—tend to recall that engraving when they think of the Boston Massacre. Do not examine the engraving until you have read the trial account closely. Can Revere's engraving help you find out what really happened that night? How does the engraving "fit" the eyewitnesses' accounts? How do the engraving and the accounts differ? Why?

Keep the central question in mind: what really happened in the Boston Massacre? Throughout this exercise,

CHAPTER 4

WHAT REALLY
HAPPENED IN
THE BOSTON
MASSACRE?
THE TRIAL OF
CAPTAIN
THOMAS
PRESTON

you will be trying to determine whether or not an order to fire was actually given. If so, by whom? If not, how can you explain why shots were fired? As commanding officer, Thomas Preston was held responsible and charged with murder. You might want to consider the evidence available to you as either a prosecution or defense attorney. Which side had the stronger case?

❧ THE EVIDENCE ❧

1. Site of the Boston Massacre, Town House Area, 1770.

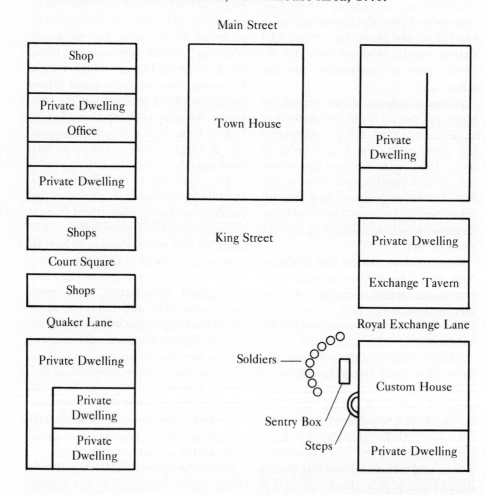

Source 2 from *Publications of The Colonial Society of Massachusetts*, Vol. VII
(Boston: The Colonial Society of Massachusetts, 1905), pp. 8–9.

2. Deposition of Captain Thomas Preston, March 12, 1770 (Excerpt).

The mob still increased and were outrageous, striking their clubs or bludgeons one against another, and calling out, come on you rascals, you bloody backs, you lobster scoundrels, fire if you dare, G-d damn you, fire and be damned, we know you dare not, and much more such language was used. At this time I was between the soldiers and the mob, parleying with, and endeavoring all in my power to persuade them to retire peaceably, but to no purpose. They advanced to the points of the bayonets, struck some of them and even the muzzles of the pieces, and seemed to be endeavoring to close with the soldiers. On which some well behaved persons asked me if the guns were charged. I replied yes. They then asked me if I intended to order the men to fire. I answered no, by no means, observing to them that I was advanced before the muzzles of the men's pieces, and must fall a sacrifice if they fired; that the soldiers were upon the half cock[6] and charged bayonets, and my giving the word fire under those circumstances would prove me to be no officer. While I was thus speaking, one of the soldiers having received a severe blow with a stick, stepped a little to one side and instantly fired. . . . On this a general attack was made on the men by a great number of heavy clubs and snowballs being thrown at them, by which all our lives were in imminent danger, some persons at the same time from behind calling out, damn your bloods—why don't you fire. Instantly three or four of the soldiers fired. . . . On my asking the soldiers why they fired without orders, they said they heard the word fire and supposed it came from me. This might be the case as many of the mob called out fire, fire, but I assured the men that I gave no such order; that my words were, don't fire, stop your firing. . . .[7]

6. The cock of a musket had to be fully drawn back (cocked) for the musket to fire. In half cock, the cock was drawn only halfway back so that priming powder could be placed in the pan. The musket, however, would not fire at half cock. This is the origin of "Don't go off half cocked." See Source 5.
7. Depositions also were taken from the soldiers, three of whom claimed, "We did our Captain's orders and if we don't obey his commands should have been confined and shot. . . ." As with Preston's deposition, the jury was not aware of that statement. In addition, ninety-six depositions were taken from townspeople.

CHAPTER 4

WHAT REALLY
HAPPENED IN
THE BOSTON
MASSACRE?
THE TRIAL OF
CAPTAIN
THOMAS
PRESTON

Source 3 from Hiller B. Zobel, ed., *The Legal Papers of John Adams*, Vol. III (Cambridge, Mass.: Belknap Press of Harvard University Press, 1965), pp. 46–98.

3. The Trial of Captain Thomas Preston (*Rex v. Preston*), October 24–29 (Excerpt).

Witnesses for the King (Prosecution)

Edward Gerrish (or Garrick)

I heard a noise about 8 o'clock and went down to Royal Exchange Lane. Saw some Persons with Sticks coming up Quaker Lane. I said [to the sentry] Capt. Goldsmith owed my fellow Apprentice. He said he was a Gentleman and would pay every body. I said there was none in the Regiment.[8] He asked for me. I went to him, was not ashamed of my face. . . . The Sentinel left his Post and Struck me. I cried. My fellow Apprentice and a young man came up to the Sentinel and called him Bloody back.[9] He called to the Main Guard. . . . There was not a dozen people when the Sentinel called the Guard.[10]

Thomas Marshall

The People kept gathering. I saw no uneasiness with the Centinel. A Party then came down from the Guard [House] I thought to relieve him. I heard one Gun. Thought it was to alarm the Barracks. A little space after another, and then several. I stood within 30 feet of the Centinel and must have seen any disturbance. . . . Between the firing the first and second Gun there was time enough for an Officer to step forward and to give the word Recover[11] if he was so minded.

Ebenezer Hinkley

Just after 9 o'clock heard the Cry of Fire. I saw the party come out of the Guard House. A Capt. cried out of the Window "fire upon 'em damn 'em." I followed 'em down before the Custom House door. Capt. Preston was out

---

8. By saying there was no gentleman in the entire regiment, Gerrish thereby insulted the sentry's superior officer, Captain Goldsmith.
9. British soldiers' coats were red. See also footnote 17.
10. Ironically, the person who had as much to do with bringing on the Boston Massacre as anyone, apprentice Edward Gerrish, was at home when the firing broke out.
11. To restore to the previous state.

and commanded 'em. They drew up and charged their Bayonets. Montgomery[12] pushed at the people advancing. In 2 or 3 minutes a Boy threw a small stick over hand and hit Montgomery on Breast. Then I heard the word fire in ¼ minute he fired. I saw some pieces of Snow as big as Egg thrown. 3 or 4 thrown at the same time of pushing on the other End of the file, before 1st gun fired. The body of People about a Rod[13] off. People said Damn 'em they durst[14] not fire don't be afraid. No threats . . . I was a Rod from Capt. Preston. Did not hear him give Order to fire. ½ minute from 1st Gun to 2d. same to 3d. The others quicker. I saw no people striking the Guns or Bayonets nor pelting 'em. I saw Preston between people and Soldiers. I did not see him when 1st firing.

Peter Cunningham

Upon the cry of fire and Bells ringing went into King Street, heard the Capt. say Turn out the Guard.[15] Saw the Centinel standing on the steps of the Custom house, pushing his Bayonet at the People who were about 30 or 40. Captain came and ordered the Men to prime and load.[16] He came before 'em about 4 or 5 minutes after and put up their Guns with his Arm. They then fired and were priming and loading again. I am pretty positive the Capt. bid 'em Prime and load. I stood about 4 feet off him. Heard no Order given to fire. The Person who gave Orders to Prime and load stood with his back to me, I did not see his face only when he put up their Guns. I stood about 10 or 11 feet from the Soldiers, the Captain about the midway between.

12. Montgomery, one of the soldiers, almost undoubtedly fired the first shot.
13. A rod equals 16.5 feet.
14. Dare.
15. To equip, dress, and outfit ready for duty.
16. Muskets were loaded with powder, wadding, a ball, and more wadding from the muzzle. Then the hammer (see Source 5) was drawn back halfway, and powder was poured into the small pan under the hammer. A small piece of flint was attached to the cock (see Source 5) so that, when the trigger was pulled, the cock would come down and the flint would make a spark that would ignite the gunpowder in the pan. The fire would then travel into the breech to ignite the powder there and fire the gun. If the powder in the pan exploded but did not ignite the powder in the breech, the result was a "flash in the pan" and a musket that did not fire.

CHAPTER 4

WHAT REALLY
HAPPENED IN
THE BOSTON
MASSACRE?
THE TRIAL OF
CAPTAIN
THOMAS
PRESTON

Alexander Cruikshanks

As the Clock struck 9 I saw two Boys abusing the Centinel. They said you Centinel, damned rascally Scoundrel Lobster[17] Son of a Bitch and desired him to turn out. He told them it was his ground and he would maintain it and would run any through who molested or attempted to drive him off. There was about a dozen standing at a little distance. They took no part. He called out Guard several times and 7 or 8 Soldiers with Swords Bayonets and one with a large Tongs[18] in his hand came. I saw the two Boys going to the Men who stood near the Centinel. They returned with a new Edition of fresh Oaths,[19] threw Snow Balls at him and he then called Guard several times as before.

William Wyatt

I heard the Bell, coming up Cornhill, saw People running several ways. The largest part went down to the North of the Townhouse. I went the South side, saw an officer leading out 8 or 10 Men. Somebody met the officer and said, Capt. Preston for Gods sake mind what you are about and take care of your Men. He went down to the Centinel, drew up his Men, bid them face about, Prime and load. I saw about 100 People in the Street huzzaing, crying fire, damn you fire. In about 10 minutes I heard the Officer say fire. The Soldiers took no notice. His back was to me. I heard the same voice say fire. The Soldiers did not fire. The Officer then stamped and said Damn your bloods fire be the consequences what it will. Immediately the first Gun was fired. I have no doubt the Officer was the same person the Man spoke to when coming down with the Guard. His back was to me when the last order was given. I was then about 5 or 6 yards off and within 2 yards at the first. He stood in the rear when the Guns were fired. Just before I heard a Stick, which I took to be upon a Gun. I did not see it. The Officer had to the best of my knowledge a cloth coloured Surtout[20] on. After the firing the Captain stepd forward before the Men and struck up their Guns. One was loading again and he damn'd 'em for firing and severely reprimanded 'em. I did not mean the Capt. had the Surtout but the Man who spoke to him when coming with the Guard.

17. The British soldiers' coats from the rear bore a slight resemblance to the back of a lobster.
18. A spike or prong (from the German *teng*).
19. More insults.
20. A certain type of overcoat.

John Cole

I saw the officer after the firing and spoke to the Soldiers and told 'em it was a Cowardly action to kill men at the end of their Bayonets. They were pushing at the People who seemed to be trying to come into the Street. The Captain came up and stamped and said Damn their bloods fire again and let 'em take the consequence. I was within four feet of him. He had no surtout but a red Coat with a Rose on his shoulder. The people were quarrelling at the head of Royal Exchange lane.[21] The Soldiers were pushing and striking with the Guns. I saw the People's Arms moving but no Sticks.

Theodore Bliss

At home. I heard the Bells for fire.[22] Went out. Came to the Town House. The People told me there was going to be a Rumpus[23] with the Soldiers. Went to the Custom house. Saw Capt. Preston there with the Soldiers. Asked him if they were loaded. He said yes. If with Ball. He said nothing. I saw the People throw Snow Balls at the Soldiers and saw a Stick about 3 feet long strike a Soldier upon the right. He sallied[24] and then fired. A little time a second. Then the other[s] fast after one another. One or two Snow balls hit the Soldier, the stick struck, before firing. I know not whether he sallied on account of the Stick or step'd back to make ready. I did not hear any Order given by the Capt. to fire. I stood so near him I think I must have heard him if he had given an order to fire before the first firing. I never knew Capt. Preston before. I can't say whether he had a Surtout on, he was dressed in red. I know him to be the Man I took to be the Officer. The Man that fired first stood next to the Exchange lane. I saw none of the People press upon the Soldiers before the first Gun fired. I did after. I aimed a blow at him myself but did not strike him. I am sure the Captain stood before the Men when the first Gun was fired. I had no apprehension[25] the Capt. did give order to fire when the first Gun was fired. I thought, after the first Gun, the Capt. did order the Men to fire but do not certainly know.

21. See Source 1 for the location of Royal Exchange Lane.
22. No town in colonial America had a municipal fire department. Whenever a fire broke out, the church bells would be rung and citizens would gather with buckets to put out the fire. In Boston, citizens were required to keep two buckets in their homes and to turn out when the bells were rung.
23. A noisy clamor; a disturbance.
24. To leap forward suddenly.
25. Doubt, as in "I had no doubt."

CHAPTER 4

WHAT REALLY
HAPPENED IN
THE BOSTON
MASSACRE?
THE TRIAL OF
CAPTAIN
THOMAS
PRESTON

I heard the word fire several times but know not whether it came from the Captain, the Soldiers or People. Two of the People struck at the Soldiers after the first Gun. I don't know if they hit 'em. There were about 100 people in the Street. The muzzles of the Guns were behind him. After the first Gun the Captain went quite to the left and I to the right.

Henry Knox

I saw the Captain coming down with his party. I took Preston by the Coat, told him for Gods sake take care of your Men for if they fire your life must be answerable. In some agitation he replied I am sensible of it. A Corporal was leading them. The Captain stopd with me and the Party proceeded to the Centinel the People crying stand by. The Soldiers with their Bayonets charged[26] pushing through the People in order to make way—make way damn your Bloods. The Captain then left me and went to the Party. I heard the Centinel say damn their bloods if they touch me I will fire. In about 3 minutes after this the party came up. I did not see any thing thrown at the Centinel. I stood at the foot of the Town house when the Guns were fired. I heard the People cry damn your bloods fire on. To the best of my recollection the Corporal had a Surtout on. I had none.

Benjamin Burdick

When I came into King Street about 9 o'Clock I saw the Soldiers round the Centinel. I asked one if he was loaded and he said yes. I asked him if he would fire, he said yes by the Eternal God and pushd his Bayonet at me. After the firing the Captain came before the soldiers and put up their Guns with his arm and said stop firing, dont fire no more or dont fire again. I heard the word fire and took it and am certain that it came from behind the Soldiers. I saw a man passing busily behind who I took to be an Officer. The firing was a little time after. I saw some persons fall. Before the firing I saw a stick thrown at the Soldiers. The word fire I took to be a word of Command. I had in my hand a highland broad Sword which I brought from home. Upon my coming out I was told it was a wrangle[27] between the Soldiers and people, upon that I went back and got my Sword. I never used to go out with a weapon. I had not my Sword drawn till after the Soldier

---

26. *Bayonets charged* was a position in the manual of arms (see Source 4) in which the musket, with bayonet fixed, was held outward and slightly upward. It would be exceedingly difficult to fire a musket accurately from this position because of the recoil upon firing.
27. A quarrel.

pushed his Bayonet at me. I should have cut his head off if he had stepd out of his Rank to attack me again. At the first firing the People were chiefly in Royal Exchange lane, there being about 50 in the Street. After the firing I went up to the Soldiers and told them I wanted to see some faces that I might swear to them another day. The Centinel in a melancholy tone said perhaps Sir you may.

Daniel Calef

I was present at the firing. I heard one of the Guns rattle.[28] I turned about and lookd and heard the officer who stood on the right in a line with the Soldiers give the word fire twice. I lookd the Officer in the face when he gave the word and saw his mouth. He had on a red Coat, yellow Jacket and Silver laced hat, no trimming on his Coat.[29] The Prisoner is the Officer I mean. I saw his face plain, the moon shone on it. I am sure of the man though I have not seen him since before yesterday when he came into Court with others. I knew him instantly. I ran upon the word fire being given about 30 feet off. The officer had no Surtout on.

Robert Goddard

The Soldiers came up to the Centinel and the Officer told them to place themselves and they formd a half moon. The Captain told the Boys to go home least[30] there should be murder done. They were throwing Snow balls. Did not go off but threw more Snow balls. The Capt. was behind the Soldiers. The Captain told them to fire. One Gun went off. A Sailor or Townsman struck the Captain. He thereupon said damn your bloods fire think I'll be treated in this manner. This Man that struck the Captain came from among the People who were seven feet off and were round on one wing. I saw no person speak to him. I was so near I should have seen it. After the Capt. said Damn your bloods fire they all fired one after another about 7 or 8 in all, and then the officer bid Prime and load again. He stood behind all the time. Mr. Lee went up to the officer and called the officer by name Capt. Preston. I saw him coming down from the Guard behind the Party. I went to Gaol[31] the next day being sworn for the Grand Jury to see

28. To make a short, sharp noise; in this context, to fire.
29. The 29th Regiment, to which Preston belonged, wore uniforms that exactly matched Calef's description.
30. Lest; for fear that.
31. Jail.

CHAPTER 4

WHAT REALLY
HAPPENED IN
THE BOSTON
MASSACRE?
THE TRIAL OF
CAPTAIN
THOMAS
PRESTON

the Captain. Then said pointing to him that's the person who gave the word to fire. He said if you swear that you will ruin me everlastingly. I was so near the officer when he gave the word fire that I could touch him. His face was towards me. He stood in the middle behind the Men. I looked him in the face. He then stood within the circle. When he told 'em to fire he turned about to me. I lookd him in the face.

Diman Morton

Between 9 and 10 I heard in my house the cry of fire but soon understood there was no fire but the Soldiers were fighting with the Inhabitants. I went to King Street. Saw the Centinel over the Gutter, his Bayonet breast high. He retired to the steps—loaded. The Boys dared him to fire. Soon after a Party came down, drew up. The Captain ordered them to load. I went across the Street. Heard one Gun and soon after the other Guns. The Captain when he ordered them to load stood in the front before the Soldiers so that the Guns reached beyond him. The Captain had a Surtout on. I knew him well. The Surtout was not red. I think cloth colour. I stood on the opposite corner of Exchange lane when I heard the Captain order the Men to load. I came by my knowledge of the Captain partly by seeing him lead the Fortification Guard.

Nathaniel Fosdick

Hearing the Bells ring, for fire I supposed I went out and came down by the Main Guard. Saw some Soldiers fixing their Bayonets on. Passed on. Went down to the Centinel. Perceived something pass me behind. Turned round and saw the Soldiers coming down. They bid me stand out of the way and damnd my blood. I told them I should not for any man. The party drew up round the Centinel, faced about and charged their Bayonets. I saw an Officer and said if there was any disturbance between the Soldiers and the People there was the Officer present who could settle it soon. I heard no Orders given to load, but in about two minutes after the Captain step'd across the Gutter. Spoke to two Men—I don't know who—then went back behind his men. Between the 4th and 5th men on the right. I then heard the word fire and the first Gun went off. In about 2 minutes the second and then several others. The Captain had a Sword in his hand. Was dressd in his Regimentals. Had no Surtout on. I saw nothing thrown nor any blows given at all. The first man on the right who fired after attempting to push the People slipped down and drop'd his Gun out of his hand. The Person who stepd in between the 4th and 5th Men I look upon it gave the orders to fire. His back was to me. I shall always think it was him. The Officer had a Wig on. I was in such a situation that I am as well satisfied there were no blows given as that the word fire was spoken.

Isaac Pierce

The Lieut. Governor asked Capt. Preston didn't you know you had no power to fire upon the Inhabitants or any number of People collected together unless you had a Civil Officer to give order. The Captain replied I was obliged to, to save my Sentry.

Joseph Belknap

The Lieut. Governor said to Preston Don't you know you can do nothing without a Magistrate. He answered I did it to save my Men.

Witnesses for the Prisoner (Preston)

Edward Hill

After all the firing Captain Preston put up the Gun of a Soldier who was going to fire and said fire no more you have done mischief enough.

Richard Palmes

Somebody there said there was a Rumpus in King Street. I went down. When I had got there I saw Capt. Preston at the head of 7 or 8 Soldiers at the Custom house drawn up, their Guns breast high and Bayonets fixed. Found Theodore Bliss talking with the Captain. I heard him say why don't you fire or words to that effect. The Captain answered I know not what and Bliss said God damn you why don't you fire. I was close behind Bliss. They were both in front. Then I step'd immediately between them and put my left hand in a familiar manner on the Captains right shoulder to speak to him. Mr. John Hickling then looking over my shoulder I said to Preston are your Soldiers Guns loaded. He answered with powder and ball. Sir I hope you dont intend the Soldiers shall fire on the Inhabitants. He said by no means. The instant he spoke I saw something resembling Snow or Ice strike the Grenadier[32] on the Captains right hand being the only one then

32. A soldier, a member of the British Grenadier Guards.

CHAPTER 4

WHAT REALLY
HAPPENED IN
THE BOSTON
MASSACRE?
THE TRIAL OF
CAPTAIN
THOMAS
PRESTON

at his right. He instantly stepd one foot back and fired the first Gun. I had then my hand on the Captains shoulder. After the Gun went off I heard the word fire. The Captain and I stood in front about half between the breech and muzzle of the Guns. I dont know who gave the word fire. I was then looking on the Soldier who fired. The word was given loud. The Captain might have given the word and I not distinguish it. After the word fire in about 6 or 7 seconds the Grenadier on the Captains left fired and then the others one after another. The Captain stood still till the second Gun was fired. After that I turned and saw the Grenadier who fired first attempting to prick me by the side of the Captain with his Bayonet. I had a large Stick in my hand. I struck over hand and hit him in his left arm. Knocked his hand from his Gun. The Bayonet struck the Snow and jarr'd the breech out of his hand. I had not before struck at any body. Upon that I turnd, thinking the other would do the same and struck at any body at first and hit Preston. In striking him my foot slip'd and my blow fell short and hit him, as he afterwards told me, on the arm. When I heard the word fire the Captains back was to the Soldiers and face to me. Before I recovered the Soldier who fired the first Gun was attempting again to push me through.[33] I tossed my Stick in his face. He fell back and I jump'd towards the land. He push'd at me there and fell down. I turn'd to catch his Gun. Another Soldier push'd at me and I ran off. Returnd soon and saw the dead carrying off and the party was gone. The Gun which went off first had scorched the nap of my Surtout at the elbow. I did not hear the Captain speak after he answered me. Was there but about ¾ of a minute in the whole. There was time enough between the first and second Gun for the Captain to have spoke to his Men. He stood leaning on the dagger in the scabbard.[34] At the time of the firing there was between 50 and 80 People at some distance not crowding upon the Soldiers and thin before them.

q. Did you situate yourself before Capt. Preston, in order that you might be out of danger, in case they fired?

a. I did not apprehend myself in any danger.

q. Did you hear Captain Preston give the word *Fire*?

a. I have told your Honors, that after the first gun was fired, I heard the word, *fire!* but who gave it, I know not.

q. Do you think it was possible Capt. Preston should give the word *fire*, and you not be certain he gave it?

a. I think it was.

33. To stab me.
34. A sheath or container for a knife or sword.

Matthew Murray

I heard no order given. I stood within two yards of the Captain. He was in front talking with a Person, I don't know who. I was looking at the Captain when the Gun was fired.

Andrew, a Negro servant to Oliver Wendell[35]

I jump'd back and heard a voice cry fire and immediately the first Gun fired. It seemed to come from the left wing from the second or third man on the left. The Officer was standing before me with his face towards the People. I am certain the voice came from beyond him. The Officer stood before the Soldiers at a sort of a corner. I turned round and saw a Grenadier who stood on the Captain's right swing his Gun and fire. I took it to be Killeroy. I look'd a little to the right and saw a Man drop. The Molatto[36] was killed by the first Gun by the Grenadier on the Captains Right. I was so frightened, after, I did not know where I was. . . .

Daniel Cornwall

Capt. Preston was within 2 yards of me—before the Men—nearest to the right—facing the Street. I was looking at him. Did not hear any order. He faced me. I think I should have heard him. I directly heard a voice say Damn you why do you fire. Don't fire. I thought it was the Captain's then. I now believe it. . . .

William Sawyer

The people kept huzzaing. Damn 'em. Daring 'em to fire. Threw Snow balls. I think they hit 'em. As soon as the Snow balls were thrown and a club a Soldier fired. I heard the Club strike upon the Gun and the corner man next the lane said fire and immediately fired. This was the first Gun. As soon as he had fired he said Damn you fire. I am so sure that I thought it was he that spoke. The next Gun fired and so they fired through pretty quick.

35. Andrew was Oliver Wendell's slave. Wendell appeared in court to testify as to Andrew's veracity.
36. Mulatto—a person of mixed Negro and Caucasian ancestry; in this case, Crispus Attucks.

CHAPTER 4

WHAT REALLY
HAPPENED IN
THE BOSTON
MASSACRE?
THE TRIAL OF
CAPTAIN
THOMAS
PRESTON

Jane Whitehouse

A Man came behind the Soldiers walked backwards and forward, encouraging them to fire. The Captain stood on the left about three yards. The man touched one of the Soldiers upon the back and said fire, by God I'll stand by you. He was dressed in dark colored clothes. . . . He did not look like an Officer. The man fired directly on the word and clap on the Shoulder. I am positive the man was not the Captain. . . . I am sure he gave no orders. . . . I saw one man take a chunk of wood from under his Coat throw it at a Soldier and knocked him. He fell on his face. His firelock[37] was out of his hand. . . . This was before any firing.

Newton Prince, a Negro, a member of the South Church

Heard the Bell ring. Ran out. Came to the Chapel. Was told there was no fire but something better, there was going to be a fight. Some had buckets and bags and some Clubs. I went to the west end of the Town House where [there] were a number of people. I saw some Soldiers coming out of the Guard house with their Guns and running down one after another to the Custom house. Some of the people said let's attack the Main Guard, or the Centinel who is gone to King street. Some said for Gods sake don't lets touch the main Guard. I went down. Saw the Soldiers planted by the Custom house two deep. The People were calling them Lobsters, daring 'em to fire saying damn you why don't you fire. I saw Capt. Preston out from behind the Soldiers. In the front at the right. He spoke to some people. The Capt. stood between the Soldiers and the Gutter about two yards from the Gutter. I saw two or three strike with sticks on the Guns. I was going off to the west of the Soldiers and heard the Guns fire and saw the dead carried off. Soon after the Guard Drums beat to arms.[38] The People whilst striking on the Guns cried fire, damn you fire. I have heard no Orders given to fire, only the people in general cried fire.

James Woodall

I saw one Soldier knocked down. His Gun fell from him. I saw a great many sticks and pieces of sticks and Ice thrown at the Soldiers. The Soldier who was knocked down took up his Gun and fired directly. Soon after the first

---

37. Musket.
38. A special drumbeat used as a signal to soldiers to arm themselves.

Gun I saw a Gentleman behind the Soldiers in velvet of blue or black plush[39] trimmed with gold. He put his hand toward their backs. Whether he touched them I know not and said by God I'll stand by you whilst I have a drop of blood and then said fire and two went off and the rest to 7 or 8. . . . The Captain, after, seemed shocked and looked upon the Soldiers. I am very certain he did not give the word fire.

Cross-Examination of Captain James Gifford

Q. Did you ever know an officer order men to fire with their bayonets charged?
A. No, Officers never give order to fire from charged bayonet. They would all have fired together, or most of them.

Thomas Handaside Peck

I was at home when the Guns were fired. I heard 'em distinct. I went up to the main guard and addressed myself to the Captain and said to him What have you done? He said, Sir it was none of my doings, the Soldiers fired of their own accord, I was in the Street and might have been shot. His character is good as a Gentleman and Soldier. I think it exceeds any of the Corps.

Lieutenant Governor Thomas Hutchinson

I was pressed by the people almost upon the Bayonets. The People cried the Governor. I called for the Officer. He came from between the Ranks. I did not know him by Moon light. I had heard no circumstances. I inquired with some emotion, How came you to fire without Orders from a Civil Magistrate? I am not certain of every word. I cannot recollect his answers. It now appears to me that it was imperfect. As if he had more to say. I remember by what he said or his actions I thought he was offended at being questioned. Before I could have his full answer the people cried to the Town house, to the Town house. A Gentleman by me (Mr. Belknap) was extremely civil. I thought he press'd my going into the Town house from a concern for my safety. I was carried by the crowd into the Council Chamber. After some hours Capt. Preston was brought there to be examined. I heard him deny giving Orders. I am very sure it did not occur to me that he had said

39. A fabric with a thick, deep pile.

CHAPTER 4

WHAT REALLY
HAPPENED IN
THE BOSTON
MASSACRE?
THE TRIAL OF
CAPTAIN
THOMAS
PRESTON

anything in answer to my question in the Street which would not consist with this denial. My intention in going up was to enquire into the affair. I have no particular intimacy with Capt. Preston. His general character is extremely good. Had I wanted an Officer to guard against a precipitate action I should have pitched upon him as soon as any in the Regiment.

The Evidence was ended.

Closing Arguments

For the Defense

[*No transcript of John Adams's closing arguments exists. From his notes, however, we can reconstruct his principal arguments. Adams began by citing cases that ruled that "it is always safer to err in acquitting rather than punishing" when there was doubt as to the defendant's guilt. He also argued that there was ample provocation and that Preston was merely defending himself and his men and was, in all, a victim of self-defense. Adams then reviewed the evidence, stating that there was no real proof that Preston had ordered his men to fire into the crowd. Adams also called into question the testimony of the prosecution witnesses, saying that Robert Goddard "is not capable of making observations" and that other witnesses were in error (he made much of the surtout). He called William Wyatt "diabolically malicious."*]

Conclusion of Prosecution's Summary to the Jury

Now Gentlemen the fact being once proved, it is the prisoner's part to justify or excuse it, for all killing is, *prima facie*,[40] Murder. They have attempted to prove, that the People were not only the aggressors, but attacked the Soldiers with so much Violence, that an immediate Danger of their own Lives, obliged them to fire upon the *Assailants*, as they are pleased to call them. Now this *violent Attack* turns out to be nothing more, than a few Snow-balls, thrown by a parcel of *Boys*; the most of them at a considerable distance, and as likely to hit the Inhabitants as the Soldiers (*all this is but* which is a common Case in the Streets of Boston at that Season of the Year, when a Number of People are collected in a Body), and one Stick, that struck Grenadier, but was not thrown with sufficient force to wound, or even sally him; whence then this Outrage, fury and abuse so much talk'd of? The Inhabitants collected, Many of them from the best of Motives, to make peace; and some out of mere Curiosity, and what was the Situation of Affairs when the Soldiers begun the fire? In addition to the

40. At first sight; on first appearance.

Testimony of many others, you may collect it from the Conduct of Mr. Palmes, a Witness on whom they principally build their Defence. Wou'd he place himself before a party of Soldiers, and risque his Life at the Muzzels of their Guns, when he thought them under a Necessity of firing to defend their Life? 'Tis absurd to suppose it; and it is impossible you should ever seriously believe, that their Situation could either justify or excuse their ... Conduct. I would contend, as much as any Man, for the tenderness and Benignity[41] of the Law; but, if upon such trifling and imaginary provocation. Men may o'er leap the Barriers of Society, and carry havock and Desolation among their defenceless Fellow Subjects; we had better resign an unmeaning title to protection in Society and range the Mountains uncontrol'd. Upon the whole Gentlemen the facts are with you, and I doubt not, you will find such a Verdict as the Laws of God, of Nature and your own Conscience will ever approve.

41. A kindly act.

CHAPTER 4

WHAT REALLY
HAPPENED IN
THE BOSTON
MASSACRE?
THE TRIAL OF
CAPTAIN
THOMAS
PRESTON

Sources 4 and 5 from Anthony D. Darling, *Red Coat and Brown Bess*, Historical Arms Series, No. 12 (Bloomfield, Ontario). Courtesy of Museum Restoration Service, © 1970, 1981.

4. The Position of "Bayonets Charged."

5. Detail of a Musket.

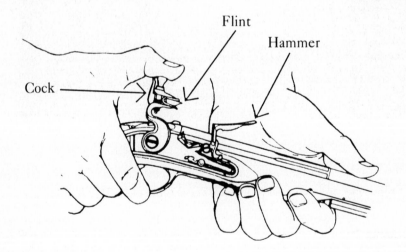

6. Paul Revere's Engraving of the Boston Massacre.

[Notice how he dubbed the Custom House "Butcher's Hall."]

☞ QUESTIONS TO CONSIDER ☜

In reconstructing the event, begin by imagining the positions of the various soldiers and witnesses. Where were the soldiers standing? Where was Captain Preston standing? Which witnesses were closest to Preston (that is, in the best positions to see and hear what happened)? Where were the other witnesses? Remember that the event took place around 9:00 P.M., when Boston was totally dark.

Next, read closely Preston's deposition and the trial testimony. What major points did Preston make in his own defense? Do you find those points plausible? More important, do the wit-

CHAPTER 4

WHAT REALLY
HAPPENED IN
THE BOSTON
MASSACRE?
THE TRIAL OF
CAPTAIN
THOMAS
PRESTON

nesses who were closest to Preston agree or disagree with his recounting, or with each other's? On what points? Be as specific as possible.

Now consider the other witnesses, those who were not so near. What did they hear? What did they see? To what degree do their testimonies agree or disagree, both with each other and with Preston and those closest to him?

Lawyers for both sides spent considerable time trying to ascertain what Captain Preston was wearing on that evening. Why did they consider this important? Based on the evidence, what do you think Preston was wearing on the evening of March 5, 1770? What conclusions could you draw from that?

The attorneys also were particularly interested in the crowd's behavior *prior to* the firing of the first musket. Why did they consider that important? How would you characterize the crowd's behavior? Are you suspicious of testimony that is at direct odds with your conclusion about this point?

Particularly damning to Preston was the testimony given by Thomas Marshall, Ebenezer Hinkley, William Wyatt, John Cole, Daniel Calef, Rob-

ert Goddard, Isaac Pierce, and Joseph Belknap. In what ways were these accounts damaging? Are there any significant flaws in their testimony?

Several witnesses (especially Jane Whitehouse) tell a quite different story. To what extent is her recounting of the event plausible? Is it corroborated by other witnesses?

We included Paul Revere's engraving, even though he probably was not an eyewitness, because by the time of Preston's trial, surely all the witnesses would have seen it and, more important, because later Americans have obtained their most lasting visual image of the event from that work. How does the engraving conform to what actually happened? How does it conflict with your determination of what actually took place? If there are major discrepancies, why do you think this is so? (Revere certainly knew a number of the eyewitnesses and could have ascertained the truth from them.)

After you have answered these questions and carefully weighed the eyewitnesses' evidence, answer the central question: what really happened in the Boston Massacre?

❧ EPILOGUE ❧

In the trial of Thomas Preston, the jury took only three hours to reach its verdict: not guilty. Some of the jurors were sympathetic to the British, and thus were determined to find Preston innocent no matter what evidence was

presented.[42] Also, the leaking of the grand jury depositions ultimately

42. This has led to the persistent claim, both at the time and later, that the jury was

helped Preston's defense, since defense attorneys knew in advance what the potentially most damaging witnesses would say in court. Finally, defense attorney John Adams's tactics (to create so much confusion in the minds of the jurors that they could not be certain what actually had taken place) were extremely effective. As it turned out, Preston had the advantage from the very beginning.

As for Thomas Preston himself, the British officer was quickly packed off to England, where he received a pension of £200 per year from the king "to compensate him for his suffering." He did not participate in the American Revolution and died in 1781. Of the eight soldiers (the sentry plus the seven men Preston brought to the Custom House), six were acquitted, and two were convicted of manslaughter and punished by being branded on the thumb. From there they disappeared into the mists of history.

On the road to the American Revolution, many events stand out as important or significant. The Boston Massacre is one such event. However, we must be careful in assessing its importance. After all, the colonists and the mother country did not finally resort to arms until five years after this dramatic event. By that time, most of those killed on King Street on March 5 had been forgotten.

Yet the Boston Massacre and other events have helped shape Americans'

attitudes as to what their own Revolution was all about. To most Americans, the British were greedy, heartless tyrants who terrorized a peaceful citizenry. More than one hundred years after the event, the Massachusetts legislature authorized a memorial honoring the "martyrs" to be placed on the site of the "massacre" (over the objections of the Massachusetts Historical Society). The Bostonians' convictions were bolstered by Irish immigrants whose ancestors had known British "tyranny" firsthand, and the Bostonians remained convinced that the American Revolution had been caused by Britain's selfishness and oppression. As we can see in the Boston Massacre, the road to the Revolution was considerably more complicated than that.

Today the site of the Boston Massacre is on a traffic island beside the Old State House (formerly called the Town House and seen in the background of Paul Revere's famous engraving) in the midst of Boston's financial district. With the exception of the State House (now a tasteful museum), the site is ringed by skyscrapers that house, among other institutions, the Bank of Boston and Fleet Bank of Massachusetts. Thousands of Bostonians and tourists stand on the Boston Massacre site every day, waiting for the traffic to abate.

Many years ago, John Adams said that "the foundation of American independence was laid" on the evening of March 5, 1770. Although he may have overstated the case, clearly many Americans have come to see the event as a crucial one in the coming of their

---

"packed." Today at least some of those jurors would have been excused by the court, since they had made up their minds before the trial began.

[95]

CHAPTER 4

WHAT REALLY
HAPPENED IN
THE BOSTON
MASSACRE?
THE TRIAL OF
CAPTAIN
THOMAS
PRESTON

Revolution against Great Britain. Now that you have examined the evidence, do you think the Boston Massacre of March 5, 1770, was a justifiable reason for rebellion against the mother country? Could the crowd action on that evening secretly have been directed by the Patriot elite, or was it a spontaneous demonstration of anti-British fury? Why was Paul Revere's engraving at such variance with what actually took place?

Few Americans have stopped to ponder what actually happened on that fateful evening. Like the American Revolution itself, the answer to that question may well be more complex than we think.

CHAPTER 5

THE FIRST AMERICAN PARTY SYSTEM: THE PHILADELPHIA CONGRESSIONAL ELECTION OF 1794

⤝ THE PROBLEM ⤞

For weeks prior to the federal congressional elections of 1794, the city of Philadelphia, the nation's temporary capital, was in a state of extreme political excitement. Not since the battle in Pennsylvania over the ratification of the United States Constitution had the city been the scene of such political tension and argument. The political factions that had appeared like small clouds over the first administration of President George Washington had grown immensely, and by 1794 in Philadelphia, they were on the verge of becoming distinct political parties.

Federalist Thomas Fitzsimons, a congressman since the beginning of the new government, was challenged by wealthy merchant and Democratic-Republican John Swanwick. Friends of the two contestants filled the air with vicious charges and countercharges in hopes of attracting voters to their respective candidates. Fitzsimons's supporters called Swanwick an "unstable, avaricious upstart who was unknown as a public figure until he 'herded with [the people's] enemies [the Democratic-Republicans], and became their tools.'" Swanwick's friends nicknamed Fitzsimons "Billy the Fidler" and portrayed him as a mindless sycophant of Secretary of the Treasury Alexander Hamilton. Meetings were held in various parts of the city to endorse one candidate or the other, and Philadelphia's newspapers were filled with charges and countercharges. Although many people were disturbed by these eruptions in what they consid-

CHAPTER 5

THE FIRST
AMERICAN
PARTY SYSTEM:
THE
PHILADELPHIA
CONGRESSIONAL
ELECTION OF
1794

ered a still fragile nation, unquestionably the growing factions had broken the political calm. Would political parties shatter the new republic or strengthen it? In Philadelphia in 1794, opinion was divided.

Challenger John Swanwick won a stunning victory over incumbent Thomas Fitzsimons, carrying seven of the city's twelve wards and collecting 56 percent of the votes cast. Federalism in Philadelphia had been dealt a severe blow.

In this chapter, you will be analyzing the evidence to determine why the lesser-known Swanwick won the election. What factors do you think were responsible for his victory? You will not be relying on just one or two types of evidence, as in previous chapters. Instead, you will be examining myriad pieces of evidence to answer that question.

∞ BACKGROUND ∞

The years between 1789 and 1801 were crucial ones for the young nation. To paraphrase a comment by Benjamin Franklin, Americans by 1789 (the first year of the Washington administration) had proved themselves remarkably adept at *destroying* governments: in the American Revolution, they had ended British rule of the thirteen colonies, and in the Constitutional Convention of 1787, they had ultimately destroyed the United States' first attempt at self-government, the Articles of Confederation. But they had yet to prove that they could *build* a central government that could protect their rights and preserve order and independence. For that reason, the period from 1789 to 1801 was important in terms of the survival of the new republic.

Many important questions confronted the nation's citizens during those difficult years. Could the new government create a financial system

that would pay off the public debt; encourage commerce, manufacturing, and investments; and establish a workable federal tax program? Was the central government strong enough to maintain order and protect citizens on the expanding frontier? Could the nation's leaders conceive a foreign policy that would maintain peace, protect international trade, and honor previous treaty commitments? To what extent should national interests overrule the interests and views of the several states?

A much larger question concerned republicanism itself. No republican experiment of this magnitude had ever been tried before, and a number of Americans expressed considerable fears that the experiment might not survive. Some people, such as Rufus King of New York,[1] wondered whether

1. Rufus King (1755–1827) was a native of Massachusetts who moved to New York in

the people possessed sufficient intelligence and virtue to be trusted to make wise decisions and choose proper leaders. Others, such as John Adams of Massachusetts, doubted that a government without titles, pomp, and ceremony would command the respect and allegiance of common men and women. Still others, such as William L. Smith of South Carolina,[2] feared that the new government was not strong enough to maintain order and enforce its will throughout the huge expanse of its domain. And finally, men such as Patrick Henry of Virginia and Samuel Adams of Massachusetts were afraid that the national government would abandon republican principles in favor of an aristocratic despotism. Hence, although most Americans were republican in sentiment, they strongly disagreed about the best ways to preserve republicanism and the dangers it faced. Some Americans openly distrusted "the people"—Alexander Hamilton of New York once called them a "headless beast." Others were wary of the government itself, even though George Washington had been chosen as its first president.

Much of the driving force of the new government came from Alexander Hamilton, the first secretary of the treasury. Hamilton used his closeness to Washington and his boldness and imagination to fashion policies that set the new nation on its initial course.

Hamilton's first task was to deal with the massive public debt. The defunct Confederation government had an unpaid debt going back to the War of Independence of more than $54 million. In addition, the various states had amassed an additional $21.5 million of their own debts. In a bold move in 1790, the secretary of the treasury proposed that the new federal government assume the debts of both its predecessor and the states, thus binding creditors to the central government. After considerable debate and some compromising, Congress passed Hamilton's plan virtually intact. At one stroke, the "credit rating" of the new government became among the best in the world.

To pay for this ambitious proposal, as well as to give the federal government operating capital, Hamilton recommended a system of taxation that rested primarily on taxes on foreign imports (tariffs) and an excise tax on selected products manufactured in the United States (tobacco products such as snuff and pipe tobacco, sugar products, and whiskey). The excise tax, however, raised considerable protest, especially in western Pennsylvania, where whiskey was an important commodity. In that area, farmers tried to prevent the collection of the tax, a protest that eventually grew into the Whiskey Rebellion of 1794. Prompted by Hamilton (see Source 4 in the Evidence section), President Washington called out fifteen thousand troops and

---

1786. He was a United States senator from 1789 to 1796 and minister to Great Britain from 1796 to 1803. He supported Alexander Hamilton's financial plans. In 1816, he was the Federalist candidate for president, losing in a landslide to James Monroe.
2. William L. Smith (1758–1812) was a Federalist congressman from South Carolina and later United States minister to Portugal. He was a staunch supporter of Alexander Hamilton.

CHAPTER 5

THE FIRST
AMERICAN
PARTY SYSTEM:
THE
PHILADELPHIA
CONGRESSIONAL
ELECTION OF
1794

dispatched them to western Pennsylvania, but the rebellion had fizzled out by the time the troops arrived.

Thus by 1794 (when he announced that he was leaving office), Hamilton had put his "system" in place. Revenue was coming into the government coffers; the debt was being serviced; and the semipublic Bank of the United States had been created in 1791 to handle government funds, make available investment capital, and expand the nation's currency in the form of bank notes. The collapse of the Whiskey Rebellion had proved that the new federal government could enforce its laws throughout the nation. Finally, by meddling in the business of Secretary of State Thomas Jefferson, Hamilton had been able to redirect American foreign policy to a more pro-British orientation. This was because Hamilton believed the new, weak republic needed British protection of its commerce, British revenue (in the form of tariffs), and a friendly neighbor to the north (Canada, a British possession). Using the popular Washington as a shield (as he later admitted), Hamilton became the most powerful figure in the new government and the one most responsible for making that new government work.

It is not surprising, however, that these issues and policies provoked sharp disagreements that eventually created two rival political factions: the Federalists (led by Hamilton) and the Democratic-Republicans (led by James Madison and Thomas Jefferson). Federalists generally advocated a strong central government, a broad interpretation of the Constitution, full payment of national and state debts,

the establishment of the Bank of the United States, encouragement of commerce, and a pro-British foreign policy. Democratic-Republicans generally favored a central government with limited powers, a strict interpretation of the Constitution, and a pro-French foreign policy; they opposed the bank.[3]

First appearing in Congress in the early 1790s, these two relatively stable factions gradually began taking their ideas to the voters, creating the seeds of what would become by the 1830s America's first political party system. Although unanticipated by the men who drafted the Constitution, this party system became a central feature of American political life, so much so that today it would probably be impossible to conduct the affairs of government or hold elections without it.

Yet Americans of the 1790s did not foresee this evolution. Many feared the rise of these political factions, believing that the new government was not strong enough to withstand their increasingly vicious battles. Most people did not consider themselves members of either political faction, and there were no highly organized campaigns or platforms to bind voters to one faction or another. It was considered bad form for candidates openly to seek office (one *stood* for office but never *ran* for office), and appeals to voters were usually made by friends or political allies of the candidates. Different property qualifications for

3. These are general tendencies. Some Federalists and Democratic-Republicans did not stand with their respective factions on all these issues.

voting in each state limited the size of the electorate, and in the 1790s, most states did not let the voters select presidential electors. All these factors impeded the rapid growth of the modern political party system.

Still, political battles during the 1790s grew more intense and ferocious. As Hamilton's economic plans and Federalism's pro-British foreign policy (the climax of which was the Jay Treaty of 1795) became clearer, Democratic-Republican opposition grew more bitter. Initially, the Federalists had the upper hand, perhaps because of that group's identification with President Washington. But gradually, the Democratic-Republicans gained strength, so much so that by 1800 their titular leader, Thomas Jefferson, was able to win the presidential election and put an end to Federalist control of the national government.

How can we explain the success of the Democratic-Republicans over their Federalist opponents? To answer this question, it is necessary to study in depth several key elections of the 1790s. Although many such contests are important for understanding the eventual Democratic-Republican victory in 1800, we have selected for further examination the 1794 race for the federal congressional seat from the city of Philadelphia. Because that seat had been held by a Federalist since the formation of the new government, this election was both an important test of strength of the rival Democratic-Republicans and representative of similar important contests being held in that same year in New York, Massachusetts, Maryland, and elsewhere. Because Philadelphia was the nation's capital in 1794, political party development was more advanced there than in other towns and cities of the young republic, thus offering us a harbinger of things to come nationwide.

❧ THE METHOD ❧

Observers of modern elections use a variety of methods to analyze political contests and determine why particular candidates won or lost. Some of the more important methods are:

1. *Study the candidates*—How a candidate projects himself or herself may be crucial to the election's outcome. Candidates have backgrounds, voting records, personalities, and idiosyncrasies voters can assess. Candidates travel extensively, are seen by voters either in person or on television, and have several opportunities to appeal to the electorate. Postelection polls have shown that many voters respond as much to the candidates as people (a strong leader, a warm person, a confident leader, and so forth) as they do to the candidates' ideas. For example, in 1952, voters responded positively to Dwight Eisenhower even though many were not sure of his positions on

CHAPTER 5

THE FIRST
AMERICAN
PARTY SYSTEM:
THE
PHILADELPHIA
CONGRESSIONAL
ELECTION OF
1794

a number of important issues. Similarly, in 1980, Ronald Reagan proved to be an extremely attractive presidential candidate, as much for his personal style as for his ideas and policies.

2. *Study the issues*—Elections often give citizens a chance to clarify their thinking on leading questions of the day. To make matters more complicated, certain groups (economic, ethnic, and interest groups, for example) respond to issues in different ways. The extent to which candidates can identify the issues that concern voters and can speak to these issues in an acceptable way can well mean the difference between victory and defeat. For example, in 1976, candidate Jimmy Carter was able to tap voters' post-Watergate disgust with corruption in the federal government and defeat incumbent Gerald Ford by speaking to that issue.

3. *Study the campaigns*—Success in devising and implementing a campaign strategy in modern times has been a crucial factor in the outcomes of elections. How does the candidate propose to deal with the issues? How are various interest groups to be lured under the party banner? How will money be raised, and how will it be spent? Will the candidate debate her or his opponent? Will the candidate make many personal appearances, or will she or he conduct a "front-porch" campaign? How will the candidate's family, friends, and political allies be used? Which areas (neighborhoods, regions, states, sections) will be targeted for special attention? To many political analysts, it is obvious that a number of superior candidates have been

unsuccessful because of poorly run campaigns. By the same token, many less-than-superior candidates have won elections because of effectively conducted campaigns.

4. *Study the voters*—Recently, the study of elections has become more sophisticated. Polling techniques have revealed that people similar in demographic variables such as age, sex, race, income, marital status, ethnic group, and religion tend to vote in similar fashions. For example, urban blacks voted overwhelmingly for Jimmy Carter in 1976.

These sophisticated polling techniques, also used for Gallup polls, Nielsen television ratings, and predicting responses to new consumer products, rest on important assumptions about human behavior. One assumption is that human responses tend to be strongly influenced (some say *determined*) by demographic variables; similar people tend to respond similarly to certain stimuli (such as candidates and campaigns). Another assumption is that these demographic patterns are constant and do not change rapidly. Finally, it is assumed that if we know how some of the people responded to certain stimuli, we can calculate how others possessing the same demographic variables will respond to those same stimuli.

Although there are many such patterns of voting behavior, they are easily observable. After the demographic variables that influence these patterns have been identified, a demographic sample of the population is created. Thus fifty white, male, middle-aged, married, Protestant, middle-income voters included in a sample might represent perhaps 100,000 people who possess these same variables. The fifty in the sample would then be polled to determine how they voted, and from this information we could infer how the 100,000 voted. Each population group in the sample would be polled in a similar fashion. By doing this, we can know with a fair amount of precision who voted for whom, thereby understanding which groups within the voting population were attracted to which candidate. Of course, the answer to why they were attracted still must be sought with one of the other methods: studying the candidates, studying the issues, and studying the campaigns.

These four approaches are methods for analyzing modern electoral contests. In fact, most political analysts use a combination of these approaches. But can these methods be used to analyze the 1794 congressional election in Philadelphia? Neither candidate openly sought the office, and neither made appearances in his own behalf. Although there certainly were important issues, neither political faction drew up a platform to explain to voters where its candidate stood on those issues. Neither political faction conducted an organized campaign. No polls were taken to determine voter concerns. At first glance, then, it appears that most if not all of these approaches to analyzing modern elections are useless in any attempt to analyze the 1794 Fitzsimons–Swanwick congressional contest.

These approaches, however, are not as useless as they initially appear. Philadelphia in 1794 was not a large

city—it contained only about 45,000 people—and many voters knew the candidates personally because both were prominent figures in the community. Their respective backgrounds were generally well known. Moreover, Fitzsimons, as the incumbent, had a voting record in Congress, and most voters would have known how Swanwick stood on the issues, either through Swanwick's friends or through the positions he took as a member of the Democratic Society. Furthermore, the Federalists and Democratic-Republicans had taken general positions on some of the important issues. In addition, we are able to establish with a fair amount of certainty which voters cast ballots for Fitzsimons and which supported Swanwick. Finally, it is possible to identify important trends and events occurring in Philadelphia. In sum, although we might not have all the evidence we would like to have (historians almost never do), intelligent uses of the evidence at our disposal enables us to analyze the 1794 election with all or most of the approaches used in analyzing modern political contests.

As you examine the various types of evidence, divide it into four groups, one group for each general approach used in analyzing elections (candidates, issues, campaign, voters). For example, there are two excerpts from Philadelphia newspapers (one Federalist and one Democratic-Republican) dealing with the excise tax and the Whiskey Rebellion in western Pennsylvania. In what group would you put this evidence? Follow this procedure for all the evidence, noting that occasionally a piece of evidence could fit

CHAPTER 5

THE FIRST
AMERICAN
PARTY SYSTEM:
THE
PHILADELPHIA
CONGRESSIONAL
ELECTION OF
1794

into more than one group. Such an arrangement of the evidence will give you four ways to analyze why the 1794 congressional election in Philadelphia turned out the way it did. Then, having examined and analyzed the evidence by groups, you will have to assess what principal factors explain Swanwick's upset victory.

∞ THE EVIDENCE ∞

1. The Candidates.

Thomas Fitzsimons (1741–1811) was born in Ireland and migrated to the colonies sometime before the Revolution, probably in 1765. He entered commerce as a clerk, worked his way up in his firm, and secured his position by marrying into the principal merchant's family. Fitzsimons served as a captain of the Pennsylvania militia during the Revolution, was a member of the Continental Congress in 1782 and 1783, and was elected to the Pennsylvania house of representatives in 1786 and 1787. He was a delegate to the Constitutional Convention in 1787, was a signer of the Constitution, and was elected to the federal House of Representatives in 1788. He was a member of the Federalist inner circle in Philadelphia and a firm supporter of Alexander Hamilton's policies. He was a strong supporter of the excise tax (see approach 2 in the "Questions to Consider" section), was an instrumental figure in the compromise that brought the national capital to Philadelphia for ten years (1790–1800), and helped draft the legislation chartering the Bank of the United States in 1791. He was one of the original founders and directors of the Bank of North America, the director and president of the Insurance Company of North America, and a key figure in dispensing federal patronage in Philadelphia. He was a Roman Catholic.

John Swanwick (1740–1798) was born in England. He and his family arrived in the colonies in the early 1770s. His father was a wagon master and minor British government official. During the Revolution, his father became a Tory and was exiled, but John Swanwick embraced the Patriot cause. In 1777, he was hired as a clerk in the merchant firm of Robert Morris. His fluency in both French and German made him invaluable to the firm, and he quickly rose to full partnership in 1783, the firm then being known as Willing, Morris & Swanwick. In 1794, he bought out Morris's share in the company. He was one of Philadelphia's leading export merchants, was a stockholder in the Bank of North America, and held a number of minor offices (under Morris) in the Confederation government. He supported the federal Constitution and Hamilton's early financial policies. Swanwick was elected to the state legislature in 1792. By 1793, he had drifted away from Federalism and had become a Democratic-Republican. In 1794, he joined the Pennsylvania Democratic Society[4] and was soon made an officer. Swanwick also was an officer in a society that aided immigrants. He opposed the excise tax but thought the Whiskey Rebellion (see approach 2 in the "Questions to Consider" section) in western Pennsylvania was the wrong method of protest. He wrote poetry and was never admitted to Philadelphia's social elite. He owned a two-hundred-acre country estate. He was a member of the Protestant Episcopal Church.

Source 2 from *Gazette of the United States* (a pro-Federalist Philadelphia newspaper), August 10, 1794.

2. A Pro-Federalist View of the Excise Tax and the Whiskey Rebellion.

. . . These Societies [the Democratic Societies], strange as it may seem, have been formed in a free elective government for the sake of *preserving liberty*. And what is the liberty they are striving to introduce? It is the liberty of reviling the rulers who are chosen by the people and the government under which they live. It is the liberty of bringing the laws into contempt and persuading people to resist them [a reference to the Whiskey Rebellion]. It is the liberty of condemning every system of Taxation because they have resolved that they will not be subject to laws—that they will not pay any taxes. To suppose that societies were formed with the purpose of opposing and with the hope of destroying government, might appear illiberal provided they had not already excited resistance to the laws and provided some of them had not publicly avowed their opinions that they *ought not to pay any taxes*. . . .

---

4. Democratic Societies were organizations composed principally of artisans and laborers and founded by Democratic-Republican leaders as political pressure groups against the Washington administration. Many Federalists believed that some Democratic Society members had been behind the Whiskey Rebellion. President Washington condemned the societies in 1794.

CHAPTER 5

THE FIRST
AMERICAN
PARTY SYSTEM:
THE
PHILADELPHIA
CONGRESSIONAL
ELECTION OF
1794

Source 3 from *General Advertiser* (a pro–Democratic-Republican Philadelphia newspaper), August 20, 1794.

3. A Pro–Democratic-Republican View of the Excise Tax and the Whiskey Rebellion.

As violent means appear the desire of high toned government men, it is to be hoped that those who derive the most benefit from our revenue laws will be the foremost to march against the Western insurgents. Let stock-holders, bank directors, speculators and revenue officers arrange themselves immediately under the banner of the treasury, and try their prowess in arms as they have done in calculation. The prompt recourse to hostilities which two certain great characters [Hamilton and Washington?] are so anxious for, will, no doubt, operate upon the knights of our country to appear in military array, and then the poor but industrious citizen will not be obliged to spill the blood of his fellow citizen before conciliatory means are tried. . . .

Source 4 from Harold C. Syrett, ed., *The Papers of Alexander Hamilton*, Vol. XVII (New York: Columbia University Press, 1972), pp. 15–19.

4. Alexander Hamilton to President Washington, August 2, 1794.

If the Judge shall pronounce that the case described in the second section of that Act exists, it will follow that a competent force of Militia should be called forth and employed to suppress the insurrection and support the Civil Authority in effectuating Obedience to the laws and punishment of Offenders.

It appears to me that the very existence of Government demands this course and that a duty of the highest nature urges the Chief Magistrate to pursue it.[5]

---

5. The Militia Act ("that Act") of 1792 required that a Supreme Court justice ("the Judge," in this case Justice James Wilson) certify that the disturbance could not be controlled by civil authorities before the president could order out the state militia. The "Chief Magistrate" referred to is President Washington. The majority of the U.S. Army was in the Northwest Territory, about to engage the Native Americans in the Battle of Fallen Timbers (August 20, 1794). Justice Wilson released his opinion that Washington could call out the troops on August 4, two days after Hamilton wrote to Washington.

Source 5 from Paul L. Ford, ed., *Writings of Thomas Jefferson*, Vol. VI (New York: G. P. Putnam's Sons, 1895), pp. 516–519.

5. Thomas Jefferson to James Madison, December 28, 1794.

And with respect to the transactions against the excise law [the Whiskey Rebellion], it appears to me that you are all swept away in the torrent of governmental opinion, or that we do not know what these transactions have been. We know of none which, according to the definitions of the law, have been anything more than riotous. . . . The excise law is an infernal one. . . . The information of our militia, returned from the Westward, is uniform, that the people there let them pass quietly; they were objects of their laughter, not of their fear.

6. Excise Tax Statistics.

There were 27 snuff and tobacco factories in Philadelphia, employing more than 400 workers. The city's sugar refineries produced 350,000 pounds of sugar in 1794. All these items came under the excise tax, which added approximately 25 percent to a product's cost.

7. Swanwick and the Democratic Society.

Swanwick was a member of the Democratic Society of Pennsylvania. The society passed a resolution opposing the excise tax. President Washington condemned the society in 1794, saying that he believed that it and other similar societies were responsible for the Whiskey Rebellion. The society endorsed Swanwick in 1794 and worked actively in his behalf.

CHAPTER 5

THE FIRST
AMERICAN
PARTY SYSTEM:
THE
PHILADELPHIA
CONGRESSIONAL
ELECTION OF
1794

Sources 8 and 9 from Billy G. Smith, *The "Lower Sort": Philadelphia's Laboring People, 1750–1800* (Ithaca, N.Y.: Cornell University Press, 1990), pp. 101, 110, 114, 116, 121, 232. For household budgets, Smith calculated the costs of food, rent, fuel, and clothing and then established how much of these items were consumed.

8. Cost of Living Index,[6] Philadelphia (Base Year 1762 = 100).

Year	Food	Rent	Firewood	Clothing	Household Budget
1788	99		74	139	123
1789	107	165[7]	76	82	115
1790	134		79	92	131
1791	130		97	92	131
1792	131		106	110	136
1793	143		111	119	144
1794	161		130	137	158

9. Index of Real Wages,[8] Philadelphia (Base Year 1762 = 100).

Year	Laborers	Sailors	Tailors	Shoemakers
1788	95	—	68	63
1789	77	—	69	63
1790	66	59	76	44
1791	74	59	63	48
1792	88	70	80	55
1793	81	84	57	143
1794	90	161	78	77

6. An index number is a statistical measure designed to show changes in a variable (such as wages or prices) over time. A base year is selected and given the value of 100. The index for subsequent years is then expressed as a percentage of the base year.
7. No other rent index is available for 1788 through 1794. The rent index in 1798, however, was 184.
8. Real wages are wages that are actually paid, adjusted for the cost of living. To find a person's real wage, one would take the index of that person's actual wage divided by the index of household budget and multiply that figure by 100. Real wages allow us to see whether a person's wages are exceeding or falling behind the cost of living.

10. Philadelphia Wards, 1794.

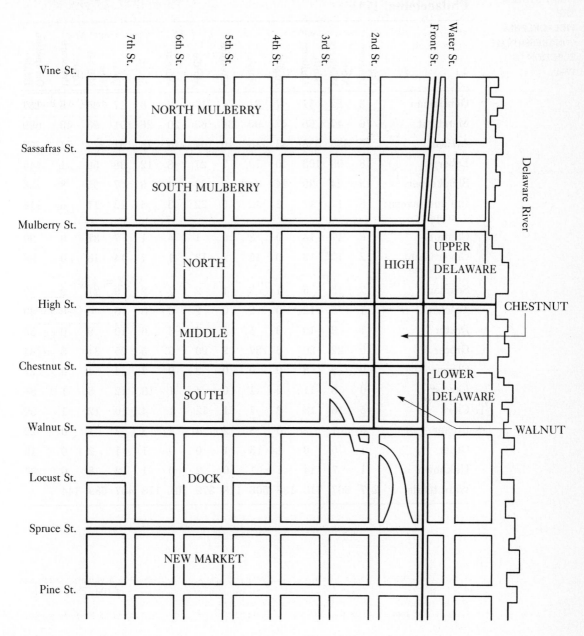

CHAPTER 5

THE FIRST
AMERICAN
PARTY SYSTEM:
THE
PHILADELPHIA
CONGRESSIONAL
ELECTION OF
1794

11. A Sample of Occupations by Ward (Males Only), Philadelphia, 1794.[9]

	Upper Delaware	North Mulberry	South Mulberry	High	North	Chestnut	Middle	Walnut	South	Dock	New Market	Lower Delaware	Occupation Totals
Gentleman	3	22	31	7	21	1	15	2	8	17	25	5	157
Merchant	76	47	65	47	90	38	63	20	26	101	83	43	699
Artisan	95	353	338	33	183	46	164	48	73	131	222	71	1,757
Laborer	18	93	103	10	70	7	27	8	12	38	56	1	443
Shopkeeper	13	24	39	24	44	9	23	4	6	7	35	8	236
Inn and tavern keeper	8	17	12	3	13	5	22	3	4	12	11	6	116
Captain	6	17	14	0	3	0	1	4	1	7	37	0	90
Government employee	2	12	13	0	16	2	13	1	7	14	18	0	98
Seaman	7	15	5	1	3	1	2	2	2	9	21	2	70
Teacher	1	5	12	0	6	0	2	0	3	5	6	0	40
Doctor	1	3	10	3	5	3	2	3	6	10	9	0	55
Grocer	10	22	20	3	37	2	20	0	5	25	34	6	184
Clergy	0	5	8	0	0	0	3	0	3	4	4	0	27
Lawyer	0	3	11	2	1	0	4	1	13	12	5	1	53
Clerk	5	16	18	3	7	1	12	1	4	10	12	1	90
Broker	0	1	2	0	3	2	4	4	3	2	1	0	22
Other	1	5	0	1	3	1	0	0	1	1	2	0	15
Unknown	1	7	14	1	1	0	2	0	1	2	8	0	37
Ward totals	247	667	715	138	506	118	379	101	178	407	589	144	

9. Sample taken from the Philadelphia city directory for 1794. Poor people were notoriously undercounted in city directories, as were nonpermanent residents, such as seamen.

Source 12 from James Hardie, *The Philadelphia Directory and Register*
(Philadelphia, 1794).

12. First-Person Account of the Yellow Fever.

Having mentioned this disorder to have occasioned great devastation in
the year 1793, a short account of it may be acceptable to several of our
readers. . . .

This disorder made its first appearance toward the latter end of July, in
a lodging house in North Water Street,[10] and for a few weeks seemed
entirely confined to that vicinity. Hence it was generally supposed to have
been imported and not generated in the city. This was the opinion of Doctors
Currie, Cathrall and many others. It was however combated by Dr. Benjamin Rush, who asserts that the contagion was generated from the stench
of a cargo of damaged coffee. . . .

But from whatever fountain we trace this poisoned stream, it has destroyed the lives of many thousands—and many of those of the most distinguished worth. . . . During the month of August the funerals amounted to
upwards of three hundred. The disease had then reached the central streets
of the city and began to spread on all sides with the greatest rapidity. In
September its malignance increased amazingly. Fear pervaded the stoutest
heart, flight became general, and terror was depicted on every countenance.
In this month 1,400 more were added to the list of mortality. The contagion
was still progressive and towards the end of the month 90 & 100 died daily.
Until the middle of October the mighty destroyer went on with increasing
havoc. From the 1st to the 17th upwards of 1,400 fell victims to the tremendous malady. From the 17th to the 30th the mortality gradually de-
creased. In the whole month, however, the dead amounted to upwards of
2,000—a dreadful number, if we consider that at this time near one half of
the inhabitants had fled. Before the disorder became so terrible, the appearance of Philadelphia must to a stranger have seemed very extraordinary. The garlic, which chewed as a preventative[,] could be smelled at
several yards distance, whilst other[s] hoped to avoid infection by a recourse
to smelling bottles, handkerchiefs dipped in vinegar, camphor bags, &c. . . .

During this melancholy period the city lost ten of her most valuable
physicians, and most of the others were sick at different times. The number
of deaths in all amounted to 4041.[11]

---

10. See Source 10. Working-class areas were particularly hard hit. On Fetter Lane (near
North Water Street), 50 percent of the residents died. See Smith, *The "Lower Sort,"* pp. 25–
26.
11. The population of Philadelphia (including its suburbs) was 42,444 in 1790.

CHAPTER 5

THE FIRST
AMERICAN
PARTY SYSTEM:
THE
PHILADELPHIA
CONGRESSIONAL
ELECTION OF
1794

Sources 13 and 14 from L. H. Butterfield, ed., *Letters of Benjamin Rush*,[12] Vol. II (Princeton, N.J.: Published for the American Philosophical Society, 1951), pp. 644–645, 657–658.

13. Benjamin Rush to Mrs. Rush, August 29, 1793, on the Yellow Fever.

Be assured that I will send for you if I should be seized with the disorder, for I conceive that it would be as much your duty not to desert me in that situation as it is now mine not to desert my patients. . . .

Its symptoms are very different in different people. Sometimes it comes on with a chilly fit and a high fever, but more frequently it steals on with headache, languor, and sick stomach. These symptoms are followed by stupor, delirium, vomiting, a dry skin, cool or cold hands and feet, a feeble slow pulse, sometimes below in frequency the pulse of health. The eyes are at first suffused with blood, they afterwards become yellow, and in most cases a yellowness covers the whole skin on the 3rd or 4th day. Few survive the 5th day, but more die on the 2 and 3rd days. In some cases the patients possess their reason to the last and discover much less weakness than in the last stage of common fevers. One of my patients stood up and shaved himself on the morning of the day he died. Livid spots on the body, a bleeding at the nose, from the gums, and from the bowels, and a vomiting of black matter in some instances close the scenes of life. The common remedies for malignant fevers have all failed. Bark, wine, and blisters make no impression upon it. Baths of hot vinegar applied by means of blankets, and the cold bath have relieved and saved some. . . .

This day I have given mercury, and I think with some advantage. . . .

12. Dr. Benjamin Rush (1745–1813) was a Pennsylvanian who was graduated from the College of New Jersey (Princeton, 1760) and studied medicine at the College of Philadelphia and the University of Edinburgh. Practicing medicine in Philadelphia, he was elected to the Continental Congress in 1776 and was a signer of the Declaration of Independence. He supported the ratification of the Constitution. By 1794, he had changed allegiances and was considered a Democratic-Republican. He participated in many reform movements, including the abolition of slavery, the end to capital punishment, temperance, an improved educational system, and prison reform. His protégé, Dr. Michael Leib, was extremely active in Democratic-Republican politics. Most physicians in Philadelphia in 1794 were Federalists. The majority fled the city when the fever broke out. Of the doctors who stayed, Rush was one of the most prominent.

14. Benjamin Rush to Mrs. Rush, September 10, 1793, on the Yellow Fever.

My dear Julia,

Hereafter my name should be Shadrach, Meshach, or Abednego, for I am sure the preservation of those men from death by fire was not a greater miracle than my preservation from the infection of the prevailing disorder. I have lived to see the close of another day, more awful than any I have yet seen. Forty persons it is said have been buried this day, and I have visited and prescribed for more than 100 patients. Mr. Willing is better, and Jno. Barclay is out of danger. Amidst my numerous calls to the wealthy and powerful, *I do not forget the poor,*[13] well remembering my dream in the autumn of 1780. . . .

15. Yellow Fever Committee.

Of the 18 people cited for contributions to the Citizens' Committee on the Fever, 9 were definitely Democratic-Republicans. Of the remaining 9, only one was an avowed Federalist.

Source 16 from J. H. Powell, *Bring Out Your Dead: The Great Plague of Yellow Fever in Philadelphia in 1793* (Philadelphia: Univ. of Pennsylvania Press, 1949), p. 123.

16. Federalist Comment on Rush.

Rush "is become the darling of the common people and his humane fortitude and exertions will render him deservedly dear."

13. Italics added.

17. Sampling of Deaths from Yellow Fever, Philadelphia, 1793 Epidemic.[14]

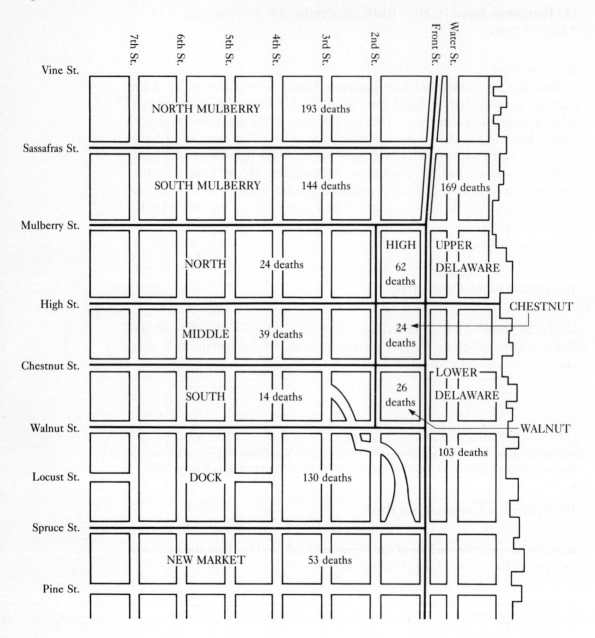

14. Sample taken from Philadelphia newspapers. After a time, officials simply stopped recording the names of those who died, except for prominent citizens. Therefore, although James Hardie reported that 4,041 people had died, one scholar has estimated the death toll at as high as 6,000, roughly one out of every seven Philadelphians.

18. Congressional Election, Philadelphia, 1794.[15]

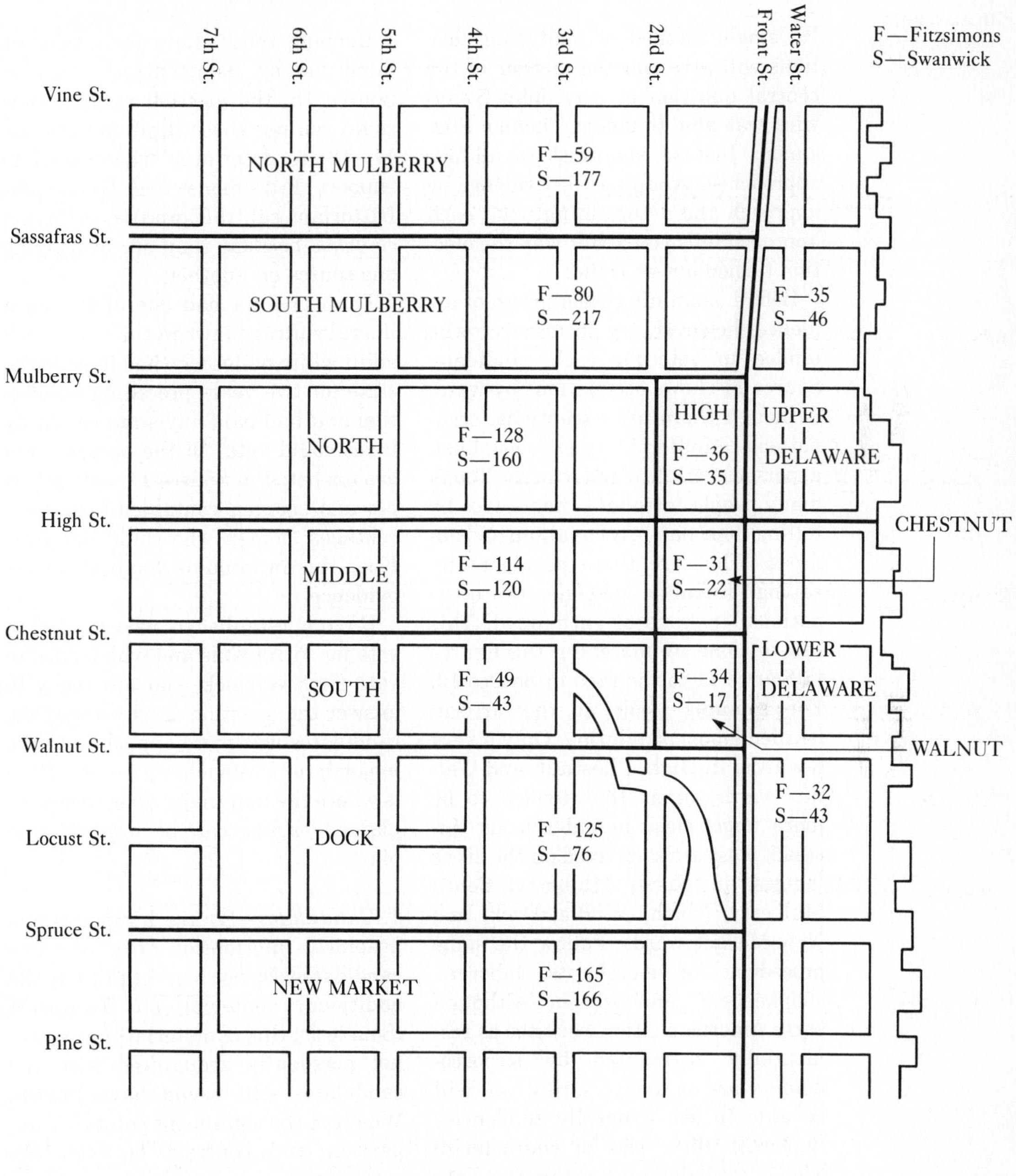

7th St.
6th St.
5th St.
4th St.
3rd St.
2nd St.
Front St.
Water St.
F—Fitzsimons
S—Swanwick
Vine St.
NORTH MULBERRY
F—59
S—177
Sassafras St.
SOUTH MULBERRY
F—80
S—217
F—35
S—46
Mulberry St.
NORTH
F—128
S—160
HIGH
F—36
S—35
UPPER
DELAWARE
High St.
CHESTNUT
MIDDLE
F—114
S—120
F—31
S—22
Chestnut St.
SOUTH
F—49
S—43
F—34
S—17
LOWER
DELAWARE
Walnut St.
WALNUT
Locust St.
DOCK
F—125
S—76
F—32
S—43
Spruce St.
NEW MARKET
F—165
S—166
Pine St.

15. Total votes: Swanwick, 1,122; Fitzsimons, 888.

CHAPTER 5

THE FIRST
AMERICAN
PARTY SYSTEM:
THE
PHILADELPHIA
CONGRESSIONAL
ELECTION OF
1794

✑ QUESTIONS TO CONSIDER ✑

No single method of analyzing elections will give you the answer to the central question of why John Swanwick was able to defeat Thomas Fitzsimons. Instead, you must use all four approaches, grouping the evidence by approach and determining what each approach tells you about why the election turned out as it did.

Before examining each group of evidence, however, try to discover who tended to vote for each candidate. Source 11 shows occupations by ward. Although there are exceptions, occupations can often be used to establish a person's wealth and status. Today many people introduce themselves by telling their name, occupation, and address. What are these people really saying? Examine carefully the occupational makeup of each ward. This can be done by matching the figures in Source 11 to the map in Source 10. For example, look at the artisan (skilled labor) population. Only a very few lived in High, Chestnut, and Walnut wards, areas that tended to be more upper-class neighborhoods. Instead, most artisans lived on the city's fringes, in North Mulberry, South Mulberry, North, Middle, Dock, and New Market wards. Follow the same procedure for merchants, laborers, shopkeepers, and so on. Although early American cities were not as residentially segregated by socioeconomic class as today's cities, you will be able to see generally tendencies that will allow you to characterize each of Philadelphia's wards in 1794.

Keeping those characterizations in mind (or by using notes), turn to Source 18, the election results. How could you use these three sources (10, 11, 18) to determine who tended to support Fitzsimons and Swanwick? Historians call this process *overlaying evidence* because they are overlaying one source on another.

Pennsylvania had one of the most liberal suffrage laws in the nation. All adult white males who had lived in the state for two years preceding an election *and* had paid any state or county taxes could vote. Of the occupational groups listed in Source 11, only laborers and seamen contained large percentages of men who could not vote. Keep this in mind as you overlay the evidence.

Having established who tended to vote for Fitzsimons and who tended to vote for Swanwick, you are ready to answer the question of why one of the candidates was more appealing to the majority of Philadelphia voters. Here is where the four major approaches explained earlier can be brought into play.

1. *Candidates*—Source 1 supplies biographical information about the two candidates. Do not neglect to study the additional material on Swanwick (Source 7); this is material that voters not personally acquainted with the candidates still would have known. What are the significant points of comparison and contrast between the candidates?

One significant point of difference is religion. Fitzsimons was a Roman Catholic, and Swanwick belonged to the Protestant Episcopal Church. Most of Philadelphia's voters were Protestant, the two largest denominations being Lutheran and Quaker. Very few voters belonged either to the Roman Catholic or to the Episcopal Church. Was religion a factor in this election? How can you prove that it was or was not?

One interesting point in Swanwick's biographical sketch is that, although wealthy, he was never admitted to Philadelphia's social elite circles, a fact that some of the voters probably knew. Do you think this was an important consideration in the voters' minds? How would you prove your point?

2. *Issues*—There were a number of issues in this election, and it was fairly clear how each faction stood on those issues. Two of the most important issues were the excise tax (Sources 2, 3, 6, 7) and the Whiskey Rebellion (Sources 4, 5).

As noted above, to raise money, Hamilton proposed, Congress passed, and President Washington signed a bill placing an excise tax on selected domestic manufactured products, an act that eventually touched off the Whiskey Rebellion of 1794. Indeed, there is some evidence that Hamilton actually anticipated such a reaction to the excise tax when he proposed it, convinced that the crushing of such an uprising would prove that the new government had the power to enforce its laws. When examining the impact of the excise tax and the Whiskey Re-

bellion on the election, use the sources to answer the following questions:

a. Which groups in Philadelphia did the excise tax affect most? How? Remember to think of people as both workers and consumers.
b. How did each candidate stand on the excise tax?
c. Which groups of Philadelphians would have been likely to favor their respective positions?
d. How did each faction stand on the Whiskey Rebellion? (See Sources 2 through 5.)
e. How did the candidates stand on this issue?
f. Which groups of Philadelphians would have been likely to favor their respective positions?
3. *Campaign*—Although there were a few mass meetings and some distribution of literature, there was no real campaign in the modern sense. In the absence of an organized campaign, how did voters make up their minds?
4. *Voters*—At the time of the election, other important trends in Philadelphia might have influenced voters. For example, review the evidence on the cost of living and on real wages compiled by Billy G. Smith (Sources 8 and 9). On cost of living, if the cost of living index in 1762 was 100, were the indices for food, firewood, and clothing rising or falling? Using household budget indices, how much more expensive was it to live in Philadelphia in 1794 than it was in 1788? (158 minus 123 equals 35, divided by 123 equals 28.5 percent)

On real wages, remember that real wages are actual wages adjusted for

CHAPTER 5

THE FIRST
AMERICAN
PARTY SYSTEM:
THE
PHILADELPHIA
CONGRESSIONAL
ELECTION OF
1794

the cost of living. As you can see, shoemakers (who were considered artisans) experienced a disastrous decline in their real wages (46.2 percent). What were the general tendencies for laborers and for tailors between 1792 and 1794? It is easily seen that sailors enjoyed an enormous increase in real wages. Keep in mind, however, that the war between Great Britain and France that broke out in 1793 made that occupation an extremely dangerous one. In sum, can the cost of living and real wage indices give you any clues to how these occupational groups might have voted?

The pieces of evidence that appear at first glance to have nothing to do with the Fitzsimons–Swanwick contest are Sources 12 through 17, on the 1793 yellow fever epidemic that virtually paralyzed the city. After all, the fever broke out more than a year prior to the election and was over by the end of October 1793. Most of those who had fled the city had returned and were in Philadelphia during the "campaign" and voting.

Yet a closer analysis of Sources 12 through 17 offers some fascinating insights, although you will have to use some historical imagination to relate them to the election. To begin with, James Hardie (Source 12) reported that the fever initially appeared "in a lodging house in North Water Street; and for a few weeks seemed entirely confined to that vicinity." Where was North Water Street (Source 10)? Who would have lived there (Sources 10 and 11)? So long as the fever was confined to that area, Hardie does not appear to have been overly concerned. What does that tell you? Hardie further reported that almost half the total population had fled the city. Which groups would have been most likely to flee (approximately 20,000 of Philadelphia's 45,000 fled)? Who could not leave? If businessmen closed their businesses when they fled, what was the situation of workers who could not afford to leave? What impact might this have had on the election a year later?

Although perhaps a bit too graphic, Dr. Benjamin Rush's August 29, 1793, letter to his wife (Source 13) is valuable because it establishes the fact that Rush, although he could have abandoned the sick, refused to do so and stayed in Philadelphia. This was an act of remarkable courage, for no one knew what caused yellow fever and people believed that it struck its victims almost completely at random. Consider, however, not what Rush *says* in Source 13 but rather *who he was* (a prominent Democratic-Republican). Refer again to footnote 12. Also examine Rush's letter of September 10, 1793 (Source 14), especially the last sentence. Do you think Rush might have been a factor in the Fitzsimons–Swanwick election? In what way?

Sources 15 and 16 attempt to tie the fever epidemic to party politics in Philadelphia. How might Philadelphia voters have reacted to the two parties (the Federalists and the Democratic-Republicans) after the fever? How might the voters have reacted to Dr. Rush (an avowed Democratic-Republican)?

Finally, examine Source 17 with some care. Where did the fever victims tend to reside? What types of people lived in those wards?

Now you are ready to answer the question of why the 1794 congres-sional election in Philadelphia turned out the way it did (Source 18). Make sure, however, that your opinion is solidly supported by evidence.

⬭ EPILOGUE ⬭

As the temporary national capital in 1794, Philadelphia was probably somewhat more advanced than the rest of the nation in the growth of political factions. However, by the presidential election of 1800, most of the country had become involved in the gradual process of party building. By that time, the Democratic-Republicans were the dominant political force, aided by more aggressive campaign techniques, their espousal of a limited national government (which most Americans preferred), their less elitist attitudes, and their ability to brand their Federalist opponents as aristocrats and pro-British monocrats.[16] Although Federalism retained considerable strength in New England and the Middle States, by 1800 it no longer was a serious challenge to the Democratic-Republicans on the national level.

For his part, John Swanwick never saw the ultimate triumph of Democratic-Republicanism because he died in the 1798 yellow fever epidemic in

16. A monocrat is a person who favors a monarchy. It was considered a disparaging term in the United States during the period.

Philadelphia. Fitzsimons never again sought political office, preferring to concentrate his energies on his already successful mercantile and banking career. Hamilton died in a duel with Aaron Burr in 1804. After he left the presidency in 1809, Jefferson retired to his estate, Monticello, to bask in the glories of being an aging founding father. He died in 1826 at the age of eighty-three.

By 1826, many of the concerns of the Federalist era had been resolved. The War of 1812 had further secured American independence, and the death of the Federalist faction had put an end to the notion of government by an entrenched (established) and favored elite. At the same time, however, new issues had arisen to test the durability of the republic and the collective wisdom of its people. After a brief political calm, party battles once again were growing fiercer, as the rise of Andrew Jackson threatened to split the brittle Jeffersonian coalition. Westward expansion was carrying Americans into territories owned by other nations, and few doubted that an almost inevitable conflict lay ahead. American

CHAPTER 5

THE FIRST
AMERICAN
PARTY SYSTEM:
THE
PHILADELPHIA
CONGRESSIONAL
ELECTION OF
1794

cities, such as Philadelphia, were growing in both population and socio-economic problems. The twin specters of slavery and sectional conflict were claiming increasing national attention. Whether the political system fashioned in the 1790s could address these crucial issues and trends and at the same time maintain its republican principles was a question that would soon have to be addressed.

CHAPTER 6

VESTED INTERESTS AND ECONOMIC DEMOCRACY: THE TANEY COURT AND THE *CHARLES RIVER BRIDGE* DECISION, 1837

❧ THE PROBLEM ❧

On July 6, 1835, John Marshall died in Philadelphia. For thirty-five years, he had been chief justice of the United States Supreme Court, and under his leadership the Court created an impressive body of constitutional doctrine. Eighty years old at the time of his death, Marshall had remained on the job in spite of the death of his wife four years earlier and a very serious operation to remove kidney stones.

The Supreme Court had begun to change long before Marshall died. The early Court appointees had leaned strongly toward the Federalist goals of a powerful central government and the protection of private property. By the time of John Quincy Adams's inauguration in 1825, however, six of

the seven Supreme Court justices[1] had been appointed by Presidents Thomas Jefferson, James Madison, and James Monroe. Furthermore, during Andrew Jackson's two terms of office, he appointed five new justices to fill vacancies on the Court created by resignations and deaths. In 1836, following Marshall's death, Jackson selected Roger Brooke Taney as chief justice. Under Taney, the Court's direction shifted toward states' rights and the relative egalitarianism of the Jeffer-

1. Prior to the twentieth century the number of justices on the Supreme Court varied. Today there are nine United States Supreme Court justices.

CHAPTER 6

VESTED
INTERESTS AND
ECONOMIC
DEMOCRACY:
THE TANEY
COURT AND THE
*CHARLES RIVER
BRIDGE*
DECISION, 1837

sonian Republicans and Jacksonian Democrats.

What kinds of reasoning formed the basis for the decisions of the so-called Jackson Court, especially in cases involving private property? More important, what role did the Supreme Court's decisions play in the broadening of opportunity, which was a major aspect of Jacksonian democracy?

 BACKGROUND

Most Americans greeted the election of Andrew Jackson to the presidency in 1828 with joy. Many believed that the "Hero of New Orleans" had been robbed of the presidency in 1824 and was finally achieving what had been rightfully his four years earlier. As one less than enthusiastic observer, Daniel Webster, noted at the time, "The shouting crowd really seems to think the country is rescued from some dreadful danger." Certainly, many voters saw Jackson as a new kind of president who would represent the interests of the "common man" rather than those of the elite.

Actually, as historian Edward Pessen has pointed out, there were some striking similarities between the Jacksonian Democrats and their political opponents. Yet, although historians no longer believe all the claims that contemporary supporters made for Jacksonian democracy, it is clear that Jackson's election was symbolic of a number of profound changes occurring in American political, economic, and social life. Universal white male suffrage and the popular election of the president, both of which were almost completely implemented by 1828, gave American politics at least the illusion of more democracy. Both the movement to revise state constitutions and the newly written constitutions of the western states signaled an egalitarian spirit that appalled and disgusted men such as John Randolph of Roanoke, Virginia, who exclaimed, "I love aristocracy; I hate democracy." But the majority of Americans were delighted with this democratic spirit. In addition, the rise of the second party system after the so-called Era of Good Feelings meant that each party aggressively courted voters and, in the process, gave them a sense of their own worth and power.

The spread of the democratic spirit, however, was the result of much more than a new political party. During this era, many Americans were troubled by the circumstances of people who were mentally ill, poor, enslaved, orphaned, uneducated, or imprisoned. A flood of reform movements followed, in which women—many of whom were newly aware of their own disadvantages in a male-dominated society—took the lead. By our standards today, some of the goals of these reform movements were questionable—for example, the establishment of poorhouses and a penitentiary system in which prisoners were kept in solitary confinement so that they could repent of their crimes. Nevertheless, many of these middle-class reformers sincerely believed that they were helping those less fortunate than themselves.

In addition to its political and social aspects, the concept of Jacksonian democracy also had economic ramifications. Just as most Jacksonians believed that politics had been dominated by a few large interest groups and juntos,[2] so they believed that the benefits of American economic progress were being enjoyed disproportionately by rich and powerful men with close connections to politicians who protected their interests. This was unfair, Jacksonians thought, to farmers, businessmen, merchants, and bankers without such connections. It was no secret, for example, that the powerful Bank of the United States regularly paid several congressmen and senators to protect the bank's position and further its policies.

Jacksonians saw the extension of the vote to all free white males as a way to democratize American politics by breaking the power of the interest groups and juntos. In the same vein, they believed that unfettered economic competition was preferable to an economic system in which the financial and political establishment received most of the benefits of the nation's economic growth. In other words, although Jacksonian Democrats did not believe that all men were equal in their potential for financial gain, they did believe that all men should have *equal opportunity* to share

in the country's economic progress. Free competition, without government favoritism and other unfair advantages, would prove which men were best.

Most Jacksonians were sharply critical of the Bank of the United States, primarily because that institution had an enormous advantage over other banks by virtue of its being chartered by the federal government and the sole repository for government funds. President Jackson himself had never trusted the bank, which he called a "Hydra-headed monster," and late in his first term, he vetoed a bill that would have extended the bank's charter for twenty more years.

After Jackson's re-election in 1832, he was determined to destroy the Bank of the United States. Although the bank was permitted to remain in business for four more years under the term of its original charter, the president ordered that government income no longer be deposited in the bank but in a number of smaller state banks, nicknamed "pet banks." At the same time, bills the government owed would continue to be paid from the old account in the Bank of the United States. Soon that account was exhausted, the link between the government and the Bank of the United States was broken, and the bank was destroyed. To his supporters, Jackson's victory made him even more a man of the people. Although we now know that this period of American history was considerably less democratic than the Jacksonians claimed, it is important to understand that most Americans believed that political, economic, and social life was becoming more

---

2. A junto is a secret political group formed to advance its members' power and interests.

CHAPTER 6

VESTED
INTERESTS AND
ECONOMIC
DEMOCRACY:
THE TANEY
COURT AND THE
*CHARLES RIVER
BRIDGE*
DECISION, 1837

democratic and that the United States was moving toward becoming a kind of utopia that all the world would admire.

Free competition and equality of opportunity in economic life would not benefit only businessmen, Jacksonians reasoned. Unfettered competition would benefit all consumers, who would be able to purchase the best goods and services at the lowest prices. Unfair advantages, such as political connections and the absence of competition, threatened the general public with inferior goods and services and with artificially high prices. Emboldened by their victory over the Bank of the United States, many Jacksonians sought to overcome all obstacles to free competition.

The United States Supreme Court, headed by John Marshall and dominated by justices with Federalist beliefs, had long seemed to many Americans another obstacle to democracy, or at least to equality of opportunity. In a series of very important cases, the Marshall Court had upheld the constitutionality of the Bank of the United States and made decisions that protected wealthy investors and advanced the rights of private property. In *Dartmouth College v. Woodward* (1819), for example, the Court had ruled that the state of New Hampshire could not amend the college's charter, which was a binding contract between the state and a private corporation.

But the president has the power to fill vacancies on the Supreme Court, with the consent of the Senate, and by the end of his second term, Jackson had appointed five justices to the seven-man Court. When the formida-

ble Marshall died, Jackson named Maryland Democrat Roger B. Taney (pronounced "Taw-nee") as the new chief justice. Taney had helped Jackson carry out his policy to destroy the Bank of the United States, and Jacksonian Democrats applauded his appointment as head of the highest court in the land.

The first major test of the new Supreme Court came with the *Charles River Bridge v. Warren Bridge* case in 1837. The Charles River Bridge Company had made enormous profits from its state-chartered toll bridge; each share of stock purchased in 1805 for $444 was worth more than $2,000 only nine years later. But in 1828, the Massachusetts legislature had granted another charter to the Warren Bridge Company, and the Charles River Bridge Company sued to prevent the completion of the new bridge. Representing the proprietors of the Charles River Bridge Company, Daniel Webster argued that its charter gave the company exclusive rights to build a bridge over the river and that protection of the company's investment was the major issue. Why, Webster asked, would men be willing to invest in an enterprise if they could not be guaranteed a sufficient profit? How could economic progress take place without continuing private investment?

The case first reached the United States Supreme Court on appeal in 1831, but a deadlocked court and then several deaths and retirements delayed the final decision until 1837. By that time, Taney was chief justice and a majority of the justices had been appointed by Jackson. After rehearing the case, Taney delivered the majority opinion.

In this problem, you will discover what the Supreme Court's decision was in the case, analyze the reasoning the Court used to reach its decision, and, most importantly, evaluate the impact of this decision on Americans.

∽ THE METHOD ∾

Decisions of the United States Supreme Court affect most people's lives, either directly or indirectly. Because of this, it is important to understand the carefully worded explanation of the reasoning behind each decision. Legal opinions are like building blocks—each section answers a specific question about one aspect of the case and must be read and understood thoroughly.

Whenever possible, courts in the United States rely on *precedents,* and the Supreme Court is no exception. Precedents are similar cases that the courts have already decided and that, taken together, form a body of constitutional doctrine or a kind of direction for the courts to follow. Infrequently, the Supreme Court may decide that some previous decisions were wrong and overturn them. The desegregation decision in *Brown v. the Board of Education of Topeka* (1954) overturned the precedents based on the "separate but equal" decision in *Plessy v. Ferguson* (1896). But usually, as in the *Charles River Bridge* case, the Supreme Court cites precedents that explain those aspects of the case that have already been settled and then goes on to answer questions that have not been decided in previous cases.

CHAPTER 6

VESTED
INTERESTS AND
ECONOMIC
DEMOCRACY:
THE TANEY
COURT AND THE
*CHARLES RIVER
BRIDGE*
DECISION, 1837

☙ THE EVIDENCE ❧

Source 1 from 11 Peters 420 (1837).

1. *The Proprietors of the Charles River Bridge v. The Proprietors of the Warren Bridge*, 1837.

[*The opinion was written by Chief Justice Roger B. Taney, and the plaintiffs to whom he refers were the proprietors of the Charles River Bridge Company.*]

The questions involved in this case are of the gravest character, and the court have[3] given to them the most anxious and deliberate consideration. The value of the right claimed by the plaintiffs is large in amount; and many persons may no doubt be seriously affected in their pecuniary interests by any decision which the court may pronounce; and the questions which have been raised as to the power of the several states, in relation to the corporations they have chartered, are pregnant with important consequences; not only to the individuals who are concerned in the corporate franchises, but to the communities in which they exist. The court are fully sensible that it is their duty, in exercising the high powers conferred on them by the constitution of the United States, to deal with these great and exclusive interests with the utmost caution; guarding, as far as they have the power to do so, the rights of property; and at the same time carefully abstaining from any encroachment on the rights reserved to the States.

[*At this point, Taney summarized the history of the issues in the* Charles River Bridge *case: the ferry monopoly granted in 1650 to Harvard College, which Harvard gave up when the bridge was chartered; the forty-year charter given to the company that built the Charles River Bridge in 1785; the requirement that the company pay a fixed amount of money to Harvard; the 1792 extension of the bridge company's charter to seventy years; and the fact that the company had fulfilled all the legislature's requirements.*]

In 1828, the legislature of Massachusetts incorporated a company by the name of "The Proprietors of the Warren Bridge," for the purpose of erecting another bridge over Charles River. This bridge is only sixteen rods,[4] at its commencement on the Charlestown side, from the commencement of the bridge of the plaintiffs; and they are about fifty rods apart at their termi-

3. Taney is following nineteenth-century grammatical usage in which the word *court* was treated as a plural noun.
4. A rod is 5.5 yards. The new bridge was only 88 yards away from the original bridge on one side of the river and about 250 yards away on the other side.

nation on the Boston side. The travellers who pass over either bridge proceed from Charlestown square, which receives the travel of many great public roads leading from the country; and the passengers and travellers who go to and from Boston, used to pass over the Charles River Bridge, from and through this square, before the erection of the Warren Bridge.

[*When the Warren Bridge charter was granted, the Charles River Bridge Company had unsuccessfully attempted to stop construction of the new bridge. After the new bridge was completed, the Charles River Bridge Company sued, claiming that it had been granted an exclusive contract to build a bridge over the river and that Massachusetts had thus broken its contract with the company. In a close decision, the Massachusetts court declared in 1829 that the contract between the state and the Charles River Bridge Company had not been impaired or violated by the legislative charter to the Warren Bridge Company. By the time the case came before the United States Supreme Court, the Warren Bridge had collected enough toll money to pay for its construction and had become a free bridge. As Chief Justice Taney pointed out, however, the original issue—whether or not Massachusetts had violated its contract with the Charles River Bridge Company—had not been settled.*]

A good deal of evidence has been offered to show the nature and extent of the ferry right granted to the college, and also to show the rights claimed by the proprietors of the [Charles River] bridge at different times by virtue of their charter, and the opinions entertained by committees of the legislature and others upon that subject. But as these circumstances do not affect the judgment of this court, it is unnecessary to recapitulate them.

The plaintiffs . . . insist mainly upon two grounds: 1. That by virtue of the grant of 1650, Harvard College was entitled, in perpetuity, to the right of keeping a ferry between Charlestown and Boston; that this right was exclusive; and that the legislature had not the power to establish another ferry on the same line of travel, because it would infringe the rights of the college; and that these rights, upon the erection of the bridge in the place of the ferry, under the charter of 1785, were transferred to, and became vested in "the proprietors of the Charles River Bridge;" and that under and by virtue of this transfer of the ferry right, the rights of the bridge company were as exclusive in that line of travel as the rights of the ferry. 2. That independently of the ferry right the acts of the legislature of Massachusetts of 1785, and 1792, by their true construction, necessarily implied that the legislature would not authorize another bridge, and especially a free one, by the side of this, and placed in the same line of travel whereby the franchise granted to the "Proprietors of the Charles River Bridge" should be rendered of no value; and the plaintiffs . . . contend that the grant of the ferry to the college, and of the charter to the proprietors of the bridge, are both contracts on the part of the State; and that the law authorizing

CHAPTER 6

VESTED
INTERESTS AND
ECONOMIC
DEMOCRACY:
THE TANEY
COURT AND THE
*CHARLES RIVER
BRIDGE*
DECISION, 1837

the erection of the Warren Bridge, in 1828, impairs the obligation of one or both of these contracts.

[*After citing two previous court cases, Taney pointed out that state legislatures can take away previously vested rights without violating the United States Constitution as long as the new laws are not ex post facto—that is, laws that punish someone for an act that was not illegal when it was committed. Therefore, Taney concluded, the company could not argue that it was unconstitutional for the legislature to have deprived the company of its vested right of property.*]

. . . Whether they claim under the ferry right, or the charter to the bridge, they must show that the title which they claim was acquired by contract, and that the terms of that contract have been violated by the charter to the Warren Bridge. In other words, they must show that the State had entered into a contract with them, or those under whom the claim, not to establish a free bridge at the place where the Warren Bridge is erected. Such, and such only, are the principles upon which the plaintiffs . . . can claim relief in this case.

[*The Court agreed that both the ferry right granted to Harvard and the charter given to the bridge company were contracts. They further agreed that the ferry right had established a monopoly.*]

. . . [S]till, [the Charles River Bridge Company] cannot enlarge the privileges granted to the bridge, unless it can be shown that the rights of Harvard College in this ferry have, by assignment, or in some other way, been transferred to the proprietors of the Charles River Bridge, and still remain in existence, vested in them, to the same extent with that in which they were held and enjoyed by the college before the bridge was built.

It has been strongly pressed upon the court, by the plaintiffs . . . that these rights are still existing, and are now held by the proprietors of the bridge. That this franchise still exists, there must be somebody possessed of the authority to use it, and to keep the ferry. Who could now lawfully set up a ferry where the old one was kept? The bridge was built in the same place, and its abutments occupied the landings of the ferry. The transportation of passengers in boats, from landing to landing, was no longer possible; and the ferry was as effectually destroyed, as if a convulsion of nature had made there a passage of dry land. The ferry then, of necessity, ceased to exist as soon as the bridge was erected; and when the ferry itself was destroyed, how can rights, which were incident to it, be supposed to survive? . . . It is clear that the incident must follow the fate of the principal, and the privilege connected with property cannot survive the destruction of the property; and if the ferry right in Harvard College was exclusive, and had been assigned to the proprietors of the bridge, the privilege of exclusion could not remain in the hands of their assignees, if those assignees destroyed the ferry.

[*Next Taney considered the question of whether the exclusive rights of the ferry monopoly had been transferred to the Charles River Bridge Company. He concluded that because Harvard College had been paid, the monopoly had gone out of existence. He also argued that the existence of the ferry monopoly granted to the college in 1650 could not have influenced the terms of the bridge charter granted to a private company 135 years later.*]

. . . Increased population longer experienced in legislation, the different character of the corporation which owned the ferry from that which owned the bridge, might well have induced a change in the policy of the State in this respect; and as the franchise of the ferry, and that of the bridge, are different in their nature, and were each established by separate grants, which have no words to connect the privileges of the one with the privileges of the other; there is no rule of legal interpretation, which would authorize the court to associate these grants together, and to infer that any privilege was intended to be given to the bridge company, merely because it had been conferred on the ferry. The charter to the bridge is a written instrument which must speak for itself, and be interpreted by its own terms.

[*At this point, Taney noted that the bridge company charters were public, or legislative, grants to private companies. American law usually followed English common law, he wrote, and the tendency of English common law was to restrain monopolies. To illustrate, Taney cited four cases that the Supreme Court had already decided. In each case, he emphasized, the Court's opinion had been that the public charters or franchises gave only specific and limited rights to companies. No* implicit *rights were contained in any of these charters.*]

Adopting the rule of construction above stated as the settled one, we proceed to apply it to the charter of 1785, to the proprietors of the Charles River Bridge. This act of incorporation is in the usual form, and the privileges such as are commonly given to corporations of that kind. It confers on them the ordinary faculties of a corporation, for the purpose of building the bridge; and establishes certain rates of toll, which the company are authorized to take. This is the whole grant. There is no exclusive privilege given to them over the waters of Charles River, above or below their bridge. No right to erect another bridge themselves, nor to prevent other persons from erecting one. No engagement from the State that another shall not be erected; and no undertaking to sanction competition, nor to make improvements that may diminish the amount of its income. Upon all these

CHAPTER 6

VESTED
INTERESTS AND
ECONOMIC
DEMOCRACY:
THE TANEY
COURT AND THE
*CHARLES RIVER
BRIDGE*
DECISION, 1837

subjects the charter is silent; and nothing is said in it about a line of travel, so much insisted on in the argument, in which they are to have exclusive privileges. No words are used, from which an intention to grant any of these rights can be inferred. If the plaintiff is entitled to them, it must be implied, simply, from the nature of the grant; and cannot be inferred from the words by which the grant is made.

[*The Warren Bridge, Taney wrote, did not block access to the Charles River Bridge, nor had the Charles River Bridge Company been prevented from charging tolls. It was simply that since the Warren River Bridge had become a free bridge, most people no longer used the Charles River Bridge. To prove their case, the Charles River Bridge Company would have to show that its own charter had granted the company monopoly rights.*]

The inquiry then is, Does the charter contain such a contract on the part of the State? Is there any such stipulation to be found in that instrument? It must be admitted on all hands that there is none,—no words that even relate to another bridge, or to the diminution of their tolls, or to the line of travel. . . . The whole community are interested in this inquiry and they have a right to require that the power of promoting their comfort and convenience, and of advancing the public prosperity, by providing safe, convenient, and cheap ways for the transportation of produce and the purposes of travel, shall not be construed to have been surrendered or diminished by the State, unless it shall appear by plain words that it was intended to be done. . . .

[*Taney then turned his attention to the extension of the Charles River Bridge charter in 1792.*]

. . . Can the legislature be presumed to have taken upon themselves an implied obligation, contrary to its own acts and declarations contained in the same law? It would be difficult to find a case justifying such an implication, even between individuals; still less will it be found where sovereign rights are concerned, and where the interests of a whole community would be deeply affected by such an implication. . . .

Indeed, the practice and usage of almost every State in the Union, old enough to have commenced the work of internal improvement, is opposed to the doctrine contended for on the part of the plaintiffs. . . . Turnpike roads have been made in succession on the same line of travel; the later ones interfering materially with the profits of the first. These corporations have, in some instances, been utterly ruined by the introduction of new and better modes of transportation and travelling. In some cases, railroads have rendered the turnpike roads on the same line of travel so entirely

useless, that the franchise of the turnpike corporation is not worth preserving. Yet in none of these cases have the corporations supposed that
their privileges were invaded, or any contract violated on the part of the
State. Amid the multitude of cases which have occurred, and have been
daily occurring for the last forty or fifty years, this is the first instance in
which an implied contract has been contended for, and this court called
upon to infer it from an ordinary act of incorporation, containing nothing
more than the usual stipulation and provisions to be found in every such
law. The absence of any such controversy, when there must have been so
many occasions to give rise to it, proves that neither States, nor individuals,
nor corporations, ever imagined that such a contract could be implied from
such charters. It shows that the men who voted for these laws, never
imagined that they were forming such a contract; and if we maintain that
they have made it, we must create it by a legal fiction, in opposition to the
truth of the fact, and the obvious intention of the party. We cannot deal
thus with the rights reserved to the States, and by legal intendments and
more technical reasoning, take away from them any portion of that power
over their own internal police and improvement, which is so necessary to
their well being and prosperity.

And what would be the fruits of this doctrine of implied contracts on the
part of the States, and of property in a line of travel by a corporation, if it
should now be sanctioned by this court? To what results would it lead us?
If it is to be found in the charter to this bridge, the same process of reasoning
must discover it in the various acts which have been passed, within the
last forty years, for turnpike companies. And what is to be the extent of
the privileges of exclusion on the different sides of the road? The counsel
who have so ably argued this case, have not attempted to define it by any
certain boundaries. How far must the new improvement be distant from
the old one? How near may you approach without invading the rights in
the privileged line? If this court should establish the principles now contended for, what is to become of the numerous railroads established on the
same line of travel with turnpike companies; and which have rendered the
franchise of the turnpike corporations of no value? Let it once be understood
that such charters carry with them these implied contracts, and give this
unknown and undefined property in a line of travelling, and you will soon
find the old turnpike corporations awakening from their sleep, and calling
upon this court to put down the improvements which have taken their
place. The millions of property which have been invested in railroads and
canals, upon lines of travel which have been before occupied by turnpike
corporations, will be put in jeopardy. We shall be thrown back to the
improvements of the last century and obliged to stand still, until the claims

CHAPTER 6

VESTED
INTERESTS AND
ECONOMIC
DEMOCRACY:
THE TANEY
COURT AND THE
*CHARLES RIVER
BRIDGE*
DECISION, 1837

of the old turnpike corporations shall be satisfied, and they shall consent to permit these States to avail themselves of the lights of modern science, and to partake of the benefit of those improvements which are now adding to the wealth and prosperity, and the convenience and comfort of every other part of the civilized world. Nor is this all. This court will find itself compelled to fix, by some arbitrary rule, the width of this new kind of property in a line of travel; for if such a right of property exists, we have no lights to guide us in marking out its extent, unless, indeed, we resort to the old feudal grants, and to the exclusive rights of ferries, by prescription, between towns; and are prepared to decide that when a turnpike road from one town to another had been made, no railroad or canal, between these two points, could afterwards be established. This court are not prepared to sanction principles which must lead to such results. . . .

The judgment of the supreme judicial court of the commonwealth of Massachusetts, dismissing the plaintiffs' bill, must, therefore, be affirmed. . . .

☙ QUESTIONS TO CONSIDER ❧

In the first paragraph of the Court's decision, Chief Justice Taney explains the significance of the case. Why was this case so important? What was the effect of the construction of the Warren Bridge on the Charles River Bridge Company?

Why did the Charles River Bridge Company sue? What were the two major grounds, or arguments, of their suit?

What were the precedents on the question of whether a legislature could take away rights it had granted previously? What did Taney argue that the Charles River Bridge Company must prove if the Court were to decide in its favor? What was the Court's reasoning and decision on this question?

What had been the general tendency of English common law with regard to monopolies? How had that influenced the American cases that Taney cited as precedents? How did he describe the charter granted to the Charles River Bridge Company in 1785?

Did the Court believe that there was an unstated, or implicit, monopoly granted in the Charles River Bridge charter? Why or why not? According to Taney, what would be the effect of such implicit monopolies? In your opinion, would the consequences that Taney forecast actually have happened? Or did he exaggerate? If so, why?

What did the Court finally decide in this case? Now you are ready to answer the central question of this exercise: what part did this decision play in the broadening of opportunity that was a major aspect of Jacksonian democracy?

⊗ **EPILOGUE** ⊗

Legal scholars consider *Charles River Bridge v. Warren Bridge* a landmark in American constitutional history. In a way, the Court went on record as saying that economic progress comes through competition and not through the protection of individual interest groups or monopolies. Yet because the decision was essentially a product of its times, the needs and ideas of future generations would necessarily alter the precedent set by the *Charles River Bridge* case. Both monopolies and oligopolies (control by a few) would increase at the end of the nineteenth century, only to encounter new antitrust laws and prosecution under Progressive era presidents Theodore Roosevelt, William Howard Taft, and Woodrow Wilson.

In our own times, the question of the proper relationship between government and private business still has not been settled. Many Americans insist on government protection of some industries, utilities, and banks, but others argue for deregulation because they believe it will bring about more competition and thus benefit consumers.

Roger B. Taney served as chief justice of the Supreme Court long after the man who had appointed him died. Taney's association with the *Dred Scott* case in 1857 made him extremely unpopular with many Americans. Northerners and many westerners were shocked by Taney's comments in this controversial case, which involved a slave's right to sue for his freedom in federal court. Essentially, Taney said that slaves were property and that property could be taken anywhere in the country. This ruling destroyed the Missouri Compromise, the Compromise of 1850, and the concept of "popular sovereignty," which allowed the citizens of a state to decide whether or not slavery would be legal in that state. At the time of his death in 1864, Taney was one of the most hated men in the country.

CHAPTER

AWAY FROM HOME: THE WORKING GIRLS OF LOWELL

◎ THE PROBLEM ◎

Just before the War of 1812, the successful New England merchant Francis Cabot Lowell toured Great Britain. Among other things, Lowell was very interested in the English textile industry. The invention of the power loom enabled spinning and weaving operations to be combined within one factory, but the factory system had spawned mill towns with overcrowded slums, horrible living conditions, and high death rates. The potential profits the new technology offered were great, yet Lowell knew that Americans already feared the Old World evils that seemed to accompany the factory system.

Back in Boston once again, Lowell and his brother-in-law built a power loom, patented it, raised money, formed a company, and built a textile factory. Realizing that their best source of available labor would be young women from the surrounding New England rural areas and that farm families would have to be persuaded to let their daughters work far from home in the new factories, the company managers developed what came to be known as the Lowell system.

In this chapter, you will be looking at what happened when people's ideas about women's "proper place" conflicted with the labor needs of the new factory system. What did the general public fear? How did the working girls react?

∞ BACKGROUND ∞

By the end of the eighteenth century, the American economy began undergoing a process that historians call modernization. This process involves a number of changes, including the rapid expansion of markets, commercial specialization, improved transportation networks, the growth of credit transactions, the proliferation of towns and cities, and the rise of manufacturing and the factory system. Quite obviously, all these factors are interrelated. Furthermore, such changes always have profound effects on people's lifestyles as well as on the pace of life itself.

While the frontier moved steadily westward, the South was primarily agrarian—tied to cash crops such as cotton and tobacco. New England's economy, however, quickly became modernized. Although agriculture was never completely abandoned in New England, by the early 1800s it was increasingly difficult to obtain land, and many small New England farms suffered from soil exhaustion. Young men, of course, could go west—in fact, so many of them left New England that soon there was a "surplus" of young women in the area. In addition, the transformation of New England agriculture and the demise of much of the "putting-out" system of the first local textile manufacturing left many single female workers underemployed or unemployed. What were these farmers' daughters supposed to do? What were their options?

At the same time that these economic developments were occurring, ideas about white middle-class women and their place in society also were changing. Even before the American Revolution, sharp distinctions between the "better sort" and the "poorer sort" were noticeable, especially in cities like Boston. The Revolution itself, with its emphasis on "republican virtues," drew many women away from their purely domestic duties and into patriotic work for the cause. The uncertainties of the early national period, which followed the Revolution, only intensified the concern about the new Republic: how could such a daring experiment in representative government succeed? An important part of the answer to this question was the concept of "republican motherhood": women would take on the important task of raising children to be responsible citizens who possessed the virtues (and value system) necessary for the success of the newly independent nation.

Those who study women's history disagree on the question of whether women's status improved or declined as a result of the emphasis on republican motherhood. Nevertheless, it was clear that the new focus on motherhood and child rearing would not only reduce the variety of roles women could play but also limit women's proper place to their own homes.

As historian Alice Kessler-Harris notes in her study of wage-earning women in the United States, there was a direct conflict for poorer or unmarried women between their need to earn money and the ideology that home and family should be central to *all* women's lives.[1] This emphasis on domestic ideology, Kessler-Harris concludes, sharpened class divisions and eroded any possibility of real independence for women. Historian Christine Stansell reaches many of the same conclusions in her study of gender and class in New York City.[2] In addition, according to Stansell, young unmarried working women often dressed and behaved in ways that directly challenged domestic ideology and women's place within the home. Such alternative ways of living, especially on the part of young, white, native-born, Protestant women, were deeply disturbing to many Americans, both male and female.

In periods of rapid change, people often try to cling to absolute beliefs and even create stereotypes that implicitly punish those who do not conform. Such a stereotype began to emerge after the American Revolution. According to this stereotype, every "true" woman was a "lady" who behaved in certain ways because of her female nature. Historian Barbara Welter has called this phenomenon "the cult of true womanhood."[3] True women possessed four virtues: piety, purity, submissiveness, and domesticity. These characteristics, it was thought, were not so much learned as

they were biologically natural, simply an inherent part of being born female. Women's magazines, etiquette books for young ladies, sermons and religious tracts, and popular short stories and novels all told women what they were like and how they should feel about themselves. Such sources are called "prescriptive literature" because they literally prescribe how people should—and should not—behave.

What, then, was expected of New England farmers' daughters and other respectable (white) women? They were supposed to be pious, more naturally religious than men (real men might occasionally swear, but real women never did). Because they were naturally logical and rational, men might pursue education, but true women should not because they might be led into error if they strayed from the Bible. As daughters, wives, or even sisters, women had the important responsibility of being the spiritual uplifters to whom men could turn when necessary.

Just as important as piety was the true woman's purity. This purity was absolute because whereas a man might "sow his wild oats" and then be saved by the love of a good woman, a "fallen woman" could never be saved. In the popular fiction of the period, a woman who had been seduced usually became insane, died, or did both. If she had a baby, it also came to a bad end. Only on her wedding night did a true woman surrender her virginity, and then out of duty rather than passion, because it was widely believed that pure women were not sexually responsive. In fact, many young women of this era knew nothing at all about

1. Alice Kessler-Harris, *Out to Work: A History of America's Wage-earning Women* (New York: Oxford, 1982).
2. Christine Stansell, *City of Women: Sex and Class in New York, 1789–1860* (New York: Knopf, 1986).
3. Barbara Welter, "The Cult of True Womanhood, 1820–1860," *American Quarterly,* vol. 18 (Summer 1966), pp. 151–174.

their own bodies or the nature of sexual intercourse until they married.

Submission and domesticity were perhaps not as vital as piety and purity. Although women who did not submit to men's leadership were destined to be unhappy (according to the thought of the day), they could correct their mistaken behavior. Men were, after all, stronger and more intelligent, the natural protectors of women. A true woman, wrote then-popular author Grace Greenwood, should be like a "perpetual child," who is always "timid, doubtful, and clingingly dependent." Such pious, pure, submissive women were particularly well suited to the important task of creating a pleasant, cheerful home—a place where men could escape from their worldly struggles and be fed, clothed, comforted, and nursed if they were ill. Even a woman who did not have very much money could create such a haven, people believed, simply by using her natural talents of sewing, cooking, cleaning, and flower arranging.

Simultaneously, then, two important trends were occurring in the early 1800s: the northern economy was modernizing, and sexual stereotypes that assigned very different roles to men and women were developing. Whereas a man should be out in the world of education, work, and politics, a woman's place was in the home, a sphere where she could be sheltered. But what would happen if the economic need for an increased supply of labor clashed with the new ideas about women's place in society? If a young unmarried woman went to work in a factory far away from her parents' farm, would she still be respectable?

Where would she live? Who would protect her? Perhaps the experience of factory work itself would destroy those special feminine characteristics all true women possessed. All these fears and more would have to be confronted in the course of the development of the New England textile industry during the 1830s and 1840s.

Although the first American textile mill using water-powered spinning machines was built in 1790, it and the countless other mills that sprang up throughout New England during the next thirty years depended heavily on the putting-out system. The mills made only the yarn, which was then distributed ("put out") to women who wove the cloth in their own homes and returned the finished products to the mills. In 1820, two-thirds of all American cloth was still being produced by women working at home. But the pace of modernization accelerated sharply with the formation of the Boston Manufacturing Company, a heavily capitalized firm that purchased a large tract of rural land in the Merrimack River valley. The Boston Associates adopted the latest technology and, more important, concentrated all aspects of cloth production inside their factories. Because they no longer put out work, they had to attract large numbers of workers, especially young women from New England farms, to their mills. Lowell, Massachusetts (the "City of Spindles"), and the Lowell mills became a kind of model, an experiment that received a good deal of attention in both Europe and America. As historian Thomas Dublin has shown, most of the young women at the Lowell mills were fifteen to thirty years old, unmarried, and from farm families that were neither the richest nor the poorest in their area. Although some of the Lowell girls occasionally sent small amounts of money back to their families, most used their wages for new clothes, education, and dowries.[4] These wages were significantly higher than those for teaching, farm labor, or domestic services, the three other major occupations open to women.

The factory girls were required to live and eat in boardinghouses run according to company rules and supervised by respectable landladies. The company partially subsidized the cost of room-and-board and also encouraged the numerous lecture series, evening schools, and church-related activities in Lowell. Girls worked together in the mills, filling the unskilled and semiskilled positions, and men (about one-fourth of the work force) performed the skilled jobs and served as overseers (foremen). Work in the mills also was characterized by strict regulations and an elaborate system of bells that signaled mealtimes and work times.

During the 1840s, factory girls occasionally published their own magazines, the most famous of which was the *Lowell Offering*. This journal grew out of a working woman's self-improvement society and was sponsored by a local Lowell minister. When the minister was transferred, the mill owners partially subsidized the magazine. The female editors, who were former mill workers, insisted that the magazine was for "literary" work rather than for labor reform. The Evidence section presents a description of Lowell mills and boardinghouses and several selections from the *Lowell Offering* and other sources. The conflict between economic modernization and the cult of true womanhood was indirectly recognized by many New Englanders and directly experienced by the Lowell mill girls. What forms did this conflict take? What fears and anxieties did it reveal? How did the mill girls attempt to cope with this tension?

❧ THE METHOD ❧

When historians use prescriptive literature as evidence, they ask (1) what message is being conveyed, (2) who is sending the message, (3) why it is being sent, and (4) for whom it is intended. All the evidence you are using

4. A dowry is the money, goods, or property that a woman brings into her marriage.

in this chapter is in some ways prescriptive—that is, it tells people how women *should* behave.

An early major criticism of the effects of factory work on young women was written by Orestes Brownson, a well-known New England editor and reformer. A sharply contrasting view appears in the excerpts from a brief, popular book about Lowell written by Reverend Henry Mills in 1845. Reverend Mills was a local Protestant minister who was asked by the textile company owners to conduct surveys into the workers' habits, health, and moral character. Depending heavily on information provided by company officials, overseers, and landladies, Reverend Mills published *Lowell, As It Was, and As It Is.*

Yet the controversy continued, because only one year later, the journal owned by the Lowell Female Labor Reform Association, *Voice of Industry,* painted a much darker picture of the factory girls' "slavery." Although purchased by a militant group of women factory workers, the *Voice* had originated as a labor reform paper. Its editorial policy always addressed larger, worker-oriented issues such as a shorter workday and dedicated a special column to women workers' concerns.

The young women who worked in the textile mills also actively participated in the debate. The evidence in the selections from the *Lowell Offering* was written by factory girls during the years 1840 to 1843. Also presented is an excerpt from a book written by Lucy Larcom, one of the few children (under age fifteen) employed in the Lowell mills in the late 1830s. She was a factory girl for more than ten years, after which she went west and obtained a college education. She became a well-known teacher and author when she returned to New England. Larcom published the book about her New England girlhood when she was sixty-five years old. The final set of evidence includes two pictures of "typical" mill girls in 1860 and letters written by mill girls and their families.

First read through the evidence, looking for elements of the cult of true womanhood in the factory girls' writings and in the Lowell system itself. Be sure to consider all four questions: What message is being conveyed? Who is sending the message? Why is it being sent? For whom is it intended? This will tell you a great deal, not only about the social standards for respectable young white women but also about the fears and anxieties aroused by a factory system that employed women away from their homes.

Reading about how people *should* behave, however, does not tell us how people actually behaved. Remember that the central question of this problem involves a clash—a conflict between ideas (the cult) and reality (the factory system). Go through the evidence again, this time trying to reconstruct what it was really like for the young women who lived and worked in Lowell. Ask yourself to what degree and in what ways they might have deviated from the ideal of "true" women. Also ask whether they could have achieved this ideal goal—and whether they really wanted to—while working and living in Lowell. In other words, try to clarify in your own mind the forms of the conflict and the reactions (of both society and the young women) to that conflict.

꧁ THE EVIDENCE ꧁

Source 1 from Orestes A. Brownson, *Boston Quarterly Review,* Vol. III (July 1840), pp. 368–370.

1. Slave Labor Versus Free Labor.

In regard to labor, two systems obtain: one that of slave labor, the other that of free labor. Of the two, the first is, in our judgment, except so far as the feelings are concerned, decidedly the least oppressive. If the slave has never been a free man, we think, as a general rule, his sufferings are less than those of the free laborer at wages. As to actual freedom, one has just about as much as the other. The laborer at wages has all the disadvantages of freedom and none of its blessings, while the slave, if denied the blessings, is freed from the disadvantages.

We are no advocates of slavery. We are as heartily opposed to it as any modern abolitionist can be. But we say frankly that, if there must always be a laboring population distinct from proprietors and employers, we regard the slave system as decidedly preferable to the system at wages.

It is no pleasant thing to go days without food; to lie idle for weeks, seeking work and finding none; to rise in the morning with a wife and children you love, and know not where to procure them a breakfast; and to see constantly before you no brighter prospect than the almshouse. . . .

It is said there is no want in this country. There may be less in some other countries. But death by actual starvation in this country is, we apprehend, no uncommon occurrence. The sufferings of a quiet, unassuming but useful class of females in our cities, in general seamstresses, too proud to beg or to apply to the almshouse, are not easily told. They are industrious; they do all that they can find to do. But yet the little there is for them to do, and the miserable pittance they receive for it, is hardly sufficient to keep soul and body together. . . .

The average life—working life, we mean—of the girls that come to Lowell, for instance, from Maine, New Hampshire, and Vermont, we have been assured, is only about three years. What becomes of them then? Few of them ever marry;[5] fewer still ever return to their native places with

---

5. According to historian Thomas Dublin (*Women at Work,* New York: Columbia University Press, 1979), the working women of Lowell tended to marry in about the same proportion as nonworking New England women, although the Lowell women married three to five years later in life and had a distinct tendency to marry men who were tradesmen or skilled workers rather than farmers.

reputations unimpaired. "She has worked in a factory" is almost enough to damn to infamy the most worthy and virtuous girl. . . .

One thing is certain: that, of the amount actually produced by the operative, [the worker] retains a less proportion than it costs the master to feed, clothe, and lodge his slave. Wages is a cunning device of the devil, for the benefit of tender consciences who would retain all the advantages of the slave system without the expense, trouble, and odium of being slaveholders.

Source 2 from Reverend Henry A. Mills, *Lowell, As It Was, and As It Is* (Lowell, Mass.: Powers, Bagley, and Dayton, 1845).

2. A Lowell Boardinghouse.

[*Reverend Mills began by describing the long blocks of boardinghouses, each three stories high, which were built in a style reminiscent of country farmhouses. Clean, well painted, and neat, these houses contained common eating rooms, parlors, and sleeping rooms for two to six boarders. The boarders, Reverend Mills observed, were sometimes a bit crowded but actually lived under better conditions than seamstresses and milliners in other towns.*]

As one important feature in the management of these houses, it deserves to be named that male operatives and female operatives do not board in the same tenement; and the following Regulations, printed by one of the companies, and given to each keeper of their houses, are here subjoined, as a simple statement of the rules generally observed by all the Corporations.

Regulations to be observed by persons occupying the Boarding-houses belonging to the Merrimack Manufacturing company.

They must not board any persons not employed by the company, unless by special permission.

No disorderly or improper conduct must be allowed in the houses.

The doors must be closed at 10 o'clock in the evening; and no person admitted after that time, unless a sufficient excuse can be given.

Those who keep the houses, when required, must give an account of the number, names, and employment of their boarders; also with regard to their general conduct and whether they are in the habit of attending public worship.

The buildings, both inside and out, and the yards about them, must be kept clean and in good order. If the buildings or fences are injured, they will be repaired and charged to the occupant.

No one will be allowed to keep swine.

The hours of taking meals in these houses are uniform throughout all the Corporations in the city, and are as follows: Dinner—always at half-past twelve o'clock. Breakfast—from November 1 to February 28, before going to work, and so early as to begin work as soon as it is light; through March at half-past seven o'clock; from April 1 to September 19, at seven o'clock; and from September 20 to October 31, at half-past seven o'clock. Supper—always after work at night, that is, after seven o'clock, from March 20 to September 19; after half-past seven o'clock, from September 20 to March 19. The time allowed for each meal is thirty minutes for breakfast, when that meal is taken after beginning work; for dinner, thirty minutes, from September 1 to April 30; and forty-five minutes from May 1 to August 31.

[*The meals might seem rushed, Mills noted, but that was common among all Americans, particularly businesspeople. Working girls could choose whichever boarding-houses they preferred, rents were very low, and their living arrangements were very respectable.*]

No tenant is admitted who has not hitherto borne a good character, and who does not continue to sustain it. In many cases the tenant has long been keeper of the house, for six, eight, or twelve years, and is well known to hundreds of her girls as their adviser and friend and second mother. . . .

The influence which this system of boarding-houses has exerted upon the good order and good morals of the place, has been vast and beneficent. It is this system to which we especially referred in our previous chapter on Waltham. By it the care and influence of the superintendent are extended over his operatives, while they are out of the mill, as well as while they are in it. Employing chiefly those who have no permanent residence in Lowell, but are only temporary boarders, upon any embarrassment of affairs they return to their country homes, and do not sink down here a helpless caste, clamouring for work, starving unless employed, and hence ready for a riot, for the destruction of property, and repeating here the scenes enacted in the manufacturing villages of England. To a very great degree the future condition of Lowell is dependent upon a faithful adhesion to this system; and it will deserve the serious consideration of those old towns which are now introducing steam mills, whether, if they do not provide boarding-houses, and employ chiefly other operatives than resident ones, they be not bringing in the seeds of future and alarming evil. . . .

To obtain this constant importation of female hands from the country, it is necessary to secure *the moral protection of their characters while they are resident in Lowell.* This, therefore, is the chief object of that moral police referred to, some details of which will now be given.

It should be stated, in the outset, that no persons are employed on the Corporations who are addicted to intemperance, or who are known to be guilty of any immoralities of conduct. As the parent of all other vices, intemperance is most carefully excluded. Absolute freedom from intoxicating liquors is understood, throughout the city, to be a prerequisite to obtaining employment in the mills, and any person known to be addicted to their use is at once dismissed. This point has not received the attention, from writers upon the moral conditions of Lowell, which it deserves; and we are surprised that the English traveller and divine, Dr. Scoresby, in his recent book upon Lowell, has given no more notice to this subject. A more strictly and universally temperate class of persons cannot be found, than the nine thousand operatives of this city; and the fact is as well known to all others living here, as it is of some honest pride among themselves. In relation to other immoralities, it may be stated, that the suspicion of criminal conduct, association with suspected persons, and general and habitual light behavior and conversation, are regarded as sufficient reasons for dismissions, and for which delinquent operatives are discharged.

[*Reverend Mills also described the discharge system at the factories. For those girls whose conduct was satisfactory and who had worked at least a year, honorable discharges were issued. Discharge letters could be used as recommendations for another job. Those who received dishonorable discharges for infractions such as stealing, lying, leaving the job without permission, or other "improper conduct" would have difficulty finding other employment.*]

So much for honorable discharges. Those dishonorable have another treatment. The names of all persons dismissed for bad conduct, or who leave the mill irregularly, are also entered in a book kept for that purpose, and these names are sent to all the counting-rooms of the city, and are there entered on *their* books. *Such persons obtain no more employment throughout the city.* The question is put to each applicant, "Have you worked before in the city, and if so, where is your discharge?" If no discharge be presented, an inquiry of the applicant's name will enable the superintendent to know whether that name stands on his book of dishonorable discharges, and he is thus saved from taking in a corrupt or unworthy hand. This system, which has been in operation in Lowell from the beginning, is of great and important effect in driving unworthy persons from our city, and in preserving the high character of our operatives.

[Male overseers, or foremen, also were closely screened and had to possess good moral character. In response to Reverend Mills's questions about the male overseers, one factory owner responded as follows.]

Lowell, May 10, 1841

Dear Sir:—

I employ in our mills, and in the various departments connected with them, thirty overseers, and as many second overseers. My overseers are married men, with families, with a single exception, and even he has engaged a tenement, and is to be married soon. Our second overseers are younger men, but upwards of twenty of them are married, and several others are soon to be married. Sixteen of our overseers are members of some regular church, and four of them are deacons. Ten of our second overseers are also members of the church, and one of them is the Super-intendent of a Sunday School. I have no hesitation in saying that in all the sterling requisites of character, in native intelligence, and practical good sense, in sound morality, and as active, useful, and exemplary citizens, they may, as a class, safely challenge comparison with any class in our com-munity. I know not, among them all, an intemperate man, nor, at this time, even what is called a moderate drinker.

[Furthermore, the girls were expected to obey numerous rules.]

Still another source of trust which a Corporation has, for the good char-acter of its operatives, is the moral control which they have over one another. Of course this control would be nothing among a generally corrupt and degraded class. But among virtuous and high-minded young women, who feel that they have the keeping of their characters, and that any stain upon their associates brings reproach upon themselves, the power of opinion becomes an ever-present, and ever-active restraint. A girl, *suspected* of immoralities, or serious improprieties of conduct, at once loses caste. Her fellow-boarders will at once leave the house, if the keeper does not dismiss the offender. In self-protection, therefore, the matron is obliged to put the of-fender away. Nor will her former companions walk with, or work with her; till at length, finding herself everywhere talked about, and pointed at, and shunned, she is obliged to relieve her fellow-operatives of a presence which they feel brings disgrace. From this power of opinion, there is no appeal; and as long as it is exerted in favor of propriety of behavior and purity of life, it is one of the most active and effectual safeguards of character.

It may not be out of place to present here the regulations, which are observed alike on all the Corporations, which are given to the operatives when they are first employed, and are posted up conspicuously in all the mills. They are as follows:—

Regulations to be observed by all persons employed by the _____
Manufacturing Company, in the Factories.

Every overseer is required to be punctual himself, and to see that those employed under him are so.

The overseers may, at their discretion, grant leave of absence to those employed under them, when there are sufficient spare hands to supply their place; but when there are not sufficient spare hands, they are not allowed to grant leave of absence unless in cases of absolute necessity.

All persons are required to observe the regulations of the room in which they are employed. They are not allowed to be absent from their work without the consent of their overseer, except in case of sickness, and then they are required to send him word of the cause of their absence.

All persons are required to board in one of the boarding-houses belonging to the company, and conform to the regulations of the house in which they board.

All persons are required to be constant in attendance on public worship, at one of the regular places of worship in this place.

Persons who do not comply with the above regulations will not be employed by the company.

Persons entering the employment of the company are considered as engaging to work one year.

All persons intending to leave the employment of the company, are required to give notice of the same to their overseer, at least two weeks previous to the time of leaving.

Any one who shall take from the mills, or the yard, any yarn, cloth, or other article belonging to the company, will be considered guilty of STEAL-ING—and prosecuted accordingly.

The above regulations are considered part of the contract with all persons entering the employment of the _____ MANUFACTURING COMPANY. All persons who shall have complied with them, on leaving the employment of the company, shall be entitled to an honorable discharge, which will serve as a recommendation to any of the factories in Lowell. No one who shall not have complied with them will be entitled to such a discharge.

_____ _____, Agent

Source 3 courtesy of Museum of American Textile History.

3. Timetable of the Lowell Mills.

TIME TABLE OF THE LOWELL MILLS,

Arranged to make the working time throughout the year average 11 hours per day.

TO TAKE EFFECT SEPTEMBER 21st., 1853.

The Standard time being that of the meridian of Lowell, as shown by the Regulator Clock of AMOS SANBORN, Post Office Corner, Central Street.

From March 20th to September 19th, inclusive.

COMMENCE WORK, at 6.30 A. M. LEAVE OFF WORK, at 6.30 P. M., except on Saturday Evenings.
BREAKFAST at 6 A. M. DINNER, at 12 M. Commence Work, after dinner, 12.45 P. M.

From September 20th to March 19th, inclusive.

COMMENCE WORK at 7.00 A. M. LEAVE OFF WORK, at 7.00 P. M., except on Saturday Evenings.
BREAKFAST at 6.30 A. M. DINNER, at 12.30 P.M. Commence Work, after dinner, 1.15 P. M.

BELLS.

From March 20th to September 19th, inclusive.

Morning Bells.	Dinner Bells.	Evening Bells.
First bell,..........4.30 A. M.	Ring out,.............12.00 M.	Ring out,............6.30 P. M.
Second, 5.30 A. M.; Third, 6.20.	Ring in,...........12.35 P. M.	Except on Saturday Evenings.

From September 20th to March 19th, inclusive.

Morning Bells.	Dinner Bells.	Evening Bells.
First bell,..........5.00 A. M.	Ring out,..........12.30 P. M.	Ring out at..........7.00 P. M.
Second, 6.00 A. M.; Third, 6.50.	Ring in,.............1.05 P. M.	Except on Saturday Evenings.

SATURDAY EVENING BELLS.

During APRIL, MAY, JUNE, JULY, and AUGUST, Ring Out, at 6.00 P. M.
The remaining Saturday Evenings in the year, ring out as follows :

SEPTEMBER.	NOVEMBER.	JANUARY.
First Saturday, ring out 6.00 P. M.	Third Saturday ring out 4.00 P. M.	Third Saturday, ring out 4.25 P. M.
Second " " 5.45 "	Fourth " " 3.55 "	Fourth " " 4.35 "
Third " " 5.30 "		
Fourth " " 5.20 "	**DECEMBER.**	**FEBRUARY.**
OCTOBER.	First Saturday, ring out 3.50 P. M.	First Saturday, ring out 4.45 P. M.
First Saturday, ring out 5.05 P. M.	Second " " 3.55 "	Second " " 4.55 "
Second " " 4.55 "	Third " " 3.55 "	Third " " 5.00 "
Third " " 4.45 "	Fourth " " 4.00 "	Fourth " " 5.10 "
Fourth " " 4.35 "	Fifth " " 4.00 "	
Fifth " " 4.25 "		**MARCH.**
NOVEMBER.	**JANUARY.**	First Saturday, ring out 5.25 P. M.
First Saturday, ring out 4.15 P. M.	First Saturday, ring out 4.10 P. M.	Second " " 5.30 "
Second " " 4.05 "	Second " " 4.15 "	Third " " 5.35 "
		Fourth " " 5.45 "

YARD GATES will be opened at the first stroke of the bells for entering or leaving the Mills.

. *SPEED GATES commence hoisting three minutes before commencing work.*

Penhallow, Printer, Wyman's Exchange, 28 Merrimack St.

Source 4 from *Voice of Industry,* January 2, 1846, in H. R. Warfel et al., eds., *The American Mind* (New York: American Book Company, 1937), p. 392.

4. "Slaver" Wagons.

We were not aware, until within a few days, of the *modus operandi* of the factory powers in this village of forcing poor girls from their quiet homes to become their tools and, like the Southern slaves, to give up their life and liberty to the heartless tyrants and taskmasters.

Observing a singular-looking "long, low, black" wagon passing along the street, we made inquiries respecting it, and were informed that it was what we term a "slaver." She makes regular trips to the north of the state [Massachusetts], cruising around in Vermont and New Hampshire, with a "commander" whose heart must be as black as his craft, who is paid a dollar a head for all he brings to the market, and more in proportion to the distance—if they bring them from such a distance that they cannot easily get back.

This is done by "hoisting false colors," and representing to the girls that they can tend more machinery than is possible, and that the work is so very neat, and the wages such that they can dress in silks and spend half their time in reading. Now, is this true? Let those girls who have been thus deceived, answer.

Let us say a word in regard to the manner in which they are stowed in the wagon, which may find a similarity only in the manner in which slaves are fastened in the hold of a vessel. It is long, and the seats so close that it must be very inconvenient.

Is there any humanity in this? Philanthropists may talk of Negro slavery, but it would be well first to endeavor to emancipate the slaves at home. Let us not stretch our ears to catch the sound of the lash on the flesh of the oppressed black while the oppressed in our very midst are crying out in thunder tones, and calling upon us for assistance.

Source 5 from *Lowell Offering,* Series I, Issue 1 (1840). Courtesy of Merrimack Valley Textile Museum.

5. Title Page of *Lowell Offering.*

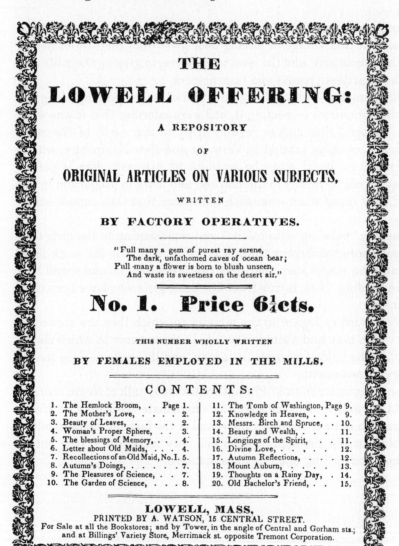

THE
LOWELL OFFERING:

A REPOSITORY

OF

ORIGINAL ARTICLES ON VARIOUS SUBJECTS,

WRITTEN

BY FACTORY OPERATIVES.

"Full many a gem of purest ray serene,
The dark, unfathomed caves of ocean bear;
Full many a flower is born to blush unseen,
And waste its sweetness on the desert air."

No. 1.   Price 6¼cts.

THIS NUMBER WHOLLY WRITTEN

BY FEMALES EMPLOYED IN THE MILLS,

CONTENTS:

LOWELL, MASS,
PRINTED BY A. WATSON, 15 CENTRAL STREET.
For Sale at all the Bookstores; and by Tower, in the angle of Central and Gorham sts.;
and at Billings' Variety Store, Merrimack st. opposite Tremont Corporation.

Source 6 from *Lowell Offering,* Series I, Issue 1 (1840), p. 16.

6. Editorial Corner.

The Lowell Offering is strictly what it purports to be, a "Repository of original articles on various subjects, written by Factory Operatives."—The objects of the publication are, to encourage the cultivation of talent; to preserve such articles as are deemed most worthy of preservation; and to correct an erroneous idea which generally prevails in relation to the intelligence of persons employed in the Mills. This number is wholly the offering of Females. . . .

We are persuaded that the citizens generally, and those engaged in the Mills particularly, will feel and manifest a lively interest in the prosperity of the Lowell Offering. That it is faultless—that the severe and captious critic will find no room for his vocation, is not to be expected. Nevertheless, while the work makes no noisy pretensions to superior excellency, it would claim no unusual indulgences. It asks only that, all the circumstances incident to its peculiar character being duly weighed, it shall be fairly and candidly judged. The Editors do not hesitate to say, that they anticipate for a favorable reception at the hands of those who have at heart the interests of that important and interesting portion of our population, whose intellectual elevation and moral welfare it aims to promote. . . .

The critical reader will doubtless discover, in many of the articles making this number of the Offering, words and phrases for which better might be substituted; and also sentences that want the freedom and smoothness of perfect composition. In explanation, the Editors have to say, that, in preparing the articles for the press, while they claimed to exercise the rights usually granted to the editorial fraternity, they resolved carefully to avoid any alteration which might affect the sentiment or style of the several writers. In consequence of this resolution a few expressions and sentences have been allowed to pass, which a less scrupulous regard for strict originality would have rejected. Nevertheless they are quite sure the rule adopted will be approved by all who shall look to the articles of the Offering as evidence of the intellectual and literary power of the writers.

An opinion extensively prevails, not merely beyond the limits of Massachusetts, that the Manufacturing city of Lowell is a nucleus of depravity and ignorance.

Confessedly, wherever there exists *any* depravity or ignorance, there is *too much* of it. We have this to testify however, that they who know least of the people of Lowell, including the Factory Operatives, entertain the most unworthy and unjust opinions of them. Close personal observation has satisfied us, that in respect of morality and intelligence, they will not suffer in comparison with the inhabitants of any part of moral and enlightened New England. We shall have occasion to speak of this subject at considerable length hereafter. We shall note the unsurpassed (if not unequaled) advantages of education enjoyed by our population; and the extensive means of information and piety furnished by popular lectures and religious institutions. We shall note the absence of theatres and kindred abominations; the care taken to exclude unworthy persons from the Corporations, &c.

And as to the intelligence of our people, we may safely present the pages of the Offering as a testimony against all revilers "who know not whereof they affirm." Editors who think proper to copy any thing therefrom, are requested to give due credit, and thus assist in the correction of an unwarranted and injurious error.

Sources 7 and 8 from *Lowell Offering,* Series II, Vol. II (1842), p. 192; Series II, Vol. III (1842), pp. 69–70.

7. Dignity of Labor.

From whence originated the idea, that it was derogatory to a lady's dignity, or a blot upon the female character, to labor? and who was the first to say, sneeringly, 'Oh, she *works* for a living'? Surely, such ideas and expressions ought not to grow on republican soil. The time has been, when ladies of the first rank were accustomed to busy themselves in domestic employment.

Homer tells us of princesses who used to draw water from the springs, and wash with their own hands the finest of the linen of their respective families. The famous Lucretia used to spin in the midst of her attendants; and the wife of Ulysses, after the siege of Troy, employed herself in weaving, until her husband returned to Ithaca. And in later times, the wife of George the Third of England, has been represented as spending a whole evening in hemming pocket-handkerchiefs, while her daughter Mary sat in the corner, darning stockings.

Few American fortunes will support a woman who is above the calls of her family; and a man of sense, in choosing a companion to jog with him through all the up-hills and down-hills of life, would sooner choose one who *had* to work for a living, than one who thought it beneath her to soil her pretty hands with manual labor, although she possessed her thousands. To be able to earn one's own living by laboring with the hands, should be reckoned among female accomplishments; and I hope the time is not far distant when none of my countrywomen will be ashamed to have it known that they are better versed in useful, than they are in ornamental accomplishments.

C.B.

8. Editorial—Home in a Boarding-House.

[*Factory boardinghouses were not really like homes, the editor pointed out. A place to eat and lodge, the boardinghouses often seemed crowded and impersonal.*]

But these are all trifles, compared with the perplexities to which we are subjected in other ways; and some of these things might be remedied by the girls themselves. We now allude to the importunities of evening visitors, such as peddlers, candy and newspaper boys, shoe-dealers, book-sellers, &c., &c., breaking in upon the only hours of leisure we can call our own, and proffering their articles with a pertinacity which will admit of no denial. That these evening salesmen are always unwelcome we will not assert, but they are too often inclined to remain where they know they are considered a nuisance. And then they often forget, if they ever knew, the rules of politeness which should regulate all transient visitors. They deal about their hints, inuendoes [*sic*], and low cunning, as though a factory boarding-house was what no boarding-house should ever be.

The remedy is entirely with the girls. Treat all of these comers with a politeness truly lady-like, when they appear as gentlemen, but let your manners change to stern formality when they forget that they are in the company of respectable females. . . .

C.B.

Sources 9 through 11 from *Lowell Offering,* Series I (1840), pp. 17–19, 61, 44–46.

9. Factory Girls.

"She has worked in a factory, *is sufficient to damn to infamy the most worthy and virtuous girl.*"

So says Mr. Orestes A. Brownson; and either this horrible assertion is true, or Mr. Brownson is a slanderer. I assert that it is *not* true, and Mr. B. may consider himself called upon to prove his words, if he can.

This gentleman has read of an Israelitish boy who, with nothing but a stone and sling, once entered into a contest with a Philistine giant, arrayed in brass, whose spear was like a weaver's beam; and he may now see what will probably appear to him quite as marvellous; and that is, that a *factory girl* is not afraid to oppose herself to the *Editor of the Boston Quarterly Review*. True, he has upon his side fame, learning, and great talent; but I have what is better than either of these, or all combined, and that is *truth*. Mr. Brownson has not said that this thing should be so; or that he is glad it is so; or that he deeply regrets such a state of affairs; but he has said it *is* so; and *I* affirm that it is *not*.

And whom has Mr. Brownson slandered? A class of girls who in this city alone are numbered by thousands, and who collect in many of our smaller towns by hundreds; girls who generally come from quiet country homes, where their minds and manners have been formed under the eyes of the worthy sons of the Pilgrims, and their virtuous partners, and who return again to become the wives of the free intelligent yeomanry of New England and the mothers of quite a portion of our future republicans. Think, for a moment, how many of the next generation are to spring from mothers doomed to infamy! "Ah," it may be replied, "Mr. Brownson acknowledges that you may still be worthy and virtuous." Then we must be a set of worthy and virtuous idiots, for no virtuous girl of common sense would choose for an occupation one that would consign her to infamy. . . .

That there has been prejudice against us, we know; but it is wearing away, and has never been so deep nor universal as Mr. B's statement will lead many to believe. Even now it may be that "the mushroom aristocracy" and "would-be fashionables" of Boston, turn up their eyes in horror at the sound of those vulgar words, *factory girls;* but *they* form but a small part of the community, and theirs are not the opinions which Mr. Brownson intended to represent. . . .

[*The prejudice against factory girls was connected to the degraded and exploited conditions of European workers, the angry letter writer asserted. "Yankee girls," she said, are independent, and although the work is hard, the wages are better than those in other kinds of employment. It is no wonder, she concluded, that so many intelligent, worthy, and virtuous young women have been drawn to Lowell.*]

The erroneous idea, wherever it exists, must be done away, that there is in factories but one sort of girls, and *that* the baser and degraded sort. There are among us *all* sorts of girls. I believe that there are few occupations which can exhibit so many gradations of piety and intelligence; but the majority may at least lay claim to as much of the former as females in other stations of life. . . . The Improvement Circles, the Lyceum and Institute, the social religious meetings, the Circulating and other libraries, can bear testimony that the little time they have is spent in a better manner. Our well filled churches and lecture halls and the high character of our clergymen and lecturers, will testify that the state of morals and intelligence is not low.

Mr. Brownson, I suppose, would not judge of our moral characters by our church-going tendencies; but as many do, a word on this subject may not be amiss. That there are many in Lowell who do not regularly attend any meeting, is as true as the correspondent of the Boston Times once represented it; but for this there are various reasons. . . .

There have also been nice calculations made, as to the small proportion which the amount of money deposited in the Savings Bank bears to that earned in the city; but this is not all that is saved. Some is deposited in Banks at other places, and some is put into the hands of personal friends. Still, much that is earned is immediately, though not foolishly, spent. Much that none but the parties concerned will ever know of, goes to procure comforts and necessaries for some lowly home, and a great deal is spent for public benevolent purposes. . . .

And now, if Mr. Brownson is a *man,* he will endeavor to retrieve the injury he has done; he will resolve that "the dark shall be light, and the wrong made right," and the assertion he has publicly made will be as publicly retracted. If he still doubts upon the subject let him come among us: let him make himself as well acquainted with us as our pastors and superintendents are; and though he will find error, ignorance, and folly among us, (and where would he find them not?) yet he would not see worthy and virtuous girls consigned to infamy, because they work in a factory.

A FACTORY GIRL

10. A Familiar Letter.

Friends and Associates:—

With indescribable emotions of pleasure, mingled with feelings of deepest gratitude to Him who is the Author of every good and perfect gift, I have perused the second and third numbers of the Lowell Offering.

As a laborer among you, (tho' least of all) I rejoice that the time has arrived when a class of laboring females (who have long been made a reproach and byword, by those whom fortune or pride has placed above the avocation by which we have subjected ourselves to the sneers and scoffs of the idle, ignorant and envious part of community,) are bursting asunder the captive chains of prejudice. . . .

I know it has been affirmed, to the sorrow of many a would-be lady, that factory girls and ladies could not be distinguished by their apparel. What a lamentable evil! and no doubt it would be a source of much gratitude to such, if the awful name of "factory girl!" were branded on the forehead of every female who is, or ever was, employed in the Mills. Appalling as the name may sound in the delicate ears of a sensitive lady, as she contrasts the music of her piano with the rumblings of the factory machinery, we would not shrink from such a token of our calling, could the treasures of the mind be there displayed, and merit, in her own unbiased form be stamped there also. . . .

Yours, in the bonds of affection,

DOROTHEA

11. Gold Watches.

It is now nearly a year since an article appeared in the Ladies' Book, in the form of a tale, though it partakes more of the character of an essay. It was written by Mrs. Hale, and exhibits her usual judgment and talent. Her object evidently was to correct the many erroneous impressions which exist in society, with regard to the folly of extravagance in dress, and all outward show. I was much pleased with all of it, with the exception of a single sentence. Speaking of the impossibility of considering dress a mark of distinction, she observed,—(addressing herself, I presume, to the *ladies* of New England,)—"How stands the difference now? Many of the factory girls wear gold watches, and an imitation, at least, of all the ornaments which grace the daughters of our most opulent citizens."

O the times! O the manners! Alas! how very sadly the world has changed! The time was when the *lady* could be distinguished from the *no-lady* by her dress, as far as the eye could reach; but now, you might stand in the same room, and judging by their outward appearance, you could not tell "which was which." Even gold watches are now no *sure* indication—for they have been worn by the lowest, even by "many of the factory girls." No *lady* need carry one now, for any other than the simple purpose of easily ascertaining the time of day, or night, if she so please! . . .

Those who do not labor for their living, have more time for the improvement of their minds, for the cultivation of conversational powers, and graceful manners; but if, with these advantages, they still need richer dress to distinguish them from *us*, the fault must be their own, and they should at least learn to honor merit, and acknowledge talent wherever they see it. . . .

And now I will address myself to my sister operatives in the Lowell factories. Good advice should be taken, from whatever quarter it may come, whether from friend or foe; and part of the advice which Mrs. Hale has given to the readers of the Ladies' Book, may be of advantage to us. Is there not among us, as a class, too much of this striving for distinction in dress? Is it not the only aim and object of too many of us, to wear something a little better than others can obtain? Do we not sometimes see the girl who has half a dozen silk gowns, toss her head, as if she felt herself six times better than her neighbor who has none? . . .

We all have many opportunities for the exercise of the kindly affections, and more than most females. We should look upon one another something as a band of orphans should do. We are fatherless and motherless: we are alone, and surrounded by temptation. Let us caution each other; let us watch over and endeavor to improve each other; and both at our boarding-houses and in the Mill, let us strive to promote each other's comfort and happiness. Above all, let us endeavor to improve ourselves by making good use of the many advantages we here possess. I say let us at least strive to do this; and if we succeed, it will finally be acknowledged that Factory Girls shine forth in ornaments far more valuable than *Gold Watches*.

A FACTORY GIRL

Source 12 from *Lowell Offering,* Series II, Vol. I (1841), p. 32. Courtesy of Merrimack Valley Textile Museum.

12. Song of the Spinners.

SONG OF THE SPINNERS.

Source 13 from Lucy Larcom, *A New England Girlhood* (Boston: Houghton Mifflin, 1889).

13. Selection from *A New England Girlhood*.

During my father's life, a few years before my birth, his thoughts had been turned towards the new manufacturing town growing up on the banks of the Merrimack. He had once taken a journey there, with the possibility in his mind of making the place his home, his limited income furnishing no adequate promise of maintenance for his large family of daughters. From the beginning, Lowell had a high reputation for good order, morality, piety, and all that was dear to the old-fashioned New Englander's heart.

After his death, my mother's thoughts naturally followed the direction his had taken; and seeing no other opening for herself, she sold her small estate, and moved to Lowell, with the intention of taking a corporation-house for mill-girl boarders. Some of the family objected, for the Old World traditions about factory life were anything but attractive; and they were current in New England until the experiment at Lowell had shown that independent and intelligent workers invariably give their own character to their occupation. My mother had visited Lowell, and she was willing and glad, knowing all about the place, to make it our home. . . .

[Because her mother could not earn enough to support the family, Lucy (age eleven) and her sister went to work in the mills.]

So I went to my first day's work in the mill with a light heart. The novelty of it made it seem easy, and it really was not hard, just to change the bobbins on the spinning-frames every three quarters of an hour or so, with half a dozen other little girls who were doing the same thing. When I came back at night, the family began to pity me for my long, tiresome day's work, but I laughed, and said,—

"Why, it is nothing but fun. It is just like play."

And for a little while it was only a new amusement; I liked it better than going to school and "making believe" I was learning when I was not. And there was a great deal of play mixed with it. We were not occupied more than half the time. The intervals were spent frolicking around among the spinning-frames, teasing and talking to the older girls, or entertaining ourselves with games and stories in a corner, or exploring, with the over-seer's permission, the mysteries of the carding-room, the dressing-room, and the weaving-room. . . .

There were compensations for being shut in to daily toil so early. The mill itself had its lessons for us. But it was not, and could not be, the right sort of life for a child, and we were happy in the knowledge that, at the longest, our employment was only to be temporary.

When I took my next three months at the grammar school, everything there was changed, and I too was changed. The teachers were kind, and thorough in their instruction; and my mind seemed to have been ploughed up during that year of work, so that knowledge took root in it easily. It was a great delight to me to study, and at the end of the three months the master told me that I was prepared for the high school.

But alas! I could not go. The little money I could earn—one dollar a week, besides the price of my board—was needed in the family, and I must return to the mill. It was a severe disappointment to me, though I did not say so at home. . . .

In the older times it was seldom said to little girls, as it always has been said to boys, that they ought to have some definite plan, while they were children, what to be and do when they were grown up. There was usually but one path open before them, to become good wives and housekeepers. And the ambition of most girls was to follow their mothers' footsteps in this direction; a natural and laudable ambition. But girls, as well as boys, must often have been conscious of their own peculiar capabilities,—must have desired to cultivate and make use of their individual powers. When I was growing up, they had already begun to be encouraged to do so. We were often told that it was our duty to develop any talent we might possess, or at least learn how to do some one thing which the world needed, or which would make it a pleasanter world. . . .

At this time I had learned to do a spinner's work, and I obtained permission to tend some frames that stood directly in front of the river-windows, with only them and the wall behind me, extending half the length of the mill,—and one young woman beside me, at the farther end of the row. She was a sober, mature person, who scarcely thought it worth her while to speak often to a child like me; and I was, when with strangers, rather a reserved girl; so I kept myself occupied with the river, my work, and my thoughts. . . .

The printed regulations forbade us to bring books into the mill, so I made my window-seat into a small library of poetry, pasting its side all over with newspaper clippings. In those days we had only weekly papers, and they had always a "poet's corner," where standard writers were well represented, with anonymous ones, also. I was not, of course, much of a critic. I chose my verses for their sentiment, and because I wanted to commit them to memory; sometimes it was a long poem, sometimes a hymn, sometimes only a stray verse. . . .

Some of the girls could not believe that the Bible was meant to be counted among forbidden books. We all thought that the Scriptures had a right to go wherever we went, and that if we needed them anywhere, it was at our work. I evaded the law by carrying some leaves from a torn Testament in my pocket.

The overseer, caring more for law than gospel, confiscated all he found. He had his desk full of Bibles. It sounded oddly to hear him say to the most religious girl in the room, when he took hers away, "I did think you had more conscience than to bring that book here." But we had some close ethical questions to settle in those days. It was a rigid code of morality under which we lived. Nobody complained of it, however, and we were doubtless better off for its strictness, in the end.

The last window in the row behind me was filled with flourishing house plants—fragrant-leaved geraniums, the overseer's pets. They gave that corner a bowery look; the perfume and freshness tempted me there often. Standing before that window, I could look across the room and see girls moving backwards and forwards among the spinning-frames, sometimes stooping, sometimes reaching up their arms, as their work required, with easy and not ungraceful movements. On the whole, it was far from being a disagreeable place to stay in. The girls were bright-looking and neat, and everything was kept clean and shining. The effect of the whole was rather attractive to strangers. . . .

One great advantage which came to these many stranger girls through being brought together, away from their own homes, was that it taught them to go out of themselves, and enter into the lives of others. Home-life, when one always stays at home, is necessarily narrowing. That is one reason why so many women are petty and unthoughtful of any except their own family's interests. We have hardly begun to live until we can take in the idea of the whole human family as the one to which we truly belong. To me, it was an incalculable help to find myself among so many working-girls, all of us thrown upon our own resources, but thrown much more upon each others' sympathies. . . .

My grandfather came to see my mother once at about this time and visited the mills. When he had entered the room, and looked around for a moment, he took off his hat and made a low bow to the girls, first toward the right, and then toward the left. We were familiar with his courteous habits, partly due to his French descent; but we had never seen anybody bow to a roomful of mill girls in that polite way, and some one of the family afterwards asked him why he did so. He looked a little surprised at the question, but answered promptly and with dignity, "I always take off my hat to ladies."

His courtesy was genuine. Still, we did not call ourselves ladies. We did not forget that we were working-girls, wearing coarse aprons suitable to our work, and that there was some danger of our becoming drudges. I know that sometimes the confinement of the mill became very wearisome to me. In the sweet June weather I would lean far out of the window, and try not to hear the unceasing clash of sound inside. Looking away to the hills, my whole stifled being would cry out

"Oh, that I had wings!"

Still I was there from choice, and

"The prison unto which we doom ourselves,
No prison is."

Source 14 courtesy of Mildred Tunis Tracey Memorial Library, New London, N.H.

14. A "Typical" Factory Girl, Delia Page, c. 1860.

Source 15 courtesy of Merrimack Valley Textile Museum.

15. Two Women Weavers, c. 1860.

Sources 16 through 21 from Thomas Dublin, ed., *Farm to Factory: Women's Letters, 1830–1860* (New York: Columbia University Press, 1981), pp. 42, 100–104, 170–172.

16. Letter from Sarah Hodgdon.

[In 1830, Sarah Hodgdon (age sixteen) and two friends went to Lowell to work in the textile mills. After approximately ten years of working in various factories, Hodgdon married a shoemaker from her hometown. This is one of her early letters to her mother.]

[June 1830]

Dear mother

I take this oppertunity to write to you to informe you that I have gone into the mill and like very well. I was here one week and three days before I went into the mill to work for my board. We boord t[o]gether. I like my boording place very well. I enjoy my health very well. I do not enjoy my mind so well as it is my desire to. I cant go to any meetings except I hire a seat therefore I have to stay home on that account.[6] I desire you pay that it may not be said of me when I come home that I have sold my soul for the gay vanitys of this world. Give my love to my father and tell him not to forget me and to my dear sister and to my brothers and to my grammother tell her I do not forget her and to my Aunts and to all my enquiring friends. I want that you should write to me as soon as you can and when you write to me I want that you should write to me the particulars about sister and Aunt Betsy. Dont fail writing. I bege you not to let this scrabling be seen.

Sarah Hodgdon

Mary Hodgdon

17. Letter from Mary Paul.

[Mary Paul left home in 1845 at age fifteen. She worked briefly and unsuccessfully as a domestic servant and then went to Lowell as a factory girl for four years. After leaving the mills, she returned home for a short while and then worked as a seamstress. Next she joined a utopian community, and finally she took a job as a housekeeper. In 1857, Paul married the son of the woman who ran the boardinghouse where she had lived in Lowell.]

6. Urban churches in this period often charged people who attended services a fee called pew rent.

Saturday, Sept. 13th 1845

Dear Father

I received your letter this afternoon by Wm Griffith. . . . I am very glad you sent my shoes. They fit very well indeed they [are] large enough.

I want you to consent to let me go to Lowell if you can. I think it would be much better for me than to stay about here. I could earn more to begin with than I can any where about here. I am in need of clothes which I cannot get if I stay about here and for that reason I want to go to Lowell or some other place. We all think if I could go with some steady girl that I might do well. I want you to think of it and make up your mind. Mercy Jane Griffith[7] is going to start in four or five weeks. Aunt Miller and Aunt Sarah think it would be a good chance for me to go if you would consent— which I want you to do if possible. I want to see you and talk with you about it.

Aunt Sarah gains slowly.

Mary

Bela Paul

18. Letter from Mary Paul.

Lowell Nov 20th 1845

Dear Father

An opportunity now presents itself which I improve in writing to you. I started for this place at the time I talked of which was Thursday. I left Whitneys at nine o'clock stopped at Windsor at 12 and staid till 3 and started again. Did not stop again for any length of time till we arrived at Lowell. Went to a boarding house and staid until Monday night. On Saturday after I got here Luthera Griffith went round with me to find a place but we were unsuccessful. On Monday we started again and were more successful. We found a place in a spinning room and the next morning I went to work. I like very well have 50 cts first payment increasing every payment as I get along in work have a first rate overseer and a very good boarding place. I work on the Lawrence Corporation. Mill is No 2 spinning room. I was very sorry that you did not come to see me start. I wanted to see you and Henry[8] but I suppose that you were otherways engaged. I hoped

7. A friend of Mary's.
8. Mary's thirteen-year-old brother.

to see Julius[9] but did not much expect to for I s[up]posed he was engaged in other matters. He got six dollars for me which I was very glad of. It cost me $3.25 to come. Stage fare was $3.00 and lodging at Windsor, 25 cts. Had to pay only 25 cts for board for 9 days after I got here before I went into the mill. Had 2.50 left with which I got a bonnet and some other small articles. Tell Harriet Burbank to send me paper. Tell her I shall send her one as soon as possible. You must write as soon as you receive this. Tell Henry I should like to hear from him. If you hear anything from William[10] write for I want to know what he is doing. I shall write to Uncle Millers folks the first opportunity. Aunt Nancy presented me with a new alpacca dress before I came away from there which I was very glad of. I think of staying here a year certain, if not more. I wish that you and Henry would come down here. I think that you might do well. I guess that Henry could get into the mill and I think that Julius might get in too. Tell all friends that I should like to hear from them.

excuse bad writing and mistakes

This from your own daughter

Mary

P.S. Be sure and direct to No. 15 Lawrence Corporation.

Bela Paul

Mary S Paul

19. Letter from Mary Paul.

Lowell Dec 21st 1845

Dear Father

I received your letter on Thursday the 14th with much pleasure. I am well which is one comfort. My life and health are spared while others are cut off. Last Thursday one girl fell down and broke her neck which caused instant death. She was going in or coming out of the mill and slipped down it being very icy. The same day a man was killed by the cars. Another had nearly all of his ribs broken. Another was nearly killed by falling down and having a bale of cotton fall on him. Last Tuesday we were paid. In all I had six dollars and sixty cents paid four dollars and sixty-eight cents for board. With the rest I got me a pair of rubbers and a pair of 50.cts shoes. Next payment I am to have a dollar a week beside my board. We have not had much snow the deepest being not more than 4 inches. It has been very

9. Mary's twenty-seven-year-old brother.
10. Mary's brother, who was married and living in Tennessee.

warm for winter. Perhaps you would like something about our regulations about going in and coming out of the mill. At 5 o'clock in the morning the bell rings for the folks to get up and get breakfast. At half past six it rings for the girls to get up and at seven they are called into the mill. At half past 12 we have dinner are called back again at one and stay till half past seven. I get along very well with my work. I can doff[11] as fast as any girl in our room. I think I shall have frames before long. The usual time allowed for learning is six months but I think I shall have frames before I have been in three as I get along so fast. I think that the factory is the best place for me and if any girl wants employment I advise them to come to Lowell. Tell Harriet that though she does not hear from me she is not forgotten. I have little time to devote to writing that I cannot write all I want to. There are half a dozen letters which I ought to write to day but I have not time. Tell Harriet I send my love to her and all of the girls. Give my love to Mrs. Clement. Tell Henry this will answer for him and you too for this time.

This from
Mary S Paul

Bela Paul
Henry S Paul

20. Letter to Delia Page.[12]

[Delia Page lived with a foster family, the Trussells, because she did not get along well with her stepmother. In 1859, at age eighteen, she went to work at a textile mill in Manchester, New Hampshire, where she fell in love with a mill worker who had evidently deserted his wife and child in Lowell. When reports of Delia's "affair" reached home, her foster family wrote her urgent letters trying to persuade her to reconsider. Eventually, in 1866, she married an eligible, respectable single man.]

New London Sept. 7, 1860

Dear Delia,

I should thank you for your very good letter. I am glad to know your health is good. I trust I shall ever feel a deep interest in your welfare.

You say you are not so much in love as we imagine; if so I am very glad of it. Not that I should not be willing you should love a worthy object but the one referred to is no doubt an *unworthy* one; and should you fix you[r] affections on him, it will cause you sorrow such as you never knew; indeed we be-

---

11. A doffer replaced empty bobbins on the spinning frames with full ones.
12. Delia Page's photograph is shown in Source 14.

lieve it would be *your ruin*. We have no reason to think, his pretensions notwithstanding, that he has any *real love for you*. Your father Trussell has told or rather written you what he has learned about him. I fear it will be hard for you to believe it, but if you will take the trouble to inquire, I think you will find it all true. He probably is incapable of even friendship, and in his apparent regard for you, is actuated by *low, base, selfish* motives.

I think you will sooner or later come to this conclusion respecting him. The sooner the better. Your reputation your happiness all you hold dear are I fear at stake. You have done well, let not your high hopes be blasted. Do the best you can, keep no company but good and you stand fair to get a good husband, one who has a real regard for you. But if you keep this man's company, the virtuous must shun you. You will not like to read this. My only excuse for writing is that I am very anxious about you. If my anxiety is unfounded so much the better. Unfounded it cannot be if you are keeping the company of an unprincipled libertine.

Your affectionate Mother Trussell

21. Letter to Delia Page.

[Sept. 7 1860]

My Dear Delia,

I am going to trouble you a little longer (I speak for the whole family now). In your situation you must necessarily form many new acquaintance[s] and amongst them there will be not a few who will assure you of their friendship and seek your confidence. The less worthy they are the more earnestly they will seek to convince you of their sincerity. You spoke of one girl whom you highly prised. I hope she is all that you think her to be. If so you are certainly fortunate in making her acquaintance.

But the best have failings & I should hardly expect one of her age a safe counciler in all cases. You must in fact rely upon a principal of morality within your own bosom and if you [are] at a loss you may depend upon the council of Mrs. Piper.[13] A safe way is not to allow yourself to say or do anything that you would not be willing anyone should know if necessary. You will say Humpf think I cant take care of myself. I have seen many who thought so and found their mistake when ruined. My dear girl. We fear much for those we love much, or the fear is in porportion [sic] to the

13. The Pipers were Trussell family friends who lived in Manchester.

Love. And although I have no reason to think that you go out nights or engage in anything that will injure your health or morrals yet the love I have for you leads me to fear lest among so much that is pleasant but evil you may be injured before you are aware of danger.

And now my Dear Girl I will finish by telling you what you must do for me.

You must take care of my little factory girl. Dont let her expose her health if you do she will be sick and loose [*sic*] all she has earned. Don't let her do any thing any time that she would be ashamed to have her father know. If you do she may loose her charracter. Try to have her improve some every day that she may be the wealthiest most respected & best beloved of all her sisters, brothers & kindred & so be fitted to make the best of husbands the best of wives.

[Luther M Trussell]

QUESTIONS TO CONSIDER

Why did Brownson (Source 1) believe that slaves were better off than free laborers? What did he imply about women who worked? What major advantages did Reverend Mills observe in the Lowell system (Source 2)? In what important ways did the system (the factories and the boardinghouses) regulate the girls' lives? How did it protect the morals of its female employees? Of course, not all girls lived up to these standards. What did they do? How were they punished? Do you think Reverend Mills presented a relatively unbiased view? Why or why not? In what ways did the author of the article in *Voice of Industry* (Source 4) believe factory girls were being exploited?

Look carefully at the title page (Source 5) and the first editorial of the *Lowell Offering* (Source 6). What do they tell you about the factory girls, their interests, and their concerns? Was C.B. (Source 7) upholding the cult of true womanhood in her article about the dignity of labor? How did "home" in the boardinghouse (Source 8) differ from the girls' real homes? Based on what you read in Reverend Mills's account, in what ways might a boardinghouse have been similar to the girls' real homes?

The next three letters were written by girls who were rather angry. How did "a factory girl" (Source 9) try to disprove Brownson's view? What fears and anxieties do this letter and the one from Dorothea (Source 10) reveal? What were these two girls trying to prove? The third letter writer (Source 11) retained her sense of humor, but she also was upset. In this case, the offensive remark to which she referred appeared in *Godey's Lady's Book,* the most popular American women's magazine of the period, and was written by the highly respected Sarah Josepha Hale (the magazine's editor and author of "Mary Had a Little Lamb"). What had Mrs. Hale written? What was the factory girl's response? What advice did she give her coworkers about fashion? About being a true woman? Even "Song of the Spinners" (Source 12) contains a message. What do the lyrics tell you about the spinners' values and attitudes toward work?

What were the other realities of factory girls' lives? What does the bell schedule (Source 3) tell you? How would you describe the image the pictures of the mill girls present (Sources 14 and 15)? What hopes (and fears) does the correspondence between the mill girls and their families (Sources 16 through 21) express? Why did Lucy Larcom (Source 13) have to go to work in the mills when she was so young? How did she feel about the work when she was a child? What contrast did she draw between young boys' and young girls' upbringing in the early nineteenth century? Did she and the other girls always obey the factory rules? What advantages did she discover in her factory experience? What were the disadvantages?

Now that you are thoroughly familiar with the ideas about how the working girls of Lowell were supposed to behave and the realities of the system under which they lived, you are ready to frame an answer to the central question: how did people react when the needs of a modernizing economy came into conflict with the ideas about women's place in society?

⌘ EPILOGUE ⌘

The Lowell system was a very real attempt to prevent the spread of the evils associated with the factory system and to make work in the textile mills "respectable" for young New England women. Working conditions in Lowell were considerably better than in most New England mill towns. However, several major strikes (or "turnouts," as they were called) occurred in the Lowell mills in the mid-1830s, and by the mid-1840s Lowell began to experience serious labor problems. To remain competitive yet at the same time maximize profits, companies introduced the "speedup" (a much faster work pace) and the "stretch-out" (one worker was put in charge of more machinery—sometimes as many as four looms). The mills also cut wages, even though boardinghouse rents were rising. In Lowell, workers first tried to have the length of the workday reduced and, as did many other American workers, united in support of the Ten-Hour Movement. When women workers joined such protests, they further challenged the ideas embodied in the cult of true womanhood—especially that of submissiveness.

Even before the strikes, the Lowell system was breaking down, as more and more mills, far larger than their predecessors, were built. Construction of private housing (especially tenements) expanded, and a much smaller proportion of mill hands lived in boardinghouses. Both housing and neighborhoods became badly overcrowded. By 1850, mill owners were looking for still other ways besides the speedup and stretch-out to reduce the cost of labor. They found their answer in the waves of Irish immigrating to America to escape the economic hardships so widespread in their own country.

Fewer and fewer "Yankee girls" were recruited for work in the textile mills. At one Lowell company, for example, the number of native-born girls declined from 737 in 1836 to 324 in 1860, although the total number of female workers remained constant. Irish men, women, and increasing numbers of children filled the gap, because as wages declined, a family income became a necessity.

By 1860, what Reverend Mills had characterized as "the moral and intellectual advantages" of the Lowell system had come to an end. Indeed, many Americans could see little or no difference between our own factory towns and those of Europe.

CHAPTER 8

THE "PECULIAR INSTITUTION": SLAVES TELL THEIR OWN STORY

⬿ THE PROBLEM ⬾

With the establishment of its new government in 1789, the United States became a virtual magnet for foreign travelers, perhaps never more so than during the three decades immediately preceding our Civil War. Middle to upper class, interested in everything from politics to prison reform to botanical specimens to the position of women in American society, these curious travelers fanned out across the United States, and almost all wrote about their observations in letters, pamphlets, and books widely read on both sides of the ocean. Regardless of their special interests, however, few travelers failed to notice—and comment on—the "peculiar institution" of African American slavery.

As were many nineteenth-century women writers, English author Harriet Martineau was especially interested in those aspects of American society that affected women and children. She was appalled by the slave system, believing it degraded marriage by allowing southern white men to exploit female slaves sexually, a practice that often produced mulatto children born into slavery.

The young Frenchman Alexis de Tocqueville came to study the American penitentiary system and stayed to investigate politics and society. In his book *Democracy in America* (1842), Tocqueville expressed his belief that American slaves had completely lost their African culture—their customs, languages, religions, and even the memories of their countries. An English novelist who was enormously popular in the United States, the crusty Charles Dickens, also visited in 1842. He spent very little time in the

[169]

CHAPTER 8

THE "PECULIAR
INSTITUTION":
SLAVES TELL
THEIR OWN
STORY

South but collected (and published) advertisements for runaway slaves that contained gruesome descriptions of their burns, brandings, scars, and iron cuffs and collars. As Dickens departed for a steamboat trip to the West, he wrote that he left "with a grateful heart that I was not doomed to live where slavery was, and had never had my senses blunted to its wrongs and horrors in a slave-rocked cradle."[1]

In the turbulent 1850s, Fredrika Bremer, a Swedish novelist, traveled throughout the United States for two years and spent considerable time in South Carolina, Georgia, and Louisiana. After her first encounters with African Americans in Charleston, Bremer wrote to her sister that "they are ugly, but appear for the most part cheerful and well-fed."[2] Her subsequent trips to the plantations of the backcountry, however, increased her sympathy for slaves and her distrust of white southerners' assertions that "slaves are the happiest people in the world."[3] In fact, by the end of her stay, Bremer was praising the slaves' morality, patience, talents, and religious practices.

These travelers—and many more—added their opinions to the growing literature about the nature of American slavery and its effects. But the overwhelming majority of this literature was written by white people. What did the slaves themselves think? How did they express their feelings about the peculiar institution of slavery?

⬦ BACKGROUND ⬦

By the time of the American Revolution, what had begun in 1619 as a trickle of Africans intended to supplement the farm labor of indentured servants from England had swelled to a slave population of approximately 500,000 people, the majority concentrated on tobacco, rice, and cotton plantations in the South. Moreover, as the African American population grew, what apparently had been a fairly loose and unregimented labor system gradually evolved into an increasingly harsh, rigid, and complete system of chattel slavery that tried to control nearly every aspect of the slaves' lives. By 1775, African American slavery had become a significant (some would have said indispensable) part of southern life.

The American Revolution did not reverse those trends. Although northern states in which African American slavery was not so deeply rooted began instituting gradual emancipation, after the Revolution, the slave system—as well as its harshness—increased in

1. Charles Dickens, *American Notes and Pictures from Italy* (London: Oxford University Press, 1957), p. 137.

2. Fredrika Bremer, *America of the Fifties: Letters of Fredrika Bremer,* ed. Adolph B. Benson (New York: American Scandinavian Foundation, 1924), p. 96.
3. Ibid., p. 100.

the South. The invention of the cotton gin, which enabled seeds to be removed from the easily grown short staple cotton, permitted southerners to cultivate cotton on the uplands, thereby spurring the westward movement of the plantation system and slavery. As a result, slavery expanded along with settlement into nearly every area of the South: the Gulf region, Tennessee, Kentucky, and ultimately Texas. Simultaneously, the slave population burgeoned, roughly doubling every 30 years (from approximately 700,000 in 1790 to 1.5 million in 1820 to more than 3.2 million in 1850). Because importation of slaves from Africa was banned in 1808 (although there was some illegal slave smuggling), most further gains in the slave population were from natural increase.

But as the slave population grew, the fears and anxieties of southern whites grew correspondingly. In 1793, a slave rebellion in the Caribbean caused tremendous consternation in the white South. Rumors of uprisings plotted by slaves were numerous. And the actual rebellion of Nat Turner in Virginia in 1831 (in which fifty-five whites were killed, many of them while asleep) only increased white insecurities and dread. In response, southern states passed a series of laws that made the system of slavery even more restrictive. Toward the end of his life, Thomas Jefferson (who did not live to see Nat Turner's uprising) agonized:

But as it is, we have the wolf by the ears, and we can neither hold him, nor safely let him go. Justice is in one scale, and self-preservation in the other. . . . I regret that I am now to

die in the belief, that the useless sacrifice of themselves by the generation of 1776, to acquire self-government and happiness to their country, is to be thrown away by the unwise and unworthy passions of their sons. . . .

By this time, however, Jefferson was nearly alone among white southerners. Most did not question the assertion that slavery was a necessity, that it was good for both the slave and the owner, and that it must be preserved at any cost.

It often has been pointed out that the majority of white southerners did not own slaves. In fact, the proportion of white southern families who did own slaves was actually declining in the nineteenth century, from one-third in 1830 to roughly one-fourth by 1860. Moreover, nearly three-fourths of these slaveholders owned fewer than ten slaves. Slaveholders, then, were a distinct minority of the white southern population, and those slaveholders with large plantations and hundreds of slaves were an exceedingly small group.

How, then, did the peculiar institution of slavery, as one southerner called it, become so embedded in the Old South? First, even though only a minority of southern whites owned slaves, nearly all southern whites were somehow touched by the institution of slavery. Fear of black uprisings prompted many nonslaveholders to support an increasingly rigid slave system that included night patrols, written passes for slaves away from plantations, supervised religious services for slaves, a law prohibiting teaching slaves to read or write, and other measures to keep slaves igno-

CHAPTER 8

THE "PECULIAR
INSTITUTION":
SLAVES TELL
THEIR OWN
STORY

rant, dependent, and always under the eyes of whites. Many nonslaveholders also were afraid that emancipation would bring them into direct economic competition with blacks, who, it was assumed, would drive down wages. Finally, although large planters represented only a fraction of the white population, they virtually controlled the economic, social, and political institutions and were not about to injure either themselves or their status by eliminating the slave system that essentially supported them.

To defend their peculiar institution, white southerners constructed a remarkably complete and diverse set of arguments. Slavery, they maintained, was actually a far more humane system than northern capitalism. After all, slaves were fed, clothed, sheltered, cared for when they were ill, and supported in their old age, whereas northern factory workers were paid pitifully low wages, used, and then discarded when no longer useful. Furthermore, many white southerners maintained that slavery was a positive good because it had introduced the "barbarous" Africans to civilized American ways and, more importantly, to Christianity. Other southern whites stressed what they believed was the childlike, dependent nature of African Americans, insisting that they could never cope with life outside the paternalistic and "benevolent" institution of slavery. In such an atmosphere, in which many of the white southern intellectual efforts went into the defense of slavery, dissent and freedom of thought were not welcome. Hence those white southerners who disagreed and might have challenged the

South's dependence on slavery remained silent, were hushed up, or decided to leave the region. In many ways, then, the enslavement of African Americans partly rested on the limitation of rights and freedoms for southern whites as well.

But how did the slaves react to an economic and social system that meant that neither they nor their children would ever experience freedom? Most white southerners assumed that slaves were happy and content. Northern abolitionists (a minority of the white population) believed that slaves continually yearned for freedom. Both groups used oceans of ink to justify and support their claims. But evidence of how the slaves felt and thought is woefully sparse. Given the restrictive nature of the slave system (which included enforced illiteracy among slaves), this pitiful lack of evidence is hardly surprising.

How, then, can we learn how slaves felt and thought about the peculiar institution? Slave uprisings were almost nonexistent, but does that mean most slaves were happy with their lot? Runaways were common, and some, such as Frederick Douglass and Harriet Jacobs, actually reached the North and wrote about their experiences as slaves. Yet how typical were their experiences? Most slaves were born, lived, and died in servitude, did not participate in organized revolts, and did not run away. How did they feel about the system of slavery?

Although most slaves did not read or write, did not participate in organized revolts, and did not attempt to run away, they did leave a remarkable amount of evidence that can help us understand their thoughts and feelings. Yet we must be imaginative in how we approach and use that evidence.

In an earlier chapter, you discovered that statistical information (about births, deaths, age at marriage, farm size, inheritance, tax rolls, and so forth) can reveal a great deal about ordinary people, such as the New Englanders on the eve of the American Revolution. Such demographic evidence can help the historian form a picture of who these people were and the socioeconomic trends of the time, even if the people themselves were not aware of those trends. In this exercise, you will be using another kind of evidence and asking different questions. Your evidence will not come from white southerners (whose stake in maintaining slavery was enormous), foreign travelers (whose own cultural biases often influenced what they reported), or even white abolitionists in the North (whose urgent need to eradicate the "sin" of slavery sometimes led them to gross exaggerations for propaganda purposes). You will be using anecdotes, stories, and songs from the rich oral tradition of African American slaves, supplemented by the narratives of two runaway slaves, to investigate the human dimensions of the peculiar institution.

Some of the oral evidence was collected and transcribed by people soon after emancipation. However, much of the evidence did not come to light until many years later, when the former slaves who were still alive were very old men and women. In fact, not until the 1920s did concerted efforts to preserve the reminiscences of these people begin. In the 1920s, Fisk University collected a good deal of evidence. In the 1930s, the government-financed Federal Writers' Project accumulated more than two thousand narratives from ex-slaves in every southern state except Louisiana and deposited them in the Library of Congress in Washington, D.C.

Much of the evidence, however, is in the form of songs and stories that slaves created and told to one another. Like the narratives of former slaves, these sources also must be used with imagination and care.

The central question you are to answer is this: how did the slaves themselves view the peculiar institution? How did they endure under a labor system that, at its very best, was still based on the total ownership of one human being by another?

∞ THE METHOD ∞

Historians must always try to be aware of the limitations of their evidence. In the Federal Writers' Project, most of the former slaves were in their eighties or nineties (quite a few were older than one hundred) at the time they were interviewed. In other words, most of the interviewees had been

CHAPTER 8

THE "PECULIAR
INSTITUTION":
SLAVES TELL
THEIR OWN
STORY

children or young people in 1860. It is also important to know that although some of the interviewers were black, the overwhelming majority were white. Lastly, although many of the former slaves had moved to another location or a different state after the Civil War, many others were still living in the same county (sometimes even on the same land) where they had been slaves. In what ways might the age of the former slave, the race of the interviewer, or the place where the former slave was living have affected the narratives?

These narratives reveal much about these people's thoughts and feelings about slavery. What direct reactions did the ex-slaves give? Why did many of them choose to be indirect? Some chose to answer questions by telling stories. Why? Remember, although some of the stories or anecdotes may not actually be true, they can be taken as representative of what the former slaves wished had happened or what they really thought about an incident. Therefore, often you must pull the true meaning from a narrative, inferring what the interviewee meant as well as what he or she said.

As for slave songs and other contemporary evidence, most slaves could never have spoken their thoughts or vented their feelings directly. Instead, they often hid their true meanings through the use of symbols, metaphors, and allegories. Here again, you must be able to read between the lines, extracting thoughts, attitudes, and feelings that were purposely hidden or concealed from all but other slaves.

Included in the evidence are two accounts of runaway slaves who escaped to the North before the Civil War. Frederick Bailey (who later changed his name to Douglass) ran away when he was about nineteen years old, but he was captured and returned. Two years later, he was able to escape, and he moved to Massachusetts, where he worked as a laborer. After joining an antislavery society and becoming a successful speaker, he published his autobiography (1845) and edited his own abolitionist newspaper, the *North Star*. Harriet Jacobs (who used the pen name Linda Brent) was twenty-seven years old when she ran away in 1845, but her narrative was not published until the beginning of the Civil War. Throughout her story, Jacobs used fictitious names and places to protect those who had helped her and to conceal the escape route she had used. Both Douglass and Jacobs were self-educated people who wrote their own books, although the abolitionist writer Lydia Maria Child made minor editorial revisions in Jacobs's manuscript.

As you examine each piece of evidence, jot down enough notes to allow you to recall that piece of evidence later. But also (perhaps in a separate column) write down the *attitude* that each piece of evidence communicates about the peculiar institution of slavery. What is the hidden message?

After you have examined each piece of evidence, look back over your notes. What attitudes about slavery stand out? What did the slaves think about the slave system?

ↀ THE EVIDENCE ↀ

Sources 1 through 16 from B. A. Botkin, Federal Writers' Project, *Lay My Burden Down: A Folk History of Slavery* (Chicago: University of Chicago Press, 1945).

1. Hog-Killing Time.

. . . I remember Mammy told me about one master who almost starved his slaves. Mighty stingy, I reckon he was.

Some of them slaves was so poorly thin they ribs would kinda rustle against each other like corn stalks a-drying in the hot winds. But they gets even one hog-killing time, and it was funny, too, Mammy said.

They was seven hogs, fat and ready for fall hog-killing time. Just the day before Old Master told off they was to be killed, something happened to all them porkers. One of the field boys found them and come a-telling the master: "The hogs is all died, now they won't be any meats for the winter."

When the master gets to where at the hogs is laying, they's a lot of Negroes standing round looking sorrow-eyed at the wasted meat. The master asks: "What's the illness with 'em?"

"Malitis," they tells him, and they acts like they don't want to touch the hogs. Master says to dress them anyway for they ain't no more meat on the place.

He says to keep all the meat for the slave families, but that's because he's afraid to eat it hisself account of the hogs' got malitis.

"Don't you all know what is malitis?" Mammy would ask the children when she was telling of the seven fat hogs and seventy lean slaves. And she would laugh, remembering how they fooled Old Master so's to get all them good meats.

"One of the strongest Negroes got up early in the morning," Mammy would explain, "long 'fore the rising horn called the slaves from their cabins. He skitted to the hog pen with a heavy mallet in his hand. When he tapped Mister Hog 'tween the eyes with the mallet, 'malitis' set in mighty quick, but it was a uncommon 'disease,' even with hungry Negroes around all the time."

2. The Old Parrot.

The mistress had an old parrot, and one day I was in the kitchen making cookies, and I decided I wanted some of them, so I tooks me out some and put them on a chair; and when I did this the mistress entered the door. I

CHAPTER 8

THE "PECULIAR
INSTITUTION":
SLAVES TELL
THEIR OWN
STORY

picks up a cushion and throws [it] over the pile of cookies on the chair, and Mistress came near the chair and the old parrot cries out, "Mistress burn, Mistress burn." Then the mistress looks under the cushion, and she had me whupped, but the next day I killed the parrot, and she often wondered who or what killed the bird.

3. The Coon and the Dog.

Every time I think of slavery and if it done the race any good, I think of the story of the coon and dog who met. The coon said to the dog, "Why is it you're so fat and I am so poor, and we is both animals?" The dog said: "I lay round Master's house and let him kick me and he gives me a piece of bread right on." Said the coon to the dog: "Better, then, that I stay poor." Them's my sentiment. I'm like the coon, I don't believe in 'buse.

4. The Partridge and the Fox.

. . . A partridge and a fox 'greed to kill a beef. They kilt and skinned it. Before they divide it, the fox said, "My wife says send her some beef for soup." So he took a piece of it and carried it down the hill, then come back and said, "My wife wants more beef for soup." He kept this up till all the beef was gone 'cept the liver. The fox come back, and the partridge says, "Now let's cook this liver and both of us eat it." The partridge cooked the liver, et its parts right quick, and then fell over like it was sick. The fox got scared and said that beef is pizen, and he ran down the hill and started bringing the beef back. And when he brought it all back, he left, and the partridge had all the beef.

5. The Rabbit and the Tortoise.

I want to tell you one story 'bout the rabbit. The rabbit and the tortoise had a race. The tortoise git a lot of tortoises and put 'em 'long the way. Ever' now and then a tortoise crawl 'long the way, and the rabbit say, "How you now, Br'er Tortoise?" And he say, "Slow and sure, but my legs very short." When they git tired, the tortoise win 'cause he there, but he never run the race, 'cause he had tortoises strowed out all 'long the way. The tortoise had other tortoises help him.

6. Same Old Thing.

The niggers didn't go to the church building; the preacher came and preached to them in their quarters. He'd just say, "Serve your masters. Don't steal your master's turkey. Don't steal your master's chickens. Don't steal your master's hogs. Don't steal your master's meat. Do whatsomever your master tells you to do." Same old thing all the time.

7. Freedom.

I been preaching the gospel and farming since slavery time. I jined the church 'most 83 years ago when I was Major Gaud's slave, and they baptizes me in the spring branch close to where I finds the Lord. When I starts preaching I couldn't read or write and had to preach what Master told me, and he say tell them niggers iffen they obeys the master they goes to Heaven; but I knowed there's something better for them, but daren't tell them 'cept on the sly. That I done lots. I tells 'em iffen they keeps praying, the Lord will set 'em free.

8. Prayers.

My master used to ask us children, "Do your folks pray at night?" We said "No," 'cause our folks had told us what to say. But the Lord have mercy, there was plenty of that going on. They'd pray, "Lord, deliver us from under bondage."

9. Hoodoo Doctor.

My wife was sick, down, couldn't do nothing. Someone got to telling her about Cain Robertson. Cain Robertson was a hoodoo doctor in Georgia. They [say] there wasn't nothing Cain couldn't do. She says, "Go and see Cain and have him come up here."

I says, "There ain't no use to send for Cain. Cain ain't coming up here because they say he is a 'two-head' nigger." (They called all them hoodoo men "two-head" niggers; I don't know why they called them two-head). "And you know he knows the white folks will put him in jail if he comes to town."

But she says, "You go and get him."

So I went.

I left him at the house, and when I came back in, he said, "I looked at your wife and she had one of them spells while I was there. I'm afraid to

CHAPTER 8

THE "PECULIAR
INSTITUTION":
SLAVES TELL
THEIR OWN
STORY

tackle this thing because she has been poisoned, and it's been going on a long time. And if she dies, they'll say I killed her, and they already don't like me and looking for an excuse to do something to me."

My wife overheard him and says, "You go on, you got to do something."

So he made me go to town and get a pint of corn whiskey. When I brought it back he drunk a half of it at one gulp, and I started to knock him down. I'd thought he'd get drunk with my wife lying there sick.

Then he said, "I'll have to see your wife's stomach." Then he scratched it, and put three little horns on the place he scratched. Then he took another drink of whiskey and waited about ten minutes. When he took them off her stomach, they were full of blood. He put them in the basin in some water and sprinkled some powder on them, and in about ten minutes more he made me get them and they were full of clear water and there was a lot of little things that looked like wiggle tails swimming around it.

He told me when my wife got well to walk in a certain direction a certain distance, and the woman that caused all the trouble would come to my house and start a fuss with me.

He said, "Yes, but it would kill my hand." He meant that he had a curing hand and that if he made anybody sick or killed them, all his power to cure would go from him.

I showed the stuff he took out of my wife's stomach to old Doc Matthews, and he said, "You can get anything into a person by putting it in them." He asked me how I found out about it, and how it was taken out, and who did it.

I told him all about it, and he said, "I'm going to see that that nigger practices anywhere in this town he wants to and nobody bothers him." And he did.

10. Buck Brasefield.

They was pretty good to us, but old Mr. Buck Brasefield, what had a plantation 'jining us'n, was so mean to his'n that 'twa'n't nothing for 'em to run away. One nigger, Rich Parker, runned off one time, and whilst he gone he seed a hoodoo man, so when he got back Mr. Brasefield took sick and stayed sick two or three weeks. Some of the darkies told him, "Rich been to the hoodoo doctor." So Mr. Brasefield got up outen that bed and come a-yelling in the field, "You thought you had old Buck, but by God he rose again." Them niggers was so scared they squatted in the field just like partridges, and some of 'em whispered, "I wish to God he had-a died."

11. The White Lady's Quilts.

Now I'll tell you another incident. This was in slave times. My mother was a great hand for nice quilts. There was a white lady had died, and they were going to have a sale. Now this is true stuff. They had the sale, and Mother went and bought two quilts. And let me tell you, we couldn't sleep under 'em. What happened? Well, they'd pinch your toes till you couldn't stand it. I was just a boy and I was sleeping with my mother when it happened. Now that's straight stuff. What do I think was the cause? Well, I think that white lady didn't want no nigger to have them quilts. I don't know what Mother did with 'em, but that white lady just wouldn't let her have 'em.

12. Papa's Death.

My papa was strong. He never had a licking in his life. He helped the master, but one day the master says, "Si, you got to have a whopping," and my poppa says, "I never had a whopping and you can't whop me." And the master says, "But I can kill you," and he shot my papa down. My mama took him in the cabin and put him on a pallet. He died.

13. Forbidden Knowledge.

None of us was 'lowed to see a book or try to learn. They say we git smarter than they was if we learn anything, but we slips around and gits hold of that Webster's old blue-back speller and we hides it till 'way in the night and then we lights a little pine torch, and studies that spelling book. We learn it too. I can read some now and write a little too.

They wasn't no church for the slaves, but we goes to the white folks' arbor on Sunday evening, and a white man he gits up there to preach to the niggers. He say, "Now I takes my text, which is, Nigger obey your master and your mistress, 'cause what you git from them here in this world am all you ever going to git, 'cause you just like the hogs and the other animals—when you dies you ain't no more, after you been throwed in that hole." I guess we believed that for a while 'cause we didn't have no way finding out different. We didn't see no Bibles.

14. Broken Families.

I seen children sold off and the mammy not sold, and sometimes the mammy sold and a little baby kept on the place and give to another woman to raise.

CHAPTER 8

THE "PECULIAR
INSTITUTION":
SLAVES TELL
THEIR OWN
STORY

Them white folks didn't care nothing 'bout how the slaves grieved when they tore up a family.

15. Burning in Hell.

We was scared of Solomon and his whip, though, and he didn't like frolicking. He didn't like for us niggers to pray, either. We never heard of no church, but us have praying in the cabins. We'd set on the floor and pray with our heads down low and sing low, but if Solomon heared he'd come and beat on the wall with the stock of his whip. He'd say, "I'll come in there and tear the hide off you backs." But some the old niggers tell us we got to pray to God that He don't think different of the blacks and the whites. I know that Solomon is burning in hell today, and it pleasures me to know it.

16. Marriage.

After while I taken a notion to marry and Massa and Missy marries us same as all the niggers. They stands inside the house with a broom held crosswise of the door and we stands outside. Missy puts a little wreath on my head they kept there, and we steps over the broom into the house. Now, that's all they was to the marrying. After freedom I gits married and has it put in the book by a preacher.

Sources 17 and 18 from Gilbert Osofsky, comp., *Puttin' on Ole Massa* (New York: Harper and Row, 1969), p. 22.

17. Pompey.

Pompey, how do I look?
O, massa, mighty.
What do you mean "mighty," Pompey?
Why, massa, you look noble.
What do you mean by "noble"?
Why, sar, you just look like one *lion*.
Why, Pompey, where have you ever seen a lion?
I see one down in yonder field the other day, massa.
Pompey, you foolish fellow, that was a *jackass*.
Was it, massa? Well you look just like him.

18. A Grave for Old Master.

Two slaves were sent out to dig a grave for old master. They dug it very deep. As I passed by I asked Jess and Bob what in the world they dug it so deep for. It was down six or seven feet. I told them there would be a fuss about it, and they had better fill it up some. Jess said it suited him exactly. Bob said he would not fill it up; he wanted to get the old man as near *home* as possible. When we got a stone to put on his grave, we hauled the largest we could find, so as to fasten him down as strong as possible.

Sources 19 through 21 from Lawrence W. Levine, "Slave Songs and Slave Consciousness: An Exploration in Neglected Sources," in *Anonymous Americans: Explorations in Nineteenth Century Social History,* ed. Tamara K. Hareven (Englewood Cliffs, N.J.: Prentice-Hall, 1971), pp. 112, 113, 121.

19.

We raise de wheat,
Dey gib us de corn;
We bake de bread,
Dey gib us de crust;
We sif de meal,
Dey gib us de huss;
We [peel] de meat,
Dey gib us de skin;
And dat's de way
Dey take us in;
We skim de pot,
Dey gib us de liquor,
And say dat's good enough for nigger.

20.

My old Mistiss promise me,
W'en she died, she'd set me free,
She lived so long dat 'er head got bal',
An, she give out'n de notion a dyin' at all.

CHAPTER 8

THE "PECULIAR
INSTITUTION":
SLAVES TELL
THEIR OWN
STORY

21.

He delivered Daniel from the lion's den,
Jonah from de belly ob de whale,
And de Hebrew children from de fiery furnace,
And why not every man?

Sources 22 and 23 from Sterling Stuckey, "Through the Prism of Folklore: The Black Ethos in Slavery," *Massachusetts Review,* vol. 9 (1968), pp. 421, 422.

22.

When I get to heaven, gwine be at ease,
Me and my God gonna do as we please.
Gonna chatter with the Father, argue with the Son,
Tell um 'bout the world I just come from.

23.

[*A song about Samson and Delilah*]

He said, 'An' if I had-'n my way,'
He said, 'An' if I had-'n my way,'
He said, 'An' if I had-'n my way,
I'd tear the build-in' down!'

Source 24 from Frederick Douglass, *Narrative of the Life of Frederick Douglass* (New York: Anchor Books, Doubleday, 1963), pp. 1–3, 13–15, 36–37, 40–41, 44–46, 74–75.

24. Autobiography of Frederick Douglass.

I was born in Tuckahoe, near Hillsborough, and about twelve miles from Easton, in Talbot county, Maryland. I have no accurate knowledge of my age, never having seen any authentic record containing it. By far the larger part of the slaves know as little of their ages as horses know of theirs, and it is the wish of most masters within my knowledge to keep their slaves thus ignorant. I do not remember to have ever met a slave who could tell of his birthday. They seldom come nearer to it than planting-time, harvesting-time, cherry-time, spring-time, or fall-time. A want of information concerning my own was a source of unhappiness to me even during childhood. The white children could tell their ages. I could not tell why I ought to be deprived of the same privilege. I was not allowed to make any inquiries of my master concerning it. He deemed all such inquiries on the part of a slave improper and impertinent, and evidence of a restless spirit. The nearest estimate I can give makes me now between twenty-seven and twenty-eight years of age. I come to this, from hearing my master say, some time during 1835, I was about seventeen years old.

My mother was named Harriet Bailey. She was the daughter of Isaac and Betsey Bailey, both colored, and quite dark. My mother was a darker complexion than either my grandmother or grandfather.

My father was a white man. He was admitted to be such by all I ever heard speak of my parentage. The opinion was also whispered that my master was my father; but of the correctness of this opinion, I know nothing; the means of knowing was withheld from me. My mother and I were separated when I was but an infant—before I knew her as my mother. It is a common custom, in the part of Maryland from which I ran away, to part children from their mothers at a very early age. . . .

I never saw my mother, to know her as such, more than four or five times in my life; and each of these times was very short in duration, and at night. She was hired by a Mr. Stewart, who lived about twelve miles from my home. She made her journeys to see me in the night, travelling the whole distance on foot, after the performance of her day's work. She was a field hand, and a whipping is the penalty of not being in the field at sunrise, unless a slave has special permission from his or her master to the contrary—a permission which they seldom get, and one that gives to him that gives it the proud name of being a kind master. I do not recollect of ever seeing my mother by the light of day. She was with me in the night. She would lie down with me, and get me to sleep, but long before I waked she was gone. Very little communication ever took place between us. Death soon ended what little we could have while she lived, and with it her hardships and suffering. She died when I was about seven years old, on one of my master's farms, near Lee's Mill. I was not allowed to be present during her illness, at her death, or burial. She was gone long before I knew any thing about it. Never having enjoyed, to any considerable extent, her soothing presence, her tender and watchful care, I received the tidings of her death with much the same emotions I should have probably felt at the death of a stranger. . . .

The slaves selected to go to the Great House Farm,[4] for the monthly allowance for themselves and their fellow-slaves, were peculiarly enthusiastic.

4. Great House Farm was the huge "home plantation" that belonged to Douglass's owner.

CHAPTER 8

THE "PECULIAR
INSTITUTION":
SLAVES TELL
THEIR OWN
STORY

While on their way, they would make the dense old woods, for miles around, reverberate with their wild songs, revealing at once the highest joy and the deepest sadness. They would compose and sing as they went along, consulting neither time nor tune. The thought that came up, came out—if not in the word, in the sound;—and as frequently in the one as in the other. . . .

I did not, when a slave, understand the deep meaning of those rude and apparently incoherent songs. I was myself within the circle; so that I neither saw nor heard as those without might see and hear. They told a tale of woe which was then altogether beyond my feeble comprehension; they were tones loud, long, and deep; they breathed the prayer and complaint of souls boiling over with the bitterest anguish. Every tone was a testimony against slavery, and a prayer to God for deliverance from chains.

I have often been utterly astonished, since I came to the north, to find persons who could speak of the singing, among slaves, as evidence of their contentment and happiness. It is impossible to conceive of a greater mistake. Slaves sing most when they are most unhappy. The songs of the slave represent the sorrows of his heart; and he is relieved by them, only as an aching heart is relieved by its tears. At least, such is my experience. I have often sung to drown my sorrow, but seldom to express my happiness. Crying for joy, and singing for joy, were alike uncommon to me while in the jaws of slavery. . . .

[*Douglass was hired out as a young boy and went to live in the city of Baltimore.*]

Very soon after I went to live with Mr. and Mrs. Auld, she very kindly commenced to teach me the A, B, C. After I had learned this, she assisted me in learning to spell words of three or four letters. Just at this point of my progress, Mr. Auld found out what was going on, and at once forbade Mrs. Auld to instruct me further, telling her, among other things, that it was unlawful, as well as unsafe, to teach a slave to read. To use his own words, further, he said, "If you give a nigger an inch, he will take an ell.[5] A nigger should know nothing but to obey his master—to do as he is told to do. Learning would *spoil* the best nigger in the world. Now," said he, "if you teach that nigger (speaking of myself) how to read, there would be no keeping him. It would forever unfit him to be a slave. He would at once become unmanageable, and of no value to his master. As to himself, it could do him no good, but a great deal of harm. It would make him discontented and unhappy." These words sank deep into my heart, stirred up sentiments

5. An ell was an English unit of measure for cloth, approximately forty-five inches.

within that lay slumbering, and called into existence an entirely new train of thought. It was a new and special revelation, explaining dark and mysterious things, with which my youthful understanding had struggled, but struggled in vain. I now understood what had been to me a most perplexing difficulty—to wit, the white man's power to enslave the black man. It was a grand achievement, and I prized it highly. From that moment, I understood the pathway from slavery to freedom. It was just what I wanted, and I got it at a time when I the least expected it. Whilst I was saddened by the thought of losing the aid of my kind mistress, I was gladdened by the invaluable instruction which, by the merest accident, I had gained from my master. Though conscious of the difficulty of learning without a teacher, I set out with high hope, and a fixed purpose, at whatever cost of trouble, to learn how to read. The very decided manner with which he spoke, and strove to impress his wife with the evil consequences of giving me instruction, served to convince me that he was deeply sensible of the truths he was uttering. It gave me the best assurance that I might rely with the utmost confidence on the results which, he said, would flow from teaching me to read. . . .

The plan which I adopted, and the one by which I was most successful, was that of making friends of all the little white boys whom I met in the street. As many of these as I could, I converted into teachers. With their kindly aid, obtained at different times and in different places, I finally succeeded in learning to read. When I was sent of errands, I always took my book with me, and by doing one part of my errand quickly, I found time to get a lesson before my return. I used also to carry bread with me, enough of which was always in the house, and to which I was always welcome; for I was much better off in this regard than many of the poor white children in our neighborhood. This bread I used to bestow upon hungry little urchins, who, in return, would give me that more valuable bread of knowledge. I am strongly tempted to give the names of two or three of those little boys, as a testimonial of the gratitude and affection I bear them; but prudence forbids;—not that it would injure me, but it might embarrass them; for it is almost an unpardonable offence to teach slaves to read in this Christian country. . . .

I was now about twelve years old, and the thought of being a *slave for life* began to bear heavily upon my heart. . . . After a patient waiting, I got one of our city papers, containing an account of the number of petitions from the north, praying for the abolition of slavery in the District of Columbia, and of the slave trade between the States. From this time I understood the words *abolition* and *abolitionist*, and always drew near when that

CHAPTER 8

THE "PECULIAR
INSTITUTION":
SLAVES TELL
THEIR OWN
STORY

word was spoken, expecting to hear something of importance to myself and fellow-slaves. The light broke in upon me by degrees. I went one day down on the wharf of Mr. Waters; and seeing two Irishmen unloading a scow of stone, I went, unasked, and helped them. When we had finished, one of them came to me and asked me if I were a slave. I told him I was. He asked, "Are ye a slave for life?" I told him that I was. The good Irishman seemed to be deeply affected by the statement. He said to the other that it was a pity so fine a little fellow as myself should be a slave for life. He said it was a shame to hold me. They both advised me to run away to the north; that I should find friends there, and that I should be free. I pretended not to be interested in what they said, and treated them as if I did not understand them; for I feared they might be treacherous. White men have been known to encourage slaves to escape, and then, to get the reward, catch them and return them to their masters. I was afraid that these seemingly good men might use me so; but I nevertheless remembered their advice, and from that time I resolved to run away. I looked forward to a time at which it would be safe for me to escape. I was too young to think of doing so immediately; besides, I wished to learn how to write, as I might have occasion to write my own pass.[6] I consoled myself with the hope that I should one day find a good chance. Meanwhile, I would learn to write.

The idea as to how I might learn to write was suggested to me by being in Durgin and Bailey's ship-yard, and frequently seeing the ship carpenters, after hewing, and getting a piece of timber ready for use, write on the timber the name of that part of the ship for which it was intended. When a piece of timber was intended for the larboard side, it would be marked thus—"L." When a piece was for the starboard side, it would be marked thus—"S." A piece for the larboard side forward, would be marked thus— "L. F." When a piece was for starboard side forward, it would be marked thus—"S. F." For larboard aft, it would be marked thus—"L. A." For starboard aft, it would be marked thus—"S. A." I soon learned the names of these letters, and for what they were intended when placed upon a piece of timber in the ship-yard. I immediately commenced copying them, and in a short time was able to make the four letters named. After that, when I met with any boy who I knew could write, I would tell him I could write as well as he. The next word would be, "I don't believe you. Let me see you try it." I would then make the letters which I had been so fortunate as to learn, and ask him to beat that. In this way I got a good many lessons in

6. In many areas, slaves were required to carry written passes stating that they had permission from their owners to travel to a certain place.

writing, which it is quite possible I should never have gotten in any other way. During this time, my copy-book was the board fence, brick wall, and pavement; my pen and ink was a lump of chalk. With these, I learned mainly how to write. I then commenced and continued copying the Italics in Webster's Spelling Book, until I could make them all without looking on the book. By this time, my little Master Thomas had gone to school, and learned how to write, and had written over a number of copy-books. These had been brought home, and shown to some of our near neighbors, and then laid aside. My mistress used to go to class meeting at the Wilk Street meetinghouse every Monday afternoon, and leave me to take care of the house. When left thus, I used to spend the time in writing in the spaces left in Master Thomas's copy-book, copying what he had written. I continued to do this until I could write a hand very similar to that of Master Thomas. Thus, after a long, tedious effort for years, I finally succeeded in learning how to write. . . .

[*After the death of his owner, Douglass was recalled to the plantation and put to work as a field hand. Because of his rebellious attitude, he was then sent to work for a notorious "slave-breaker" named Covey. When Covey tried to whip Douglass, who was then about sixteen years old, Douglass fought back.*]

We were at it for nearly two hours. Covey at length let me go, puffing and blowing at a great rate, saying that if I had not resisted, he would not have whipped me half so much. The truth was, that he had not whipped me at all. I considered him as getting entirely the worst end of the bargain; for he had drawn no blood from me, but I had from him. The whole six months afterwards, that I spent with Mr. Covey, he never laid the weight of his finger upon me in anger. He would occasionally say, he didn't want to get hold of me again. "No," thought I, "you need not; for you will come off worse than you did before."

This battle with Mr. Covey was the turning point in my career as a slave. It rekindled the few expiring embers of freedom, and revived within me a sense of my own manhood. It recalled the departed self-confidence, and inspired me again with a determination to be free. The gratification afforded by the triumph was a full compensation for whatever else might follow, even death itself. He only can understand the deep satisfaction which I experienced, who has himself repelled by force the bloody arm of slavery. I felt as I never felt before. It was a glorious resurrection, from the tomb of slavery, to the heaven of freedom. My long-crushed spirit rose, cowardice departed, bold defiance took its place; and I now resolved that, however long I might remain a slave in form, the day had passed forever when I could be a slave

CHAPTER 8

THE "PECULIAR
INSTITUTION":
SLAVES TELL
THEIR OWN
STORY

in fact. I did not hesitate to let it be known of me, that the white man who expected to succeed in whipping, must also succeed in killing me.

From this time I was never again what might be called fairly whipped, though I remained a slave four years afterwards. I had several fights, but was never whipped.

It was for a long time a matter of surprise to me why Mr. Covey did not immediately have me taken by the constable to the whipping-post, and there regularly whipped for the crime of raising my hand against a white man in defense of myself. And the only explanation I can now think of does not entirely satisfy me; but such as it is, I will give it. Mr. Covey enjoyed the most unbounded reputation for being a first-rate overseer and negro-breaker. It was of considerable importance to him. That reputation was at stake; and had he sent me—a boy about sixteen years old—to the public whipping-post, his reputation would have been lost; so, to save his reputation, he suffered me to go unpunished. . . .

[*During the Civil War, Douglass actively recruited African American soldiers for the Union, and he worked steadfastly after the war for African American civil rights. Douglass also held a series of federal jobs that culminated in his appointment as the United States minister to Haiti in 1888. He died in 1895 at the age of seventy-eight.*]

Source 25 from Linda Brent, *Incidents in the Life of a Slave Girl* (New York: Harcourt Brace Jovanovich, 1973), pp. xiii–xiv, 7, 9–10, 26–28, 48–49, 54–55, 179, 201–203, 207.

25. Autobiography of Linda Brent (Harriet Jacobs).

I wish I were more competent to the task I have undertaken. But I trust my readers will excuse deficiencies in consideration of circumstances. I was born and reared in Slavery; and I remained in a Slave State twenty-seven years. Since I have been at the North, it has been necessary for me to work diligently for my own support, and the education of my children. This has not left me much leisure to make up for the loss of early opportunities to improve myself; and it has compelled me to write these pages at irregular intervals, whenever I could snatch an hour from household duties.

When I first arrived in Philadelphia, Bishop Paine advised me to publish a sketch of my life, but I told him I was altogether incompetent to such an undertaking. Though I have improved my mind somewhat since that time, I still remain of the same opinion; but I trust my motives will excuse what might otherwise seem presumptuous. I have not written my experiences in order to attract attention to myself; on the contrary, it would have been more pleasant to me to have been silent about my own history. Neither do I care to excite sympathy for my own sufferings. But I do earnestly desire to arouse the women of the North to a realizing sense of the condition of two millions of women at the South, still in bondage, suffering what I suffered, and most of them far worse. I want to add my testimony to that of abler pens to convince the people of the Free States what Slavery really is. Only by experience can any one realize how deep, and dark, and foul is that pit of abominations. May the blessing of God rest on this imperfect effort in behalf of my persecuted people!

I was born a slave; but I never knew it till six years of happy childhood had passed away. My father was a carpenter, and considered so intelligent and skilful in his trade, that when buildings out of the common line were to be erected, he was sent for from long distances, to be head workman. On condition of paying his mistress two hundred dollars a year, and supporting himself, he was allowed to work at his trade, and manage his own affairs. His strongest wish was to purchase his children; but, though he several times offered his hard earnings for that purpose, he never succeeded. In complexion my parents were a light shade of brownish yellow, and were termed mulattoes. They lived together in a comfortable home; and, though we were all slaves, I was so fondly shielded that I never dreamed I was a piece of merchandise, trusted to them for safe keeping, and liable to be demanded of them at any moment. I had one brother, William, who was two years younger than myself—a bright, affectionate child. I had also a great treasure in my maternal grandmother, who was a remarkable woman in many respects. . . .

[*When Linda Brent was six years old, her mother died, and six years later the kind mistress to whom Brent's family belonged also died. In the will, Brent was bequeathed to the mistress's five-year-old niece, Miss Emily Flint.*]

Dr. Flint, a physician in the neighborhood, had married the sister of my mistress, and I was now the property of their little daughter. It was not without murmuring that I prepared for my new home; and what added to my unhappiness, was the fact that my brother William was purchased by the same family. My father, by his nature, as well as by the habit of transacting business as a skilful mechanic, had more of the feelings of a freeman than is common among slaves. My brother was a spirited boy; and being brought up under such influences, he early detested the name of master and mistress. One day, when his father and his mistress both happened to call

CHAPTER 8

THE "PECULIAR
INSTITUTION":
SLAVES TELL
THEIR OWN
STORY

him at the same time, he hesitated between the two; being perplexed to know which had the strongest claim upon his obedience. He finally concluded to go to his mistress. When my father reproved him for it, he said, "You both called me, and I didn't know which I ought to go to first."

"You are *my* child," replied our father, "and when I call you, you should come immediately, if you have to pass through fire and water."

Poor Willie! He was now to learn his first lesson of obedience to a master. Grandmother tried to cheer us with hopeful words, and they found an echo in the credulous hearts of youth. . . .

My grandmother's mistress had always promised her that, at her death, she would be free; and it was said that in her will she made good the promise. But when the estate was settled, Dr. Flint told the faithful old servant that, under existing circumstances, it was necessary she should be sold.

On the appointed day, the customary advertisement was posted up, proclaiming that there would be a "public sale of negroes, horses, &c." Dr. Flint called to tell my grandmother that he was unwilling to wound her feelings by putting her up at auction, and that he would prefer to dispose of her at private sale. My grandmother saw through his hypocrisy; she understood very well that he was ashamed of the job. She was a very spirited woman, and if he was base enough to sell her, when her mistress intended she should be free, she was determined the public should know it. She had for a long time supplied many families with crackers and preserves; consequently, "Aunt Marthy," as she was called, was generally known, and every body who knew her respected her intelligence and good character. Her long and faithful service in the family was also well known, and the intention of her mistress to leave her free. When the day of sale came, she took her place among the chattels, and at the first call she sprang upon the auction-block. Many voices called out, "Shame! Shame! Who is going to sell *you*, aunt Marthy? Don't stand there! That is no place for *you*." Without saying a word, she quietly awaited her fate. No one bid for her. At last, a feeble voice said, "Fifty dollars." It came from a maiden lady, seventy years old, the sister of my grandmother's deceased mistress. She had lived forty years under the same roof with my grandmother; she knew how faithfully she had served her owners, and how cruelly she had been defrauded of her rights; and she resolved to protect her. The auctioneer waited for a higher bid; but her wishes were respected; no one bid above her. She could neither read nor write; and when the bill of sale was made out, she signed it with a cross. But what consequence was that, when she had a big heart overflowing with human kindness? She gave the old servant her freedom. . . .

During the first years of my service in Dr. Flint's family, I was accustomed to share some indulgences with the children of my mistress. Though this seemed to me no more than right, I was grateful for it, and tried to merit the kindness by the faithful discharge of my duties. But I now entered on my fifteenth year—a sad epoch in the life of a slave girl. My master began to whisper foul words in my ear. Young as I was, I could not remain ignorant of their import. I tried to treat them with indifference or contempt. The master's age, my extreme youth, and the fear that his conduct would be reported to my grandmother, made him bear this treatment for many months. He was a crafty man, and resorted to many means to accomplish his purposes. . . . The mistress, who ought to protect the helpless victim, has no other feelings towards her but those of jealousy and rage. . . . Even the little child, who is accustomed to wait on her mistress and her children, will learn, before she is twelve years old, why it is that her mistress hates such and such a one among the slaves. . . . She listens to violent outbreaks of jealous passion, and cannot help understanding what is the cause. She will become prematurely knowing in evil things. Soon she will learn to tremble when she hears her master's footfall. She will be compelled to realize that she is no longer a child. If God has bestowed beauty upon her, it will prove her greatest curse. That which commands admiration in the white woman only hastens the degradation of the female slave. . . .

I longed for some one to confide in. I would have given the world to have laid my head on my grandmother's faithful bosom, and told her all my troubles. But Dr. Flint swore he would kill me, if I was not as silent as the grave. Then, although my grandmother was all in all to me, I feared her as well as loved her. I had been accustomed to look up to her with a respect bordering upon awe. I was very young, and felt shamefaced about telling her such impure things, especially as I knew her to be very strict on such subjects. Moreover, she was a woman of a high spirit. She was usually very quiet in her demeanor; but if her indignation was once roused, it was not very easily quelled. . . . I dreaded the consequences of a violent outbreak; and both pride and fear kept me silent. . . . It was lucky for me that I did not live on a distant plantation, but in a town not so large that the inhabitants were ignorant of each other's affairs. Bad as are the laws and customs in a slave-holding community, the doctor, as a professional man, deemed it prudent to keep up some outward show of decency. . . .

[*Dr. Flint was enraged when he found out that Brent had fallen in love with a young, free African American carpenter. The doctor redoubled his efforts to seduce Brent and told her terrible stories about what happened to slaves who ran away. For a long time, she was afraid to try to escape because of stories such as the one she recounts here.*]

CHAPTER 8

THE "PECULIAR
INSTITUTION":
SLAVES TELL
THEIR OWN
STORY

In my childhood I knew a valuable slave, named Charity, and loved her, as all children did. Her young mistress married, and took her to Louisiana. Her little boy, James, was sold to a good sort of master. He became involved in debt, and James was sold again to a wealthy slaveholder, noted for his cruelty. With this man he grew up to manhood, receiving the treatment of a dog. After a severe whipping, to save himself from further infliction of the lash, with which he was threatened, he took to the woods. He was in a most miserable condition—cut by the cowskin, half naked, half starved, and without the means of procuring a crust of bread.

Some weeks after his escape, he was captured, tied, and carried back to his master's plantation. This man considered punishment in his jail, on bread and water, after receiving hundreds of lashes, too mild for the poor slave's offence. Therefore he decided, after the overseer should have whipped him to his satisfaction, to have him placed between the screws of the cotton gin, to stay as long as he had been in the woods. This wretched creature was cut with the whip from his head to his feet, then washed with strong brine, to prevent the flesh from mortifying. . . . He was then put into the cotton gin, which was screwed down, only allowing him room to turn on his side when he could not lie on his back. Every morning a slave was sent with a piece of bread and bowl of water, which were placed within reach of the poor fellow. The slave was charged, under penalty of severe punishment, not to speak to him.

Four days passed, and the slave continued to carry the bread and water. On the second morning, he found the bread gone, but the water untouched. When he had been in the press four days and five nights, the slave informed his master that the water had not been used for four mornings, and that a horrible stench came from the gin house. The overseer was sent to examine into it. When the press was unscrewed, the dead body was found partly eaten by rats and vermin. . . .

[*Dr. Flint's jealous wife watched his behavior very closely, so Flint decided to build a small cabin out in the woods for Brent, who was now sixteen years old. Still afraid to run away, she became desperate.*]

And now, reader, I come to a period in my unhappy life, which I would gladly forget if I could. The remembrance fills me with sorrow and shame. It pains me to tell you of it; but I have promised to tell you the truth, and I will do it honestly, let it cost me what it may. I will not try to screen myself behind the plea of compulsion from a master; for it was not so. Neither can I plead ignorance or thoughtlessness. For years, my master had done his utmost to pollute my mind with foul images, and to destroy the pure principles inculcated by my grandmother, and the good mistress of my childhood. The influences of slavery had had the same effect on me that they had on other young girls; they had made me prematurely knowing, concerning the evil ways of the world. I knew what I did, and I did it with deliberate calculation. . . .

I have told you that Dr. Flint's persecutions and his wife's jealousy had given rise to some gossip in the neighborhood. Among others, it chanced that a white unmarried gentleman had obtained some knowledge of the circumstances in which I was placed. He knew my grandmother, and often spoke to me in the street. He became interested for me, and asked questions about my master, which I answered in part. He expressed a great deal of sympathy, and a wish to aid me. He constantly sought opportunities to see me, and wrote to me frequently. I was a poor slave girl, only fifteen years old.

So much attention from a superior person was, of course, flattering; for human nature is the same in all. I also felt grateful for his sympathy, and encouraged by his kind words. It seemed to me a great thing to have such a friend. By degrees, a more tender feeling crept into my heart. He was an educated and eloquent gentleman; too eloquent, alas, for the poor slave girl who trusted in him. Of course I saw whither all this was tending. I knew the impassable gulf between us; but to be an object of interest to a man who is not married, and who is not her master, is agreeable to the pride and feelings of a slave, if her miserable situation has left her any pride or sentiment. It seems less degrading to give one's self, than to submit to compulsion. There is something akin to freedom in having a lover who has no control over you, except that which he gains by kindness and attachment. A master may treat you as rudely as he pleases, and you dare not speak; moreover, the wrong does not seem so great with an unmarried man, as with one who has a wife to be made unhappy. There may be sophistry in all this; but the condition of a slave confuses all principles of morality, and, in fact, renders the practice of them impossible.

[Brent had two children, Benjy and Ellen, as a result of her relationship with Mr. Sands, the white "gentleman." Sands and Brent's grandmother tried to buy Brent, but Dr. Flint rejected all their offers. However, Sands was able (through a trick) to buy his two children and Brent's brother, William. After he was elected to Congress, Sands married a white woman. William escaped to the North, and Brent spent seven years hiding in the tiny attic of a shed attached to her grandmother's house. Finally, Brent and a friend escaped via ship to Philadelphia. She then went to New York City, where she found work as a nursemaid for a kind family, the Bruces, and was reunited with her two children. However, as a fugitive slave, she was not really safe, and she used to read the newspapers every day to see whether Dr. Flint or any of his relatives were visiting New York.]

CHAPTER 8

THE "PECULIAR
INSTITUTION":
SLAVES TELL
THEIR OWN
STORY

But when summer came, the old feeling of insecurity haunted me. It was necessary for me to take little Mary[7] out daily, for exercise and fresh air, and the city was swarming with Southerners, some of whom might recognize me. Hot weather brings out snakes and slaveholders, and I like one class of the venomous creatures as little as I do the other. What a comfort it is, to be free to *say* so! . . .

I kept close watch of the newspapers for arrivals; but one Saturday night, being much occupied, I forgot to examine the Evening Express as usual. I went down into the parlor for it, early in the morning, and found the boy about to kindle a fire with it. I took it from him and examined the list of arrivals. Reader, if you have never been a slave, you cannot imagine the acute sensation at my heart, when I read the names of Mr. and Mrs. Dodge,[8] at a hotel in Courtland Street. It was a third-rate hotel, and that circumstance convinced me of the truth of what I had heard, that they were short of funds and had need of my value, as *they* valued me; and that was by dollar and cents. I hastened with the paper to Mrs. Bruce. Her heart and hand were always open to every one in distress, and she always warmly sympathized with mine. It was impossible to tell how near the enemy was. He might have passed and repassed the house while we were sleeping. He might at that moment be waiting to pounce upon me if I ventured out of doors. I had never seen the husband of my young mistress, and therefore I could not distinguish him from any other stranger. A carriage was hastily ordered; and, closely veiled, I followed Mrs. Bruce, taking the baby again with me into exile. After various turnings and crossings, and returnings, the carriage stopped at the house of one of Mrs. Bruce's friends, where I was kindly received. Mrs. Bruce returned immediately, to instruct the domestics what to say if any one came to inquire for me.

It was lucky for me that the evening paper was not burned up before I had a chance to examine the list of arrivals. It was not long after Mrs. Bruce's return to her house, before several people came to inquire for me. One inquired for me, another asked for my daughter Ellen, and another said he had a letter from my grandmother, which he was requested to deliver in person.

They were told, "She *has* lived here, but she has left."

"How long ago?"

"I don't know, sir."

"Do you know where she went?"

"I do not, sir." And the door was closed. . . .

7. Mary was the Bruces' baby.
8. Emily Flint and her husband.

[*Mrs. Bruce was finally able to buy Brent from Mr. Dodge, and she immediately gave Brent her freedom.*]

Reader, my story ends with freedom; not in the usual way, with marriage. I and my children are now free! We are as free from the power of slaveholders as are the white people of the north; and though that, according to my ideas, is not saying a great deal, it is a vast improvement in *my* condition. The dream of my life is not yet realized. I do not sit with my children in a home of my own. I still long for a hearthstone of my own, however humble. I wish it for my children's sake far more than for my own. But God so orders circumstances as to keep me with my friend Mrs. Bruce. Love, duty, gratitude, also bind me to her side. It is a privilege to serve her who pities my oppressed people, and who has bestowed the inestimable boon of freedom on me and my children. . . .

[*Harriet Jacobs's story was published in 1861, and during the Civil War she did relief work with the newly freed slaves behind the Union army lines. For several years after the war ended, she worked tirelessly in Georgia to organize orphanages, schools, and nursing homes. Finally, she returned to the North, where she died in 1897 at the age of eighty-four.*]

✂ QUESTIONS TO CONSIDER ✂

The evidence in this chapter falls into three categories: reminiscences from former slaves, culled from interviews conducted in the 1930s (Sources 1 through 18); songs transcribed soon after the Civil War, recalled by runaway slaves, or remembered years after (Sources 19 through 23); and the autobiographies of two slaves who escaped to the North: Frederick Douglass and Harriet Jacobs (Sources 24 and 25).

These categories are artificial at best, and you might want to rearrange the evidence in a way that may suit your purposes better.

The evidence contains a number of subtopics, and arrangement into those subtopics may be profitable. For example:

1. How did slaves feel about their masters and/or mistresses?
2. How did slaves feel about their work? Their families? Their religion?
3. How did they feel about freedom?
4. How did slaves feel about themselves?

By regrouping the evidence into subtopics and then using each piece of evidence to answer the question for that subtopic, you should be able to answer the central question: what did slaves (or former slaves) think and feel about the peculiar institution of slavery?

CHAPTER 8

THE "PECULIAR
INSTITUTION":
SLAVES TELL
THEIR OWN
STORY

As mentioned, some of the slaves and former slaves chose to be direct in their messages (see, for example, Source 19), but many more chose to communicate their thoughts and feelings more indirectly or obliquely. Several of the symbols and metaphors used are easy to figure out (see Source 23), but others will take considerably more care. The messages are there, however.

Frederick Douglass and Harriet Jacobs wrote their autobiographies for northern readers. Furthermore, both these runaway slaves were active in abolitionist work. Do these facts mean that this evidence is worthless? Not at all, but the historian must be very careful when analyzing such obviously biased sources. Which parts of Douglass's and Jacobs's stories seem to be exaggerated or unlikely to be true? What do these writers say about topics such as their work, religious beliefs, and families? Does any other evidence from the interviews, tales, or songs corroborate what Douglass and Jacobs wrote?

One last point you might want to consider: why have historians neglected this kind of evidence for so long?

⬾ EPILOGUE ⬿

Even before the Civil War formally ended, thousands of African Americans began casting off the shackles of slavery. Some ran away to meet the advancing Union armies (who often treated them no better than their former masters and mistresses). Others drifted into cities, where they hoped to find work opportunities for themselves and their families. Still others stayed on the land, perhaps hoping to become free farmers. At the end of the war, African Americans were quick to establish their own churches and enrolled in schools established by the Freedmen's Bureau. For most former slaves, the impulse seems to have been to look forward and not backward into the agonizing past of slavery.

Yet memories of slavery were not forgotten and often were passed down orally, from generation to generation.

In 1976, Alex Haley's book *Roots* and the twelve-part television miniseries based on it stunned an American public that had assumed that blacks' memories of their origins and of slavery had been for the most part either forgotten or obliterated.[9] Although much of Haley's work contains the author's artistic license, the skeleton of the book was the oral tradition transmitted by his family since the capture of his ancestor Kunta Kinte in West Africa in the late eighteenth century. Not only had Haley's family remembered its African origins, but stories about slavery had not been lost—they had been passed down through the generations.

9. A condensed version of *Roots* appeared in 1974 in *Reader's Digest.*

While Haley was engaged in his twelve years of research and writing, historian Henry Irving Tragle proposed to compile a documentary history of the Nat Turner rebellion of 1831. Talking to black people in 1968 and 1969 in Southampton County, Virginia, where the rebellion occurred, Tragle discovered that in spite of numerous attempts to obliterate Turner from the area's historical memory, Turner's action had become part of the oral history of the region. As the surprised Tragle wrote, "I believe it possible to say with certainty that Nat Turner did exist as a folk-hero to several generations of black men and women who have lived and died in Southampton County since 1831."[10] Again, oral history had persisted and triumphed over time, and professional historians began looking with a new eye on what in the past many had dismissed as unworthy of their attention.

Folk music, customs, religious practices, stories, and artifacts also received new attention. Increasingly, students of history have been able to reconstruct the lives, thoughts, and feelings of people once considered inarticulate. Of course, these people were not inarticulate, but it took imagination to let their evidence speak.

Many people have argued about the impact of slavery on blacks and whites alike, and that question may never be answered fully. What we *do* know is that an enormous amount of historical evidence about slavery exists, from the perspectives of both African Americans and whites. And the memory of that institution lingers. It is part of what one southern white professional historian calls the "burden of southern history," a burden to be overcome but never completely forgotten.

10. Henry Irving Tragle, *The Southampton Slave Revolt of 1831: A Compilation of Source Material* (Amherst: University of Massachusetts Press, 1971), p. 12.

CHAPTER 9

MAKING VALUE JUDGMENTS:
THOREAU, DOUGLAS, POLK,
AND THE MEXICAN WAR

∞ THE PROBLEM ∞

On July 23 or 24, 1846, Henry David Thoreau[1] walked into the village of Concord, Massachusetts, from his cabin on the shore of Walden Pond to have a shoe repaired by the local cobbler. In the village, he encountered Sam Staples, Concord's constable, tax collector, and jailer. Staples stopped Thoreau, reminding him that he had not paid his poll tax[2] for several years. Thoreau replied that he had no intention of paying the tax, to which Staples in turn remarked that eventually he would have to take Thoreau to jail. "As well now as any time, Sam" was Thoreau's rejoinder, so the two men marched to the Concord jail, where Thoreau was incarcerated with a man accused of having burned down a barn.

Later that evening, a hooded figure[3] appeared at Staples's home to pay Thoreau's tax for him. Staples, however, refused to return to the jail to release his prisoner, so Thoreau spent one night in the Concord jail. Upon being released the next morning, Thoreau (according to Staples) was "mad

1. At his birth in 1817, Thoreau was named David Henry Thoreau and was called Henry. After his graduation from Harvard in 1837, he reversed his first and middle names.
2. The poll tax was a tax on all males in Massachusetts between the ages of twenty and seventy. The tax was one dollar per year, used primarily to keep up the roads and fund public schools.

3. Most Thoreau scholars believed that Thoreau's Aunt Maria was the hooded figure, although others assert that it might have been his mother, one of his sisters, or even Ralph Waldo Emerson.

as the devil" that someone had ruined his act of protest by paying his tax for him and refused to leave the jail. Somewhat confused by this turn of events, the jailer threatened to throw Thoreau out, whereby the former prisoner left the jail, collected his mended shoe, and went to pick berries.

Eighteen months later, in response to questions concerning his nonpayment of the poll tax, Thoreau delivered a lecture to the Concord Lyceum[4] titled "The Rights and Duties of the Individual in Relation to Government," published in 1849 as "Resistance to Civil Government" and later (in 1866, four years after Thoreau's death) with its now-famous title "Civil Disobedience."

Although Thoreau had not paid his poll tax for six years, he justified his resistance in part because of his opposition to the United States' declaration of war on Mexico, which had taken place only six weeks prior to his brief imprisonment (on May 11, 1846). On May 13, two days after Congress's declaration of war, a brisk debate erupted in the House of Representatives, led by antiwar Whig party stalwart Columbus Delano[5] of Ohio. Rising to counter Delano's and others' attacks on the war as "unholy, unrighteous, and damnable" was Stephen A. Douglas, a young Democratic congressman from Illinois. Not only did Douglas defend Democratic president James K. Polk's actions, but he also sharply criticized Americans who opposed the Mexican War.

Approximately seven months after Douglas's impassioned defense of Polk (and slightly more than five months after Thoreau's symbolic act of defiance), the president spoke for himself, delivering (in writing) his Second Annual Message to Congress on December 8, 1846. Like Douglas, not only did Polk attempt to justify the United States' war against Mexico, but the president also commented briefly on those citizens who opposed the conflict.

Your first task in this chapter is to analyze the ideas of Henry David Thoreau, Stephen A. Douglas, and President James K. Polk regarding the rights and responsibilities of American citizens, especially during times of war. In Thoreau's opinion, what responsibilities did American citizens owe to their government? What rights did citizens have? What did he believe should happen when responsibilities and individual conscience were in conflict? As for Douglas and Polk, what did they believe were citizens' responsibilities to their government in wartime? In their view, what rights did citizens have (or *not* have) in times of war?

Your second task in this chapter is considerably more difficult. After having analyzed the ideas of Thoreau, Douglas, and Polk, you are asked to make value judgments regarding those ideas and to support your value judgments in an intelligent manner. Answer the following questions:

4. The lyceum movement in America, begun in the early nineteenth century, was a pioneer attempt at community education. Open to all members of a community, the lyceum's typical activities centered on public lectures, concerts, and debates. The Concord Lyceum was established in 1829.
5. Columbus Delano (1809–1896) was a first-term Whig congressman from Ohio.

CHAPTER 9

MAKING VALUE
JUDGMENTS:
THOREAU,
DOUGLAS, POLK,
AND THE
MEXICAN WAR

1. What does it mean to be a citizen?
2. Because citizens enjoy certain benefits by virtue of being citizens, what (if anything) do they owe in return?
3. Should citizens support their government in times of crisis even if the citizens perceive the actions of that government as wrong?
4. Should the majority *always* rule? When should it *not* rule?
5. What makes a government's actions legitimate or illegitimate? Who should make those decisions?
6. With regard to Douglas and Polk, were they correct that Americans should support their government during wartime in spite of their individual beliefs?

These questions have never been resolved, and they arise again and again, most often when the United States perceives itself as being in some sort of crisis.

BACKGROUND

Ever since colonial times, Americans had viewed the West as the key to both their individual and their collective futures. To land companies and investors, the West held out the promise of great riches, fortunes made in either land speculation or trade. To southern planters, who often exhausted the soil growing cash crops like tobacco, it offered the chance to repeat their successes on rich, virgin land. To European immigrants and people from the overpopulated northeastern farming communities, the West was seen as a Garden of Eden where they could make a new start. To Thomas Jefferson, it represented an "Empire of Liberty" that would prevent the rise of unwholesome cities and social conflict in the young republic. Hence it is easy to see why most Americans came to equate national progress with westward expansion. In this atmosphere, the ceding of western lands by the new states to the national government in the 1780s and the Louisiana Purchase of 1803 were seen as the ensurers of national greatness. And in a society in which private property was venerated and the acquisition of land had become for many almost a cultural imperative, westward expansion was very nearly inevitable.

Although there were a number of obstacles to westward expansion, at most they proved temporary. The Indian nations offered brisk opposition, but they could fight only a holding action against the more numerous and technologically superior Caucasians. When the United States put its mind to it, the Indians were quickly, and sometimes mercilessly, eradicated or gathered onto reservations, where they were forced to become dependent on the United States government for their existence. For their part, the Spanish (in the Floridas), French (in the Louisiana Territory), and British (in the Northwest) could not bring sufficient military power to bear so far from home and ultimately preferred to sell or give up through treaty their territorial claims. Even the Republic of Mexico, which did choose to fight, was no match for its expansion-minded neighbor.

The demographic, economic, and social imperatives to expand and the absence of powerful opposition gradually convinced many Americans that westward expansion was both a right and a duty, approved by God for "His people." As one editor explained, it was America's "manifest destiny to overspread the continent allotted by Providence for the free development of our yearly multiplying millions." Another contemporary envisaged a time when the American eagle would have its beak in Canada, its talons in Mexico, and its wings flapping in the two oceans. Although there is more than a trace of arrogance and feeling of superiority in both statements, it is important to note that a vast number of American Caucasians sincerely believed in those claims, much as many white southerners in the same era sincerely believed that most slaves were happy with their collective lot.

By the 1830s, the westward expansion of Americans had gone beyond the Louisiana Territory into Texas (owned by the Republic of Mexico) and Oregon (jointly occupied by the United States and Great Britain since 1818). In Texas, settlers from the United States regularly ignored Mexican laws and officials. For example, Mexico's prohibition of slavery did not stop settlers from bringing slaves into Texas.

Mexican laws, which required that all settlers convert to Roman Catholicism, were scoffed at and almost universally broken. When the Mexican government attempted to enforce these and other laws in 1836, American migrants to Texas (numbering approximately thirty thousand) rebelled.

Mexico attempted to crush the rebellion. At the Alamo, Mexican general Santa Anna killed all the defenders (he spared women and children and, according to legend, at least one male native Mexican) and then stacked their bodies like cordwood and burned them. Later, Mexicans shot every defender at Goliad, even though a formal surrender had been arranged with an agreement that survivors would be spared. Still, the Texans under General Sam Houston prevailed, and by the end of 1836, Texas was an independent nation. Most Texans, however, did not want Texas to remain independent; they wanted to become part of the United States.

Whether to annex Texas to the United States was an issue that divided Americans for the next eight years. Some people in the North and Midwest opposed the annexation of Texas, fearing that it would tip the political balance in Congress in favor of the slave states and (prophetically, as it turned out) that annexation would precipitate a war with Mexico. That nation had never relinquished its claim to its lost province. Moreover, Texans maintained that the southern boundary of the Lone Star Republic[6]

6. This was the nickname for the Republic of Texas, derived from its flag with one star.

CHAPTER 9

MAKING VALUE
JUDGMENTS:
THOREAU,
DOUGLAS, POLK,
AND THE
MEXICAN WAR

was the Rio Grande, whereas Mexico continued to insist that the border was the Nueces River. Border clashes between Texans and Mexicans in the disputed territory were common. Meanwhile, the non-Indian population of Texas swelled from approximately 38,000 in 1836 to about 142,000 ten years later.[7]

In the United States, Presidents Jackson and Van Buren cautiously avoided the annexation issue (Jackson did not even recognize the Republic of Texas until after the 1836 presidential election), whereas Tyler (1841–1845) was rebuffed by the United States Senate when he proposed annexation in 1844. Finally, on March 1, 1845, three days before Polk's inauguration as president, a joint congressional resolution approved the inclusion of Texas in the United States. Mexico promptly broke off diplomatic relations.

There is little doubt that Polk sided with the expansionists. During the presidential campaign of 1844, he had made it clear that he approved of his party's pro-expansion platform and that he would move aggressively to fulfill it. Indeed, it is likely that Polk's and the Democrats' stand on westward expansion was in part responsible for their 1844 victory. The presidential election was a surprisingly close one, with Polk winning 50 percent of the popular vote and 170 electoral votes to Henry Clay's 48 percent of the popular vote and 105 electoral votes. Expan-

sionism could well have made the difference.

In spite of his party's pro-expansion platform and its rather bellicose rhetoric, once in office Polk worked diligently to acquire territory by negotiation rather than war. On the Oregon question, the president privately informed the British ambassador that he would accept a compromise that would set the Oregon–Canadian boundary at the forty-ninth parallel.[8] Troubled by difficulties at home, Great Britain also was eager to compromise, and the two nations reached an agreement in 1846.

Polk's efforts to acquire California and New Mexico from Mexico did not end so amicably. Even before his inauguration, Polk had his eye on California. Unstable political conditions in Mexico City had prevented Mexico from exercising much power in the area, and by 1841 most semblances of Mexican authority in California had vanished. Such a power vacuum made it likely that another nation would try to acquire California. Many Americans—including Polk—believed that both England and France were anxious to establish footholds in the region. If either nation were to acquire California (which in 1845 contained only a few hundred United States citizens), the United States' "manifest destiny" would be thwarted. With European nations showing increasing interest and Mexico so internally unsta-

7. In 1835, United States citizens who had emigrated to Texas numbered approximately 30,000, whereas the population of Mexican origin was around 7,800.

8. The original American claim was considerably north of the forty-ninth parallel, at 54°40′, thus leading to the popular Democratic party slogan in the 1844 presidential race of "Fifty-four forty or fight!"

ble, Polk was determined to move swiftly.

As with the Oregon question, Polk would have preferred to acquire California by negotiation. If negotiations were to break down, however, he was fully prepared to take that territory by force. On the day after Polk learned that his special emissary, John Slidell, had not been received by the Mexican government (January 13, 1846), he ordered General Zachary Taylor and his troops to occupy a position in the disputed territory between the Rio Grande and the Nueces Rivers. Clearly, the president hoped that Taylor's force would provoke an attack by Mexico, thereby giving the United States an excuse to declare war and seize the territory it wanted.

As weeks passed and no such incident occurred, Polk grew impatient and (according to his diary) was determined to declare war on Mexico without an attack. During the evening of May 9, 1846, however, he received word that Mexican soldiers had fired on American troops in the disputed area. Two days later, Polk asked Congress for a declaration of war. Al-though the vote in Congress was by no means unanimous (144–77 in the House, 30–24 in the Senate), the United States was now at war with the Republic of Mexico.

Polk did not lead a united nation into war. Opposition to the Mexican War was strong, especially among the Whigs (such as Abraham Lincoln, who denounced Polk in a speech in the House of Representatives) and in the Northeast (which feared a further erosion of its power by the admission of more western states). Newspapers in New York City, Charleston, Cincinnati, Boston, Richmond, and other cities condemned the conflict. Abolitionists were convinced that the war was a slaveholders' plot to expand the peculiar institution. Opposition to the war clearly irritated Polk, so much so that he addressed that question in his Second Annual Message. No matter what the president said, however, the Mexican War forced many Americans to choose between their loyalty to their government and their consciences. Henry David Thoreau was such a person.

∽ THE METHOD ∽

The question of whether historians should make value judgments about past people and events is extremely controversial. Many historians firmly believe that they have neither the right nor the obligation to make value judgments. To these historians, the story of the past should be value neutral, a chronicle of the trends, events, and people of the past without the insertion of value judgments by the tellers of the story. Other historians (a considerably larger group) assert with equal forcefulness that it is both wrong and unhistorical to judge people of the past by the values of the pres-

CHAPTER 9

MAKING VALUE
JUDGMENTS:
THOREAU,
DOUGLAS, POLK,
AND THE
MEXICAN WAR

ent. For example, these historians might say that it is unfair to expect the Founding Fathers to have included women and African Americans when they proclaimed in 1776 that "all men are created equal." Finally, a third group of historians claim that it is the duty of those who tell the story of the past to use history to teach and strengthen those values that we hold dear: liberty, justice, tolerance, and so on. There is little doubt that this controversy will continue as long as people learn, teach, and write about the past.

What is often ignored in the heat of this controversy is that both teachers and students make value judgments all the time, often without even realizing it. It is one thing, for example, to offer the opinion that Captain Thomas Preston was innocent (or guilty) of the charge that he ordered his men to fire during the so-called Boston Massacre. That is *not* a value judgment; it is a hypothesis that can be proven or disproven using the weight of testimony given by eyewitnesses at the trial *Rex v. Preston*. It is quite another matter, however, to assert that the British were tyrants when it came to their rule of the colonies. *That* is a value judgment—a statement of belief grounded not in evidence but in the value system of the person making the assertion. If you listen carefully to political leaders, business figures, religious advocates, and others (including historians), you will discover that what these people claim to be proven hypotheses often are value judgments instead.

As making value judgments is almost inevitable, where does that leave those of us attempting to understand America's past? To begin with, we must be able to recognize the difference between a hypothesis (which can be proven using factual evidence) and a value judgment (which cannot). For example, the statement that women did not possess rights equal to those of men during the 1820s and 1830s (during the so-called democratic era) is a hypothesis, and an examination of laws, court cases, prescriptive literature, and the like would prove that statement to be true. To state, however, that women should have had equal rights is a value judgment that is based less on evidence than on the system of beliefs of the claimant. Thus we must begin by recognizing the difference between a hypothesis and a value judgment.

Second, when we make value judgments (as you will be asked to do in this chapter), we must do so with considerable sensitivity and care. For one thing, we must be fair to the people of the past. Although we may make a value judgment about a historical person's words or actions, we also must try to understand why that person might have spoken or acted in the way that he or she did and never simply dismiss that person out of hand as stupid, crazy, or evil. Rather, we should attempt to understand the context in which that person spoke or acted. This is not to say that we cannot make value judgments about a person's words or actions, but we must do so carefully.

Finally, as we make value judgments about a past person's words or actions, we must recognize that there may be others around us (fellow students, for instance) who could very well make very different value judgments. A value judgment is not a hypothesis, and neither side can amass a preponderance of evidence to prove its point. To avoid having such a situation deteriorate into a meaningless wrangle, the two (or more) sides must agree on a common set of questions that both sides will attempt to answer. Each person also must listen to others fully and respectfully, allowing them sufficient uninterrupted time to make their points.

Your first (and least difficult) task in this chapter is to analyze the conflicting ideas of Henry David Thoreau, Stephen A. Douglas, and President James K. Polk on the rights and duties of American citizens, especially during times of war. By now you should be able to do this with ease: (1) What are the main points each person made? (2) How did each person support those points? In the case of Thoreau, you will have to read his essay with some care, for his points are like building blocks, constructed one on top of another. As for Douglas and Polk, their main points and supporting arguments are extremely brief and much easier to analyze.

Your second task (making value judgments regarding the arguments of Thoreau, Douglas, and Polk), if done well, is not so easy. After you analyze the men's arguments, you must make value judgments by answering the following questions:

1. In your view, what does it mean to be a citizen?
2. Since citizens enjoy certain benefits by virtue of being citizens, what (if anything) do they owe in return?
3. Should citizens support their government in times of crisis, even if the actions of that government are perceived by the citizens as wrong?
4. Should the majority *always* rule? When should the majority *not* rule (if ever)?
5. What makes a government's actions legitimate or illegitimate? Who should make those decisions?
6. As for Thoreau, was his position responsible or irresponsible? What criteria would you use in answering that question?
7. As for Douglas and Polk, were they correct that Americans should support their government during wartime in spite of citizens' individual beliefs? What if dissenters are in the minority?

CHAPTER 9

MAKING VALUE
JUDGMENTS:
THOREAU,
DOUGLAS, POLK,
AND THE
MEXICAN WAR

∞ **THE EVIDENCE** ∞

Source 1 from Henry David Thoreau, *Walden and Civil Disobedience: Authoritative Texts,* ed. Owen Thomas (New York: W. W. Norton and Co., 1966), pp. 224–243.

1. "Civil Disobedience" by Henry David Thoreau.

I heartily accept the motto,—"That government is best which governs least;" and I should like to see it acted up to more rapidly and systematically. Carried out, it finally amounts to this, which also I believe,—"That government is best which governs not at all;" and when men are prepared for it, that will be the kind of government which they will have. Government is at best but an expedient; but most governments are usually, and all governments are sometimes, inexpedient. The objections which have been brought against a standing army, and they are many and weighty, and deserve to prevail, may also at last be brought against a standing government. The standing army is only an arm of the standing government. The government itself, which is only the mode which the people have chosen to execute their will, is equally liable to be abused and perverted before the people can act through it. Witness the present Mexican war, the work of comparatively a few individuals using the standing government as their tool; for, in the outset, the people would not have consented to this measure.

This American government,—what is it but a tradition, though a recent one, endeavoring to transmit itself unimpaired to posterity, but each instant losing some of its integrity? It has not the vitality and force of a single living man; for a single man can bend it to his will. It is a sort of wooden gun to the people themselves; and, if ever they should use it in earnest as a real one against each other, it will surely split. But it is not the less necessary for this; for the people must have some complicated machinery or other, and hear its din, to satisfy that idea of government which they have. Governments show thus how successfully men can be imposed on, even impose on themselves, for their own advantage. It is excellent, we must all allow; yet this government never of itself furthered any enterprise, but by the alacrity with which it got out of its way. *It* does not keep the country free. *It* does not settle the West. *It* does not educate. The character inherent in the American people has done all that has been accomplished; and it would have done somewhat more, if the government had not sometimes got in its way. For government is an expedient by which men would fain succeed in letting one another alone; and, as has been said, when it is most expedient, the governed are most let alone by it. Trade and commerce, if they were not made of India rubber, would never manage to bounce over the obstacles which legislators are continually putting in their way; and, if one were to judge these men wholly by the effects of their actions, and not partly by their intentions, they would deserve to be classed and punished with those mischievous persons who put obstructions on the railroads.

But, to speak practically and as a citizen, unlike those who call themselves no-government men, I ask for, not at once no government, but *at once* a better government. Let every man make known what kind of government would command his respect, and that will be one step toward obtaining it.

After all, the practical reason why, when the power is once in the hands of the people, a majority are permitted, and for a long period continue, to rule, is not because they are most likely to be in the right, nor because this seems fairest to the minority, but because they are physically the strongest. But a government in which the majority rule in all cases cannot be based on justice, even as far as men understand it. Can there not be a government in which majorities do not virtually decide right and wrong, but conscience?—in which majorities decide only those questions to which the rule of expediency is applicable? Must the citizen ever for a moment, or in the least degree, resign his conscience to the legislator? Why has every man a conscience, then? I think that we should be men first, and subjects afterward. It is not desirable to cultivate a respect for the law, so much as for the right. The only obligation which I have a right to assume, is to do at any time what I think right. It is truly enough said, that a corporation has no conscience; but a corporation of conscientious men is a corporation *with* a conscience. Law never made men a whit more just; and, by means of their respect for it, even the well-disposed are daily made the agents of injustice. A common and natural result of an undue respect for law is, that you may see a file of soldiers, colonel, captain, corporal, privates, powder-monkeys[9] and all, marching in admirable order over hill and dale to the wars, against their wills, aye, against their common sense and consciences, which makes it very steep marching indeed, and produces a palpitation of the heart. They have no doubt that it is a damnable business in which they are concerned; they are all peaceably inclined. Now, what are they? Men at all? or small moveable forts and magazines, at the service of some unscrupulous man in power? Visit the Navy Yard, and behold a marine, such a man as an

9. Powder monkeys were young boys who carried gunpowder casks to the guns.

CHAPTER 9

MAKING VALUE
JUDGMENTS:
THOREAU,
DOUGLAS, POLK,
AND THE
MEXICAN WAR

American government can make, or such as it can make a man with its black arts, a mere shadow and reminiscence of humanity, a man laid out alive and standing, and already, as one may say, buried under arms with funeral accompaniments, though it may be

> "Not a drum was heard, nor a funeral note,
>   As his 'corse to the ramparts we hurried;
> Not a soldier discharged his farewell shot
>   O'er the grave where our hero we buried."[10]

The mass of men serve the State thus, not as men mainly, but as machines, with their bodies. They are the standing army, and the militia, jailers, constables, *posse comitatus*,[11] &c. In most cases there is no free exercise whatever of the judgment or of the moral sense; but they put themselves on a level with wood and earth and stones; and wooden men can perhaps be manufactured that will serve the purpose as well. Such command no more respect than men of straw, or a lump of dirt. They have the same sort of worth only as horses and dogs. Yet such as these even are commonly esteemed good citizens. Others, as most legislators, politicians, lawyers, ministers, and office-holders, serve the State chiefly with their heads; and, as they rarely make any moral distinctions, they are as likely to serve the devil, without intending it, as God. A very few, as heroes, patriots, martyrs, reformers in the great sense, and *men,* serve the State with their consciences also, and so necessarily resist it for the most part, and they are commonly treated by it as enemies. A wise man will only be useful as a man, and will not submit to be "clay," and "stop a hole to keep the wind away,"[12] but leave that office to his dust at least:—

> "I am too high-born to be propertied,
> To be a secondary at control,
> Or useful serving-man and instrument
> To any sovereign state throughout the world."[13]

He who gives himself entirely to his fellow-men appears to them useless and selfish; but he who gives himself partially to them is pronounced a benefactor and philanthropist.

How does it become a man to behave toward this American government to-day? I answer that he cannot without disgrace be associated with it. I

---

10. Charles Wolfe, "The Burial of Sir John Moore at Corunna."
11. A body of men summoned by a sheriff. In America, it was known as a posse.
12. William Shakespeare, *Hamlet,* act 5, sc. 1, lines 236–237.
13. William Shakespeare, *King John,* act 5, sc. 2, lines 79–82.

cannot for an instant recognize that political organization as *my* government which is the *slave's* government also.

All men recognize the right of revolution; that is, the right to refuse allegiance to and to resist the government, when its tyranny or its inefficiency are great and unendurable. But almost all say that such is not the case now. But such was the case, they think, in the Revolution of '75.[14] If one were to tell me that this was a bad government because it taxed certain foreign commodities brought to its ports, it is most probable that I should not make an ado about it, for I can do without them: all machines have their friction; and possibly this does enough good to counterbalance the evil. At any rate, it is a great evil to make a stir about it. But when the friction comes to have its machine, and oppression and robbery are organized, I say, let us not have such a machine any longer. In other words, when a sixth of the population of a nation which has undertaken to be the refuge of liberty are slaves, and a whole country is unjustly overrun and conquered by a foreign army, and subjected to military law, I think that it is not too soon for honest men to rebel and revolutionize. What makes this duty the more urgent is the fact, that the country so overrun is not our own, but ours is the invading army.

Paley,[15] a common authority with many on moral questions, in his chapter on the "Duty of Submission to Civil Government," resolves all civil obligation into expediency; and he proceeds to say, "that so long as the interest of the whole society requires it, that is, so long as the established government cannot be resisted or changed without public inconveniency, it is the will of God that the established government be obeyed, and no longer."—"This principle being admitted, the justice of every particular case of resistance is reduced to a computation of the quantity of the danger and grievance on the one side, and of the probability and expense of redressing it on the other." Of this, he says, every man shall judge for himself. But Paley appears never to have contemplated those cases to which the rule of expediency does not apply, in which a people, as well as an individual, must do justice, cost what it may. If I have unjustly wrested a plank from a drowning man, I must restore it to him though I drown myself. This, according to Paley, would be inconvenient. But he that would save his life, in such a case, shall lose it. This people must cease to hold slaves, and to make war on Mexico, though it cost them their existence as a people.

14. The American Revolution.
15. William Paley (1743–1805) was a British philosopher.

CHAPTER 9

MAKING VALUE
JUDGMENTS:
THOREAU,
DOUGLAS, POLK,
AND THE
MEXICAN WAR

In their practice, nations agree with Paley; but does any one think that Massachusetts does exactly what is right at the present crisis? . . .

Practically speaking, the opponents to a reform in Massachusetts are not a hundred thousand politicians at the South, but a hundred thousand merchants and farmers here, who are more interested in commerce and agriculture than they are in humanity, and are not prepared to do justice to the slave and to Mexico, *cost what it may*. I quarrel not with far-off foes, but with those who, near at home, co-operate with, and do the bidding of those far away, and without whom the latter would be harmless. We are accustomed to say, that the mass of men are unprepared; but improvement is slow, because the few are not materially wiser or better than the many. It is not so important that many should be as good as you, as that there be some absolute goodness somewhere; for that will leaven the whole lump. There are thousands who are *in opinion* opposed to slavery and to the war, who yet in effect do nothing to put an end to them; who, esteeming them-selves children of Washington and Franklin, sit down with their hands in their pockets, and say that they know not what to do, and do nothing; who even postpone the question of freedom to the question of free-trade, and quietly read the prices-current along with the latest advices from Mexico, after dinner, and, it may be, fall asleep over them both. What is the price-current of an honest man and patriot to-day? They hesitate, and they regret, and sometimes they petition; but they do nothing in earnest and with effect. They will wait, well disposed, for others to remedy the evil, that they may no longer have it to regret. At most, they give only a cheap vote, and a feeble countenance and God-speed, to the right, as it goes by them. There are nine hundred and ninety-nine patrons of virtue to one virtuous man; but it is easier to deal with the real possessor of a thing than with the temporary guardian of it.

All voting is a sort of gaming, like chequers or backgammon, with a slight moral tinge to it, a playing with right and wrong, with moral ques-tions; and betting naturally accompanies it. The character of the voters is not staked. I cast my vote, perchance, as I think right; but I am not vitally concerned that that right should prevail. I am willing to leave it to the majority. Its obligation, therefore, never exceeds that of expediency. Even voting *for the right* is *doing* nothing for it. It is only expressing to men feebly your desire that it should prevail. A wise man will not leave the right to the mercy of chance, nor wish it to prevail through the power of the majority. There is but little virtue in the action of masses of men. When the majority shall at length vote for the abolition of slavery, it will be because they are indifferent to slavery, or because there is but little slavery left to be abolished by their vote. *They* will then be the only slaves. Only *his* vote can hasten the abolition of slavery who asserts his own freedom by his vote. . . .

It is not a man's duty, as a matter of course, to devote himself to the eradication of any, even the most enormous wrong; he may still properly have other concerns to engage him; but it is his duty, at least, to wash his hands of it, and, if he gives it no thought longer, not to give it practically his support. If I devote myself to other pursuits and contemplations, I must first see, at least, that I do not pursue them sitting upon another man's shoulders. I must get off him first, that he may pursue his contemplations too. See what gross inconsistency is tolerated. I have heard some of my townsmen say, "I should like to have them order me out to help put down an insurrection of the slaves, or to march to Mexico,—see if I would go;" and yet these very men have each, directly by their allegiance, and so indirectly, at least, by their money, furnished a substitute. The soldier is applauded who refuses to serve in an unjust war by those who do not refuse to sustain the unjust government which makes the war; is applauded by those whose own act and authority he disregards and sets at nought; as if the State were penitent to that degree that it hired one to scourge it while it sinned, but not to that degree that it left off sinning for a moment. Thus, under the name of order and civil government, we are all made at least to pay homage to and support our own meanness. After the first blush of sin, comes its indifference; and from immoral it becomes, as it were, *un*moral, and not quite unnecessary to that life which we have made. . . .

I do not hesitate to say, that those who call themselves abolitionists should at once effectually withdraw their support, both in person and property, from the government of Massachusetts, and not wait till they constitute a majority of one, before they suffer the right to prevail through them. I think that it is enough if they have God on their side, without waiting for that other one. Moreover, any man more right than his neighbors, constitutes a majority of one already.

I meet this American government, or its representative the State government, directly, and face to face, once a year, no more, in the person of its tax-gatherer; this is the only mode in which a man situated as I am necessarily meets it; and it then says distinctly, Recognize me; and the simplest, the most effectual, and, in the present posture of affairs, the indispensablest mode of treating with it on this head, of expressing your little satisfaction with and love for it, is to deny it then. My civil neighbor, the tax-gatherer, is the very man I have to deal with,—for it is, after all, with men and not with parchment that I quarrel,—and he has voluntarily chosen to be an agent of the government. How shall he ever know well

CHAPTER 9

MAKING VALUE
JUDGMENTS:
THOREAU,
DOUGLAS, POLK,
AND THE
MEXICAN WAR

what he is and does as an officer of the government, or as a man, until he is obliged to consider whether he shall treat me, his neighbor, for whom he has respect, as a neighbor and well-disposed man, or as a maniac and disturber of the peace, and see if he can get over this obstruction to his neighborliness without a ruder and more impetuous thought or speech corresponding with his action? I know this well, that if one thousand, if one hundred, if ten men whom I could name,—if ten *honest* men only,— aye, if *one* HONEST man, in this State of Massachusetts, *ceasing to hold slaves,* were actually to withdraw from this copartnership, and be locked up in the county jail therefor, it would be the abolition of slavery in America. For it matters not how small the beginning may seem to be: what is once well done is done for ever. But we love better to talk about it: that we say is our mission. Reform keeps many scores of newspapers in its service, but not one man. If my esteemed neighbor, the State's ambassador,[16] who will devote his days to the settlement of the question of human rights in the Council Chamber, instead of being threatened with the prisons of Carolina, were to sit down the prisoner of Massachusetts, that State which is so anxious to foist the sin of slavery upon her sister,—though at present she can discover only an act of inhospitality to be the ground of a quarrel with her,—the Legislature would not wholly waive the subject the following winter.

Under a government which imprisons any unjustly, the true place for a just man is also a prison. The proper place to-day, the only place which Massachusetts has provided for her freer and less desponding spirits, is in her prisons, to be put out and locked out of the State by her own act, as they have already put themselves out by their principles. It is there that the fugitive slave, and the Mexican prisoner on parole, and the Indian come to plead the wrongs of his race, should find them; on that separate, but more free and honorable ground, where the State places those who are not *with* her but *against* her,—the only house in a slave-state in which a free man can abide with honor. If any think that their influence would be lost there, and their voices no longer afflict the ear of the State, that they would not be as an enemy within its walls, they do not know by how much truth is stronger than error, nor how much more eloquently and effectively he can combat injustice who has experienced a little in his own person. Cast your whole vote, not a strip of paper merely, but your whole influence. A minority is powerless while it conforms to the majority; it is not even a

16. Samuel Hoar (1778–1856), a congressman from Concord, was sent to Charleston, South Carolina, to protest the treatment accorded Negro seamen from Massachusetts. Hoar was expelled from Charleston by the legislature of South Carolina.

minority then; but it is irresistible when it clogs by its whole weight. If the alternative is to keep all just men in prison, or give up war and slavery, the State will not hesitate which to choose. If a thousand men were not to pay their tax-bills this year, that would not be a violent and bloody measure, as it would be to pay them, and enable the State to commit violence and shed innocent blood. This is, in fact, the definition of a peaceable revolution, if any such is possible. If the tax-gatherer, or any other public officer, asks me, as one has done, "But what shall I do?" my answer is, "If you really wish to do any thing, resign your office." When the subject has refused allegiance, and the officer has resigned his office, then the revolution is accomplished. But even suppose blood should flow. Is there not a sort of blood shed when the conscience is wounded? Through this wound a man's real manhood and immortality flow out, and he bleeds to an everlasting death. I see this blood flowing now.

I have contemplated the imprisonment of the offender, rather than the seizure of his goods,—though both will serve the same purpose,—because they who assert the purest right, and consequently are most dangerous to a corrupt State, commonly have not spent much time in accumulating property. To such the State renders comparatively small service, and a slight tax is wont to appear exorbitant, particularly if they are obliged to earn it by special labor with their hands. If there were one who lived wholly without the use of money, the State itself would hesitate to demand it of him. But the rich man—not to make any invidious comparison—is always sold to the institution which makes him rich. Absolutely speaking, the more money, the less virtue; for money comes between a man and his objects, and obtains them for him; and it was certainly no great virtue to obtain it. It puts to rest many questions which he would otherwise be taxed to answer; while the only new question which it puts is the hard but superfluous one, how to spend it. Thus his moral ground is taken from under his feet. The opportunities of living are diminished in proportion as what are called the "means" are increased. The best thing a man can do for his culture when he is rich is to endeavour to carry out those schemes which he entertained when he was poor. Christ answered the Herodians[17] according to their condition. "Show me the tribute-money," said he;—and one took a penny out of his pocket;—If you use money which has the image of Cæsar on it, and which he has made current and valuable, that is, *if you are men of the State,* and gladly enjoy the advantages of Cæsar's govern-

---

17. Followers of Herod Antipas, tetrarch of Galilee from 4 B.C. to A.D. 40. Herod appears in the Christians' New Testament as the figure who taxed the Israelites and was searching for the infant Jesus.

CHAPTER 9

MAKING VALUE
JUDGMENTS:
THOREAU,
DOUGLAS, POLK,
AND THE
MEXICAN WAR

ment, then pay him back some of his own when he demands it; "Render therefore to Cæsar that which is Cæsar's, and to God those things which are God's,"—leaving them no wiser than before as to which was which; for they did not wish to know.

When I converse with the freest of my neighbors, I perceive that, whatever they may say about the magnitude and seriousness of the question, and their regard for the public tranquillity, the long and the short of the matter is, that they cannot spare the protection of the existing government, and they dread the consequences of disobedience to it to their property and families. For my own part, I should not like to think that I ever rely on the protection of the State. But, if I deny the authority of the State when it presents its tax-bill, it will soon take and waste all my property, and so harass me and my children without end. This is hard. This makes it impossible for a man to live honestly and at the same time comfortably in outward respects. It will not be worth the while to accumulate property; that would be sure to go again. You must hire or squat somewhere, and raise but a small crop, and eat that soon. You must live within yourself, and depend upon yourself, always tucked up and ready for a start, and not have many affairs. A man may grow rich in Turkey even, if he will be in all respects a good subject of the Turkish government. Confucius said,—"If a State is governed by the principles of reason, poverty and misery are subjects of shame; if a State is not governed by the principles of reason, riches and honors are the subjects of shame." No: until I want the protection of Massachusetts to be extended to me in some distant southern port, where my liberty is endangered, or until I am bent solely on building up an estate at home by peaceful enterprise, I can afford to refuse allegiance to Massachusetts, and her right to my property and life. It costs me less in every sense to incur the penalty of disobedience to the State, than it would to obey. I should feel as if I were worth less in that case.

Some years ago, the State met me in behalf of the church, and commanded me to pay a certain sum toward the support of a clergyman whose preaching my father attended, but never I myself. "Pay it," it said, "or be locked up in the jail." I declined to pay. But, unfortunately, another man saw fit to pay it. I did not see why the schoolmaster should be taxed to support the priest, and not the priest the schoolmaster; for I was not the State's schoolmaster, but I supported myself by voluntary subscription. I did not see why the lyceum should not present its tax-bill, and have the State to back its demand, as well as the church. However, at the request of the selectmen, I condescended to make some such statement as this in writing:—"Know all men by these presents, that I, Henry Thoreau, do not wish to be regarded as a member of any incorporated society which I have not joined." This I gave to the town-clerk; and he has it. The State, having thus learned that I did not wish to be regarded as a member of that church, has never made a like demand on me since; though it said that it must adhere to its original presumption that time. If I had known how to name them, I should then have signed off in detail from all the societies which I never signed on to; but I did not know where to find a complete list.

I have paid no poll-tax for six years. I was put into a jail once on this account, for one night; and, as I stood considering the walls of solid stone, two or three feet thick, the door of wood and iron, a foot thick, and the iron grating which strained the light, I could not help being struck with the foolishness of that institution which treated me as if I were mere flesh and blood and bones, to be locked up. I wondered that it should have concluded at length that this was the best use it could put me to, and had never thought to avail itself of my services in some way. I saw that, if there was a wall of stone between me and my townsmen, there was a still more difficult one to climb or break through, before they could get to be as free as I was. I did not for a moment feel confined, and the walls seemed a great waste of stone and mortar. I felt as if I alone of all my townsmen had paid my tax. They plainly did not know how to treat me, but behaved like persons who are underbred. In every threat and in every compliment there was a blunder; for they thought that my chief desire was to stand the other side of that stone wall. I could not but smile to see how industriously they locked the door on my meditations, which followed them out again without let or hinderance, and *they* were really all that was dangerous. As they could not reach me, they had resolved to punish my body; just as boys, if they cannot come at some person against whom they have a spite, will abuse his dog. I saw that the State was half-witted, that it was timid as a lone woman with her silver spoons, and that it did not know its friends from its foes, and I lost all my remaining respect for it, and pitied it.

Thus the State never intentionally confronts a man's sense, intellectual or moral, but only his body, his senses. It is not armed with superior wit or honesty, but with superior physical strength. I was not born to be forced. I will breathe after my own fashion. Let us see who is the strongest. What force has a multitude? They only can force me who obey a higher law than I. They force me to become like themselves. I do not hear of *men* being *forced* to live this way or that by masses of men. What sort of life were that to live? When I meet a government which says to me, "Your money or your life," why should I be in haste to give it my money? It may be in a great strait, and not know what to do: I cannot help that. It must help itself; do as I do. It is not worth the while to snivel about it. I am not responsible for the successful workings of the machinery of society. I am

CHAPTER 9

MAKING VALUE
JUDGMENTS:
THOREAU,
DOUGLAS, POLK,
AND THE
MEXICAN WAR

not the son of the engineer. I perceive that, when an acorn and a chestnut fall side by side, the one does not remain inert to make way for the other, but both obey their own laws, and spring and grow and flourish as best they can, till one, perchance, overshadows and destroys the other. If a plant cannot live according to its nature, it dies; and so a man.

The night in prison was novel and interesting enough. The prisoners in their shirt-sleeves were enjoying a chat and the evening air in the door-way, when I entered. But the jailer said, "Come, boys, it is time to lock up;" and so they dispersed, and I heard the sound of their steps returning into the hollow apartments. My room-mate was introduced to me by the jailer, as "a first-rate fellow and a clever man." When the door was locked, he showed me where to hang my hat, and how he managed matters there. The rooms were whitewashed once a month; and this one, at least, was the whitest, most simply furnished, and probably the neatest apartment in the town. He naturally wanted to know where I came from, and what brought me there; and, when I had told him, I asked him in my turn how he came there, presuming him to be an honest man, of course; and, as the world goes, I believe he was. "Why," said he, "they accuse me of burning a barn; but I never did it." As near as I could discover, he had probably gone to bed in a barn when drunk, and smoked his pipe there; and so a barn was burnt. He had the reputation of being a clever man, had been there some three months waiting for his trial to come on, and would have to wait as much longer; but he was quite domesticated and contented, since he got his board for nothing, and thought that he was well treated.

He occupied one window, and I the other; and I saw, that if one stayed there long, his principal business would be to look out the window. I had soon read all the tracts that were left there, and examined where former prisoners had broken out, and where a grate had been sawed off, and heard the history of the various occupants of that room; for I found that even here there was a history and a gossip which never circulated beyond the walls of the jail. Probably this is the only house in the town where verses are composed, which are afterward printed in a circular form, but not published. I was shown quite a long list of verses which were composed by some young men who had been detected in an attempt to escape, who avenged themselves by singing them.

I pumped my fellow-prisoner as dry as I could, for fear I should never see him again; but at length he showed me which was my bed, and left me to blow out the lamp.

It was like travelling into a far country, such as I had never expected to behold, to lie there for one night. It seemed to me that I never had heard the town-clock strike before, nor the evening sounds of the village; for we slept with the windows open, which were inside the grating. It was to see my native village in the light of the middle ages, and our Concord was turned into a Rhine stream, and visions of knights and castles passed before me. They were the voices of old burghers that I heard in the streets. I was an involuntary spectator and auditor of whatever was done and said in the kitchen of the adjacent village-inn,—a wholly new and rare experience to me. It was a closer view of my native town. I was fairly inside of it. I never had seen its institutions before. This is one of its peculiar institutions; for it is a shire town. I began to comprehend what its inhabitants were about.

In the morning, our breakfasts were put through the hole in the door, in small oblong-square tin pans, made to fit, and holding a pint of chocolate, with brown bread, and an iron spoon. When they called for the vessels again, I was green enough to return what bread I had left; but my comrade seized it, and said that I should lay that up for lunch or dinner. Soon after, he was let out to work at haying in a neighboring field, whither he went every day, and would not be back till noon; so he bade me good-day, saying that he doubted if he should see me again.

When I came out of prison,—for some one interfered, and paid the tax,—I did not perceive that great changes had taken place on the common, such as he observed who went in a youth, and emerged a tottering and gray-headed man; and yet a change had to my eyes come over the scene,—the town, and State, and country,—greater than any that mere time could effect. I saw yet more distinctly the State in which I lived. I saw to what extent the people among whom I lived could be trusted as good neighbors and friends; that their friendship was for summer weather only; that they did not greatly purpose to do right; that they were a distinct race from me by their prejudices and superstitions, as the Chinamen and Malays are; that, in their sacrifices to humanity, they ran no risks, not even to their property; that, after all, they were not so noble but they treated the thief as he had treated them, and hoped, by a certain outward observance and a few prayers, and by walking in a particular straight though useless path from time to time, to save their souls. This may be to judge my neighbors harshly; for I believe that most of them are not aware that they have such an institution as the jail in their village.

It was formerly the custom in our village, when a poor debtor came out of jail, for his acquaintances to salute him, looking through their

CHAPTER 9

MAKING VALUE
JUDGMENTS:
THOREAU,
DOUGLAS, POLK,
AND THE
MEXICAN WAR

fingers, which were crossed to represent the grating of a jail window, "How do ye do?" My neighbors did not thus salute me, but first looked at me, and then at one another, as if I had returned from a long journey. I was put into jail as I was going to the shoemaker's to get a shoe which was mended. When I was let out the next morning, I proceeded to finish my errand, and, having put on my mended shoe, joined a huckleberry party, who were impatient to put themselves under my conduct; and in half an hour,—for the horse was soon tackled,[18]—was in the midst of a huckleberry field, on one of our highest hills, two miles off; and then the State was nowhere to be seen.

This is the whole story of "My Prisons."

I have never declined paying the highway tax, because I am as desirous of being a good neighbor as I am of being a bad subject; and, as for supporting schools, I am doing my part to educate my fellow-countrymen now. It is for no particular item in the tax-bill that I refuse to pay it. I simply wish to refuse allegiance to the State, to withdraw and stand aloof from it effectually. I do not care to trace the course of my dollar, if I could, till it buys a man, or a musket to shoot one with,—the dollar is innocent,—but I am concerned to trace the effects of my allegiance. In fact, I quietly declare war with the State, after my fashion, though I will still make what use and get what advantage of her I can, as is usual in such cases.

If others pay the tax which is demanded of me, from a sympathy with the State, they do but what they have already done in their own case, or rather they abet injustice to a greater extent than the State requires. If they pay the tax from a mistaken interest in the individual taxed, to save his property or prevent his going to jail, it is because they have not considered wisely how far they let their private feelings interfere with the public good.

This, then, is my position at present. But one cannot be too much on his guard in such a case, lest his action be biassed by obstinacy, or an undue regard for the opinions of men. Let him see that he does only what belongs to himself and to the hour. . . .

The authority of government, even such as I am willing to submit to,— for I will cheerfully obey those who know and can do better than I, and in many things even those who neither know nor can do so well,—is still an impure one: to be strictly just, it must have the sanction and consent of the governed. It can have no pure right over my person and property but what I concede to it. The progress from an absolute to a limited monarchy, from

18. Harnessed.

a limited monarchy to a democracy, is a progress toward a true respect for the individual. Is a democracy, such as we know it, the last improvement possible in government? Is it not possible to take a step further towards recognizing and organizing the rights of man? There will never be a really free and enlightened State, until the State comes to recognize the individual as a higher and independent power, from which all its own power and authority are derived, and treats him accordingly. I please myself with imagining a State at last which can afford to be just to all men, and to treat the individual with respect as a neighbor; which even would not think it inconsistent with its own repose, if a few were to live aloof from it, not meddling with it, nor embraced by it, who fulfilled all the duties of neighbors and fellow-men. A State which bore this kind of fruit, and suffered it to drop off as fast as it ripened, would prepare the way for a still more perfect and glorious State, which also I have imagined, but not yet anywhere seen.

Source 2 from *Appendix to the Congressional Globe, for the First Session, Twenty-ninth Congress: Containing Speeches and Important State Papers* (Washington, D.C.: Blair and Rives, 1846), pp. 903–905.

2. Speech by Stephen A. Douglas, May 13, 1846.

THE MEXICAN WAR.

SPEECH OF MR. S. A. DOUGLASS,[19]

OF ILLINOIS,

IN THE HOUSE OF REPRESENTATIVES,

May 13, 1846.

The Bill making appropriations for the support of the Army, &c., being under consideration in Committee of the Whole—

Mr. DOUGLASS rose to reply to the speech of the gentleman from Ohio [Mr. DELANO] who had just taken his seat. Several members proposed that the committee rise, with a view to adjournment, that he might speak in the morning, if he preferred that course. He declined to avail himself of their courtesy, as his remarks would necessarily be desultory and without preparation, and directed principally to the points which had already been

19. The family name was originally Douglass. Stephen dropped the second "s" sometime in 1846. See Robert W. Johannsen, *Stephen A. Douglas* (New York: Oxford University Press, 1973), p. 876 n. 7.

CHAPTER 9

MAKING VALUE
JUDGMENTS:
THOREAU,
DOUGLAS, POLK,
AND THE
MEXICAN WAR

touched in the discussion. My object (said he) is to vindicate our Government and country from the aspersions and calumnies which have been cast upon them by several gentlemen in the course of this debate, in connexion with the causes which have led to the existing war with Mexico. I prefer to meet and repel those charges at once, while they are fresh in our minds, and to demonstrate, so far as my feeble abilities will enable me to do so, that our Government has not been in the wrong, and Mexico in the right, in the origin and progress of the pending controversy. The gentleman from Ohio has been so kind as to herald my expected advent before my arrival, and to announce that I was about to follow him in the debate. I suppose he drew such an inference from the fact that I entered the hall while he was speaking, took a seat near him, and listened to his speech with the most respectful attention. He certainly had no other authority for the announcement. Acting on this supposition, he has addressed a large portion of his remarks to me, and invited a special answer from me to the main points of his argument. I propose to gratify him in this respect; and, while I shall speak with freedom and boldness of his positions and arguments, I shall endeavor to observe that courtesy towards him, individually, which is consistent with an appropriate reply to such an extraordinary speech. . . .

[Here Douglas recited what he considered to be sufficient justification for war, especially emphasizing Mexico's repeated insults to the United States.]

The facts which I have briefly recited are accessible to, if not within the knowledge of, every gentleman who feels an interest in examining them. Their authenticity does not depend upon the weight of my authority. They are to be found in full, and in detail, in the public documents on our tables and in our libraries. With a knowledge of the facts, or, at least, professing to know them, gentlemen have the hardihood to tell us that the President has unwisely and unnecessarily precipitated the country into an unjust and unholy war. They express great sympathy for Mexico; profess to regard her an injured and persecuted nation—the victim of American injustice and aggression. They have no sympathy for the widows and orphans, whose husbands and fathers have been robbed and murdered by the Mexican authorities—no sympathy with our own countrymen who have dragged out miserable lives within the walls of her dungeons, without crime and without trial—no indignation at the outrages upon our commerce and shipping, and the insults to our national flag—no resentment at the violation of treaties, and the invasion of our territory! . . .

I commend the patriotism, if not the morality, of the sentiment which he quoted at the beginning, and repeated several times during the course of his remarks: "I go for my country, right or wrong." I fear, however, that this sentiment, once so much applauded by our countrymen, is about to be brought into ridicule and contempt, by the use which that gentleman and his coadjutors are now disposed to make of it. They tell us that they go for their country, right or wrong; but they insist that their country is, and has been, all the time in the wrong. They profess to support the war; but they vote against the law which recognises its existence and provides the means—the money and the men—to expel a hostile army that has invaded our country and butchered our citizens. They profess great anxiety for the triumph of our arms; but they denounce the war—the cause in which our country is engaged—as *"unholy unrighteous, and damnable."*

Mr. J. W. HOUSTON.[20] Who made use of that expression? Was it any gentleman on this side of the House?

Mr. DOUGLASS. Yes, sir. The gentleman from Ohio, [Mr. DELANO,] who has just taken his seat, made use of the identical words, and repeated them several times, with great emphasis, in the course of his speech, while the great body of his political friends listened with the most profound respect, and gave every indication of approbation and encouragement, by expressions, looks, and nods of assent. Even now I see the venerable gentleman from Massachusetts nodding his approval of the sentiment.

Mr. J. Q. ADAMS.[21] Yes, sir. I approve and endorse every word and syllable of it.

Mr. DOUGLASS. So I supposed, from the marked indications of approbation which that gentleman and his friends gave to all the attacks which have been made, during this discussion, upon the rights, interests, and honor of our country. He is more bold and less politic in the expression of his opinions. They, after a little reflection, discover the expediency of concealment; but the lamentable fact is too palpable, that their feelings and sympathies are in perfect unison. Since he has had the hardihood to avow the sentiment, I suppose they will consider its profanity and moral treason perfectly consistent with their professions of Christianity and patriotism. What reliance shall we place on the sincerity of gentlemen's professions, that they are for their country, right or wrong, when they exert all their power and influence to put their country in the wrong in the eyes of Christendom, and invoke the wrath of Heaven upon us for our manifold national crimes and aggressions? With professions of patriotism on their

20. John Wallace Houston (1814–1896) was a first-term Whig congressman from Delaware.
21. John Quincy Adams (1767–1848) was the former president of the United States (1825–1829) and a Whig member of the House of Representatives from 1831 until his death in 1848.

CHAPTER 9

MAKING VALUE
JUDGMENTS:
THOREAU,
DOUGLAS, POLK,
AND THE
MEXICAN WAR

lips, do they not show that their hearts are with the enemy? They appeal to the consciences and religious scruples of our countrymen to unite in execration of our Government for supporting what they denounce as an unholy, unrighteous, and damnable cause. They predict that the vengeance of God will fall upon us; that sickness, and carnage, and death, will be our portion; that defeat and disgrace will attend our arms! Is there not treason in the heart that can feel, and poison in the breath that can utter, such sentiments against their own country, when forced to take up arms in self-defence, to repel the invasion of a brutal and perfidious foe? They for their country, right or wrong! who tell our people, if they rally under their country's standard, their bones will bleach on the plains of Mexico, and the enemy will look down from the mountain-top to behold the destruction of our armies by disease, and all those mysterious elements of death, which Divine Providence employs to punish a wicked people for prosecuting an unholy and unjust war! Sir, I tell these gentlemen that it requires more charity than falls to the lot of frail man to believe that the expression of such sentiments is consistent with the sincerity of their professions—with patriotism, honor, and duty to their country. Patriotism emanates from the heart; it fills the soul; inspires the whole man with a devotion to his country's cause, and speaks and acts the same language. America wants no friends, acknowledges the fidelity of no citizen, who, after war is declared, condemns the justice of her cause, and sympathizes with the enemy. All such are traitors in their hearts, and it only remains for them to commit some overt act for which they may be dealt with according to their deserts. . . .

Source 3 from James D. Richardson, ed., *A Compilation of the Messages and Papers of the Presidents, 1789–1897,* Vol. IV (Washington, D.C.: U.S. Government Printing Office, 1897), pp. 471–473.

3. Second Annual Message to Congress by President James K. Polk.

SECOND ANNUAL MESSAGE.

WASHINGTON, *December 8, 1846.*

Fellow-Citizens of the Senate and of the House of Representatives:
    In resuming your labors in the service of the people it is a subject of congratulation that there has been no period in our past history when all the elements of national prosperity have been so fully developed. Since your

last session no afflicting dispensation has visited our country. General good health has prevailed, abundance has crowned the toil of the husbandman, and labor in all its branches is receiving an ample reward, while education, science, and the arts are rapidly enlarging the means of social happiness. The progress of our country in her career of greatness, not only in the vast extension of our territorial limits and the rapid increase of our population, but in resources and wealth and in the happy condition of our people, is without an example in the history of nations.

As the wisdom, strength, and beneficence of our free institutions are unfolded, every day adds fresh motives to contentment and fresh incentives to patriotism.

Our devout and sincere acknowledgments are due to the gracious Giver of All Good for the numberless blessings which our beloved country enjoys.

It is a source of high satisfaction to know that the relations of the United States with all other nations, with a single exception, are of the most amicable character. Sincerely attached to the policy of peace early adopted and steadily pursued by this Government, I have anxiously desired to cultivate and cherish friendship and commerce with every foreign power. The spirit and habits of the American people are favorable to the maintenance of such international harmony. In adhering to this wise policy, a preliminary and paramount duty obviously consists in the protection of our national interests from encroachment or sacrifice and our national honor from reproach. These must be maintained at any hazard. They admit of no compromise or neglect, and must be scrupulously and constantly guarded. In their vigilant vindication collision and conflict with foreign powers may sometimes become unavoidable. Such has been our scrupulous adherence to the dictates of justice in all our foreign intercourse that, though steadily and rapidly advancing in prosperity and power, we have given no just cause of complaint to any nation and have enjoyed the blessings of peace for more than thirty years. From a policy so sacred to humanity and so salutary in its effects upon our political system we should never be induced voluntarily to depart.

The existing war with Mexico was neither desired nor provoked by the United States. On the contrary, all honorable means were resorted to to avert it. After years of endurance of aggravated and unredressed wrongs on our part, Mexico, in violation of solemn treaty stipulations and of every principle of justice recognized by civilized nations, commenced hostilities, and thus by her own act forced the war upon us. Long before the advance of our Army to the left bank of the Rio Grande we had ample cause of war against Mexico, and had the United States resorted to this extremity we might have appealed to the whole civilized world for the justice of our

CHAPTER 9

MAKING VALUE
JUDGMENTS:
THOREAU,
DOUGLAS, POLK,
AND THE
MEXICAN WAR

cause. I deem it to be my duty to present to you on the present occasion a condensed review of the injuries we had sustained, of the causes which led to the war, and of its progress since its commencement. This is rendered the more necessary because of the misapprehensions which have to some extent prevailed as to its origin and true character. The war has been represented as unjust and unnecessary and as one of aggression on our part upon a weak and injured enemy. Such erroneous views, though entertained by but few, have been widely and extensively circulated, not only at home, but have been spread throughout Mexico and the whole world. A more effectual means could not have been devised to encourage the enemy and protract the war than to advocate and adhere to their cause, and thus give them "aid and comfort." It is a source of national pride and exultation that the great body of our people have thrown no such obstacles in the way of the Government in prosecuting the war successfully, but have shown themselves to be eminently patriotic and ready to vindicate their country's honor and interests at any sacrifice. The alacrity and promptness with which our volunteer forces rushed to the field on their country's call prove not only their patriotism, but their deep conviction that our cause is just. . . .

[*Most of the remainder of Polk's Second Annual Message is a chronological listing of the "wrongs which we have suffered from Mexico" that, in Polk's opinion, made the United States' declaration of war a justifiable act.*]

∽ QUESTIONS TO CONSIDER ∽

Begin by extracting the main points from the selections by Thoreau, Douglas, and Polk. According to Thoreau, what should the *real* role of government be? (Note that he said it was *not* the government that had kept the country free, settled the West, and so on.) How does Thoreau address the issue of obeying the laws of a government in which the majority rules (and thus has determined those laws)? How does he compare the obligations of a citizen with those of a soldier?

Thoreau placed the American citizen in a curious dilemma. What did he think of the "hundred thousand merchants and farmers" in Massachusetts who did not oppose either slavery or the Mexican War? In contrast, what did he think of the reformers (those who devoted themselves "to the eradication of any, even the most enormous wrong")? What was Thoreau's alternative? Did he believe that people who disagree with laws made by the majority should obey them and work to change them later? In that vein, what did he think the abolitionists should do?

Thoreau spoke of a "higher law" that all people should obey. What, in his view, was that higher law? What did he think of politicians and orators? Finally, what did he see as the ideal government (the "really free and enlightened State")?

Douglas was a fiery orator who filled the galleries of the House of Representatives whenever he spoke.[22] On Wednesday, May 13, 1846, he was at his best. He began by saying that his object was "to vindicate our Government and country" from the critics of the war. In the portion of the speech reproduced here, how does he attempt to do that? How would Douglas have defined the word *patriotism*? Can you think of some actions that he would have labeled as treason? What would Douglas have thought about Thoreau's higher law?

In President Polk's opinion, who was to blame for the Mexican War? Does it follow that all Americans should have supported their nation during that war? Polk offers two rea-sons why Americans should not oppose the war effort. What are these reasons? One is quite easily seen, but the other is somewhat disguised (see his sentence beginning "It is a source of national pride . . .").

Having extracted the main points from each selection, you are now ready to make value judgments regarding those points. Refer back to the questions in the Method section of this chapter. The first five questions (having to do with the rights and responsibilities of citizenship and with the concept of majority rule) can be answered without direct references to the points of Thoreau, Douglas, or Polk. You should try, however, to use their points as well as your own to support your answers to those questions. Questions 6 and 7 require going considerably beyond the arguments made by the three men. Was Thoreau's position responsible or irresponsible? How do you define those terms? Responsible to whom? Answering question 6 will determine how you answer question 7 on Douglas's and Polk's opinions of dissenters.

---

22. Describing one of Douglas's speeches, long-time political foe John Quincy Adams wrote, "He now raved out his hour in abusive invective upon the members. . . . His face was convulsed, his gesticulations frantic, and he lashed himself into such a heat that if his body had been made out of combustible matter, it would have burnt out." Quoted in Gerald M. Capers, *Stephen A. Douglas, Defender of the Union* (Boston: Little, Brown, 1959), p. 18.

CHAPTER 9

MAKING VALUE
JUDGMENTS:
THOREAU,
DOUGLAS, POLK,
AND THE
MEXICAN WAR

⚬ EPILOGUE ⚬

From the United States' point of view, it won the Mexican War with a minimum of effort because Mexico was badly overmatched. Troops under General Zachary Taylor moved across the Rio Grande, winning important battles at Monterrey and Buena Vista. Simultaneously, General Winfield Scott landed at Vera Cruz and marched inland to Mexico City. In California, a combined force of army and navy easily scattered the weak Mexican resistance. In all, the war lasted less than twenty-one months and cost the United States only thirteen thousand men.

The United States gained a great deal from its lopsided victory. Perhaps most important, the nation added significantly to its size (more than 529,000 square miles, an increase of approximately 30 percent), thus further ensuring its power and world influence. Untold billions of dollars worth of natural resources, beginning with the discovery of gold in California one month before the end of the Mexican War, have been tapped in that area. In search of gold, land, or opportunity, millions of Americans migrated to the area gained in the war, until by the late twentieth century, the state of California (which in 1912 had a population smaller than that of Georgia) had become the most populous state in the Union. If, as one editorialist suggested, this was the United States' "manifest destiny," it was one that Americans themselves took a most active part in achieving.

Several individuals benefited from the war as well. Zachary Taylor and Winfield Scott became war heroes. Indeed, Taylor won the presidency in 1848 almost solely on the basis of being a military hero. He had never even voted, and it has been said that he refused to accept the notification of his nomination for the presidency because the letter had postage due. Many younger men also made their military reputations during the Mexican War and gained valuable combat experience. For example, most of the generals on both sides of the Civil War (including Ulysses S. Grant and Robert E. Lee) saw action in that conflict.

And yet if the United States' victory in the Mexican War was as significant as it was inevitable, that victory thrust upon the nation immensely difficult problems. The extent to which the issue of slavery had intruded into American life can be seen in the debate over the future of the territory taken from Mexico. How that territory was to be organized and whether or not slavery would be permitted there were subjects of intense discussion that the Compromise of 1850 only temporarily alleviated. As Americans would come to realize, the linking of the issues of slavery and territorial expansion proved tragic. Ultimately, only the Civil War—and the loss of 600,000 lives—would settle that question.

The Mexican War also left a residue of bad feelings between the United States and Mexico that has never really disappeared. The southwesterners' treatment of Mexicans as inferiors was not much different from the white southerners' treatment of African Americans and the far westerners' treatment of Orientals. President Woodrow Wilson's invasion of Mexico (1914–1917) hardly furthered better relations. More recently, many Mexicans believe that the growing anger in the United States over the issue of illegal aliens is particularly directed at them. Equally offensive to many is the habit people of the United States have of referring to themselves as "Americans," as if no one else in the Western Hemisphere deserves that name. Overall, the relationship between the two nations has been less than harmonious, and it has been strained even further by the free-trade talks between Washington and Mexico City during the 1990s.

Henry David Thoreau's symbolic protest had, as he no doubt expected, no appreciable effect on the government's conduct of the Mexican War. One week after his lecture to the Concord Lyceum, the peace treaty was signed between the United States and Mexico. Indeed, even some of Thoreau's friends turned against him. Sometime patron Ralph Waldo Emerson privately commented that Thoreau's protest was "mean and skulking, and in bad taste," a comment that no doubt got back to Thoreau. Thoreau received modest renown for his book *Walden* (1854) but never really achieved the literary reputation he craved. He died of tuberculosis in 1862. Only in the twentieth century, thanks to the homages of Mohandas

"Mahatma" Gandhi, Martin Luther King, Jr., and the Vietnam War protesters, did Thoreau become a major literary figure.

When Stephen A. Douglas rose on the House floor on May 13, 1846, he was at the beginning of what was to be a short but distinguished political career. Elevated from the House of Representatives to the Senate in 1847, he became a major figure in that body and a powerful force in the Democratic party. He was regularly mentioned as a possible candidate for the presidency. Yet Douglas's two principal goals—the preservation of the Union and the presidency—both eluded him. As the issue of slavery and its expansion became a more important issue to Americans (an issue, ironically, that was inflamed by the Mexican War that Douglas supported), the Democratic party—and Douglas himself—could not retain unity and strength. The party finally collapsed at its 1860 convention in Charleston, South Carolina, just as Douglas was within reach of the White House. Nominated later by a convention of Northern Democrats, he lost to Abraham Lincoln in the 1860 presidential election and died on June 3, 1861. His last words were instructions to his sons "to obey the laws and support the constitution of the United States." He was only forty-eight years old.

It is unlikely that James K. Polk ever heard of Thoreau. His criticism of dissenters during the Mexican War was directed not at Thoreau but at Whig congressmen and political figures within his own Democratic party. He retired from the presidency in

CHAPTER 9

MAKING VALUE
JUDGMENTS:
THOREAU,
DOUGLAS, POLK,
AND THE
MEXICAN WAR

1849, satisfied that he had achieved all his goals. He died less than a year after leaving office.

As students of the American past look back on the ideas of Thoreau, Douglas, and Polk, they realize that no one of them was entirely right or entirely wrong. Such an assessment, however, cannot be supported with hard factual evidence. Rather, we are required to make value judgments, a slippery ground on which many historians would like not to tread but on which they inevitably do.

CHAPTER 10

THE PRICE FOR VICTORY:
THE DECISION TO USE
AFRICAN AMERICAN TROOPS

∽ THE PROBLEM ∽

With the outbreak of war at Fort Sumter in April 1861, many northern African Americans volunteered for service in the Union army. President Abraham Lincoln, however, initially rejected black petitions to become soldiers. On April 29, Secretary of War Simon Cameron wrote one of many letters to African American volunteers; it curtly stated that "this Department has no intention at present to call into the service of the Government any colored soldiers."[1] Later, in July 1862, when Congress passed the

Confiscation Act (part of which authorized the president to use escaped slaves for the suppression of the rebellion "in such manner as he may judge best") and the Militia Act (which authorized him to enroll African Americans for military service), Lincoln virtually ignored both laws, arguing that the two acts *authorized* him to recruit blacks but did not *require* him to do so.

Curiously, in the South, too, free blacks and some slaves petitioned to be included in the newly formed Confederate army, perhaps hoping that such service might improve their conditions or even win them freedom. Like Lincoln, Confederate president Jefferson Davis rejected African American volunteers for military ser-

1. The letter was addressed to "Jacob Dodson (colored)" and is in *The War of the Rebellion: A Compilation of the Official Records of the Union and Confederate Armies*, Series III, Vol. I (Washington, D.C.: U.S. Government Printing Office, 1899), p. 133.

CHAPTER 10

THE PRICE FOR
VICTORY: THE
DECISION TO
USE AFRICAN
AMERICAN
TROOPS

vice and consistently opposed their use. Yet ultimately both chief executives changed their minds and accepted African Americans into the armed forces, although in Davis's case, the policy reversal came too late for black units to see action on the Confederate side. And although the recruitment of African American soldiers by the South might have prolonged the conflict, it probably would not have altered the ultimate outcome. In this chapter, you will examine the evidence so as to answer the following questions:

1. What were the arguments in the North and South against arming African Americans and using them as regular soldiers? What were the arguments in favor of this move? How did the reasons in the North and South differ? How were they similar?

2. What do you think were the principal reasons why both the United States and the Confederate States of America changed their policies? How did the reasons in the North and South differ? How were they similar?

∽ BACKGROUND ∾

Although many leaders in both the North and South studiously tried to avoid public discussion of the issue, the institution of slavery unquestionably played a major role in bringing on the American Civil War. As slavery intruded into the important issues and events of the day (such as westward expansion, the Mexican War, the admission of new states to the Union, the course charted for the proposed transcontinental railroad, and the right of citizens to petition Congress), as well as into all the major institutions (churches and schools, for example), an increasing number of northerners and southerners came to feel that the question of slavery must be settled, and settled on the battlefield. Therefore, when news arrived of the firing on Fort Sumter, many greeted the announcement with relief. Lincoln's call for seventy-five thousand volunteers

was answered with an enormous response. A wave of patriotic fervor swept across the northern states, as crowds greeted Union soldiers marching south to "lick the rebels." In the South, too, the outbreak of war was greeted with great enthusiasm. In Charleston, South Carolina, a day of celebration was followed by a night of parades and fireworks. Many southerners compared the upcoming war to the American Revolution, when, so the thinking went, an outnumbered but superior people had been victorious over the tyrant.

Yet for a number of reasons, most northern and southern leaders carefully avoided the slavery issue even after the war had begun. To Abraham Lincoln, the debate over the abolition of slavery threatened to divert northerners from what he considered the war's central aim: preserving the

Union and denying the South's right to secede. In addition, Lincoln realized that a great number of northern whites, including himself, did not view African Americans as equals and might well oppose a war designed to liberate slaves from bondage. Finally, in large parts of Virginia, North Carolina, Kentucky, and Tennessee and in other pockets in the South, Union sentiment was strong, largely because of the antiplanter bias in these states. But anti-Negro sentiment also was strong in these same areas. With the border states so crucial to the Union both politically and militarily (as points of invasion into the South), it is not surprising that Lincoln purposely discouraged any notion that the war was for the purpose of emancipating slaves. Therefore, when influential editor Horace Greeley publicly called on Lincoln in August 1862 to make the Civil War a war for the emancipation of slaves, the president replied that the primary purpose of the war was to preserve the Union. "My paramount object in this struggle," Lincoln wrote, "is *not* either to save or destroy slavery" (italics added).

> If I could save the Union without freeing *any* slave I would do it, and if I could save it by freeing *all* the slaves I would do it; and if I could save it by freeing some and leaving others alone I would also do that. What I do about slavery, and the colored race, I do because I believe it helps to save the Union; and what I forbear, I forbear because I do *not* believe it would help to save the Union.[2]

2. Lincoln to Greeley, August 22, 1862, in Roy P. Basler, ed., *The Collected Works of*

Hence President Lincoln, in spite of his "*personal* wish that all men everywhere could be free" (italics added), strongly resisted all efforts to turn the Civil War into a moral crusade to, in his words, "destroy slavery."

On the Confederate side, President Jefferson Davis also had reasons to avoid making slavery (in this case, its preservation) a primary war aim. Davis feared, correctly, that foreign governments would be unwilling to recognize or aid the Confederacy if the preservation of slavery was the most important southern reason for fighting. In addition, the majority of white southerners did not own slaves, often disliked people who did, and, Davis feared, might not fight if the principal war aim was to defend the peculiar institution. Therefore, while Lincoln was explaining to northerners that the war was being fought to preserve the Union, Davis was trying to convince southerners that the struggle was for independence and the defense of constitutional rights.

Yet as it became increasingly clear that the Civil War was going to be a long and costly conflict, issues concerning slavery and the use of African Americans in the war effort continually came to the surface. In the North, reports of battle casualties in 1862 caused widespread shock and outrage, and some fear that the United States would be exhausted before the Confederacy was finally subdued—if it was to be subdued at all.[3]

Abraham Lincoln, Vol. V (New Brunswick, N.J.: Rutgers University Press, 1953), pp. 388–389. Italics added.
3. The following is an estimate of Union cas-

CHAPTER 10

THE PRICE FOR
VICTORY: THE
DECISION TO
USE AFRICAN
AMERICAN
TROOPS

Also, many northerners came to feel that emancipation could be used as both a political and diplomatic weapon. Those European nations (especially England, which had ended slavery throughout its own empire in 1833) that had been technically neutral but were leaning toward the Confederacy might, northerners reasoned, be afraid to oppose a government committed to such a worthy cause as emancipation. Some northerners also hoped that a proclamation of emancipation would incite widespread slave rebellions in the South that would cripple the Confederacy. Not to be overlooked, however, are those northerners (a minority) who sincerely viewed slavery as a stain on American society and whose eradication was a moral imperative.

Gradually, President Lincoln came to favor the emancipation of slaves, although never to the extent that the abolitionists wanted. In early 1862, the president proposed the gradual emancipation of slaves by the states, with compensation for the slave owners and colonization of the former slaves outside the boundaries of the United States. When Congress mandated that Lincoln go further than that, by passing the Confiscation Act of 1862, which explicitly called for the permanent emancipation of all slaves in the Confederacy, the president simply ignored the law, choosing not to

enforce it.[4] But political and diplomatic considerations prompted Lincoln to alter his course and support the issuing of the Preliminary Emancipation Proclamation in September 1862. So that his action would not be interpreted as one of desperation, the president waited until after the Union "victory" at the Battle of Antietam. Although the proclamation (scheduled to take effect on January 1, 1863) actually freed slaves only in areas still under Confederate control (hence immediately freeing no one), the act was a significant one regarding a shift in war aims. The final Emancipation Proclamation was issued on January 1, 1863.[5]

The second important issue that Lincoln and other northern leaders had to face was whether or not to arm African Americans and make them regular soldiers in the Union Army. Blacks had seen service in the American Revolution and the War of 1812, prompting abolitionist Frederick Douglass, a former slave, to criticize the United States' initial policy of excluding African Americans from the army in the Civil War, saying in February 1862,

Colored men were good enough to fight under Washington. They are not good

---

ualties (the sum of those killed, wounded, and missing) for the principal engagements of 1862; Shiloh (April, 13,000 casualties), Seven Pines (May, 6,000), Seven Days (June, 16,000), Antietam (September, 12,400), Fredericksburg (December, 12,000).

4. It was this action of Lincoln that prompted the exchange between Greeley and the president in August 1862.
5. The Preliminary Emancipation Proclamation was issued to test public opinion in the North and to give southern states the opportunity to retain slavery by returning to the Union before January 1, 1863. No state in the Confederacy took advantage of Lincoln's offer, and the final proclamation was issued and took effect on January 1, 1963.

enough to fight under McClellan. They were good enough to fight under Andrew Jackson. They are not good enough to fight under Gen. Halleck. They were good enough to help win American Independence, but they are not good enough to help preserve that independence against treason and rebellion.[6]

Emancipation of slaves in the South was one thing, but making blacks United States soldiers was another.

Such a decision would imply that white northerners recognized African Americans as equals. Although most abolitionists preached the dual message of emancipation and racial equality, most northern whites did not look on African Americans as equals, a belief that they shared with their president. Would whites fight alongside blacks even in racially separated units? Were blacks, many northern whites asked, courageous enough to stand and hold their positions under fire? What would African Americans want as a price for their aid? Throughout 1862, northern leaders carried on an almost continual debate over whether to accept African Americans into the Union army, an issue that had a number of social, ideological, and moral implications.

In the Confederacy, the issue of arming African Americans for the southern war effort was also a divisive one. The northern superiority in population, supplemented by continued immigration from Europe, put the South at a terrific numerical disadvantage, a disadvantage that could be lessened by the enlistment of at least a portion of the approximately four million slaves. Southern battle casualties also had been fearfully high, in some battles higher than those of the Union.[7] How long could the Confederacy hold out as its numbers continually eroded? If the main goal of the war was southern independence, shouldn't Confederate leaders use all available means to secure that objective? It was known that some northern whites, shocked by Union casualty figures, were calling on Lincoln to let the South go in peace. If the Confederacy could hold out, many southerners hoped, northern peace sentiments might grow enough to force the Union to give up. If slaves could help in that effort, some reasoned, why not arm them? Yet, as in the North, the question of whether or not to arm African Americans had significance far beyond military considerations. Except for the promise of freedom, what would motivate the slaves to fight for their masters? If freedom was to be offered, then what, many surely would argue, was the war being fought over in the first place? Would southern whites fight with blacks? Would some African Americans, once armed, then turn against their masters? And finally, if southern whites were correct in their insistence

6. Quoted in James M. McPherson, *The Negro's Civil War: How American Negroes Felt and Acted During the War for the Union* (New York: Pantheon Books, 1965), p. 163.

7. The following are estimates of Confederate casualties for the principal engagements of 1862–1863; Seven Days (June 1862, 20,000), Antietam (September 1862, 13,700), Fredericksburg (December 1862, 5,000), Gettysburg (July 1863, 28,000).

CHAPTER 10

THE PRICE FOR
VICTORY: THE
DECISION TO
USE AFRICAN
AMERICAN
TROOPS

that African Americans were essentially docile, childlike creatures, what conceivable support could they give to the war effort? Interestingly, there were some remarkable similarities in the points debated by the northern and southern policymakers and citizens.

❧ THE METHOD ❧

In this chapter, you are confronted with two series of speeches—private and official correspondence, reports, newspaper articles and editorials, and laws and proclamations. One series concerns the argument in the North over whether to arm blacks, and the other series deals with the same question in the South. Read and analyze each series separately. Take notes as you go along, always being careful not to lose track of your central objectives.

By now you should be easily able to identify and list the major points, pro and con, in a debate. Jotting down notes as you read the evidence is extremely helpful. Be careful, however, because some reports, articles, and letters contain more than one argument.

Several earlier chapters required that you read between the lines—that is, identify themes and issues that are implied though never directly stated. What emotional factors can you iden-

tify on both sides of the question? How important would you say these factors were in the final decision? For example, you will see from the evidence that at no time in the debate being carried on in the North were battle casualties mentioned. Were casualties therefore of no importance in the debate? How would you go about answering this question?

In some cases, the identity of the author of a particular piece (if known) can give you several clues as to that person's emotions, fears, anxieties, and needs. In other cases, where the identity of the author is not known, you may have to exercise a little historical imagination. What might this person really have meant when he or she said (or failed to say) something? Can you infer from the context of the argument any emotions that are not explicitly stated?

❧ THE EVIDENCE ❧

NORTH

Source 1 from James M. McPherson, *The Negro's Civil War: How American Negroes Felt and Acted During the War for the Union* (New York: Pantheon Books, 1965), p. 33.

1. Petition of Some Northern Blacks to President Lincoln, October 1861.

We, the undersigned, respectfully represent to Your Excellency that we are native citizens of the United States, and that, notwithstanding much injustice and oppression which our race have suffered, we cherish a strong attachment for the land of our birth and for our Republican Government. We are filled with alarm at the formidable conspiracy for its overthrow, and lament the vast expense of blood and treasure which the present war involves. . . . We are anxious to use our power to give peace to our country and permanence to our Government.

We are strong in numbers, in courage, and in patriotism, and in behalf of our fellow countrymen of the colored race, we offer to you and to the nation a power and a will sufficient to conquer rebellion, and establish peace on a permanent basis. We pledge ourselves, upon receiving the sanction of Your Excellency, that we will immediately proceed to raise an efficient number of regiments, and so fast as arms and equipments shall be furnished, we will bring them into the field in good discipline, and ready for action.

Source 2 from Bell Irvin Wiley, *The Life of Billy Yank: The Common Soldier of the Union* (Baton Rouge: Louisiana State University Press, 1971), p. 109.

2. A. Davenport (a Union Soldier from New York) to His Home Folk, June 19, 1861.

I think that the best way to settle the question of what to do with the darkies would be to shoot them.

CHAPTER 10

THE PRICE FOR
VICTORY: THE
DECISION TO
USE AFRICAN
AMERICAN
TROOPS

Source 3 from McPherson, *The Negro's Civil War*, p. 162.

3. Newspaper Editorial by Frederick Douglass, *Douglass' Monthly*, September 1861.

Our Presidents, Governors, Generals and Secretaries are calling, with almost frantic vehemence, for men—"Men! men! send us men!" they scream, or the cause of the Union is gone; . . . and yet these very officers, representing the people and Government, steadily and persistently refuse to receive the very class of men which have a deeper interest in the defeat and humiliation of the rebels, than all others. . . . What a spectacle of blind, unreasoning prejudice and pusillanimity[8] is this! The national edifice is on fire. Every man who can carry a bucket of water, or remove a brick, is wanted; but those who have the care of the building, having a profound respect for the feeling of the national burglars who set the building on fire, are determined that the flames shall only be extinguished by Indo-Caucasian[9] hands, and to have the building burnt rather than save it by means of any other. Such is the pride, the stupid prejudice and folly that rules the hour.

Why does the Government reject the negro? Is he not a man? Can he not wield a sword, fire a gun, march and countermarch, and obey orders like any other? . . . If persons so humble as we can be allowed to speak to the President of the United States, we should ask him if this dark and terrible hour of the nation's extremity is a time for consulting a mere vulgar and unnatural prejudice? . . . We would tell him that this is no time to fight with one hand, when both are needed; that this is no time to fight only with your white hand, and allow your black hand to remain tied. . . . While the Government continues to refuse the aid of colored men, thus alienating them from the national cause, and giving the rebels the advantage of them, it will not deserve better fortunes than it has thus far experienced.—Men in earnest don't fight with one hand, when they might fight with two, and a man drowning would not refuse to be saved even by a colored hand.

8. Cowardice.
9. Douglass meant European American.

Source 4 from Roy P. Basler, ed., *The Collected Works of Abraham Lincoln*, Vol. V (New Brunswick, N.J.: Rutgers University Press, 1953), p. 222.

4. Lincoln's Proclamation Revoking General Hunter's Order of Military Emancipation of May 9, 1862.[10]

May 19, 1862

I, Abraham Lincoln, president of the United States, proclaim and declare, that the government of the United States, had no knowledge, information, or belief, of an intention on the part of General Hunter to issue such a proclamation; nor has it yet, any authentic information that the document is genuine. And further, that neither General Hunter, nor any other commander, or person, has been authorized by the Government of the United States, to make proclamations declaring the slaves of any State free; and that the supposed proclamation, now in question, whether genuine or false, is altogether void, so far as respects such declaration.

Sources 5 and 6 from *Diary and Correspondence of Salmon P. Chase*,[11] in Vol. II of *Annual Report of the American Historical Association for the Year 1902* (Washington, D.C.: U.S. Government Printing Office, 1903), pp. 45–46, 48–49.

5. Diary of Salmon P. Chase, Entry for July 21, 1862.

. . . I went at the appointed hour, and found that the President had been profoundly concerned at the present aspect of affairs, and had determined to take some definitive steps in respect to military action and slavery. He had prepared several Orders, the first of which contemplated authority to Commanders to subsist their troups in the hostile territory—the second, authority to employ negroes as laborers—the third requiring that both in the case of property taken and of negroes employed, accounts should be kept with such degrees of certainty as would enable compensation to be made in proper cases—another provided for the colonization of negroes in some tropical country.

---

10. On April 12, 1862, General David Hunter organized the first official regiment of African American soldiers. On May 9, Hunter proclaimed that slaves in Georgia, Florida, and South Carolina were free. Lincoln overruled both proclamations, and the regiment was disbanded without pay. Observers reported that the regiment, composed of former slaves, was of poor quality. Do you think those reports influenced Lincoln's thinking? Lincoln also overruled similar proclamations by General John C. Frémont in Missouri.
11. Chase was Lincoln's secretary of the treasury from 1861 until 1864.

CHAPTER 10

THE PRICE FOR
VICTORY: THE
DECISION TO
USE AFRICAN
AMERICAN
TROOPS

A good deal of discussion took place upon these points. The first Order was universally approved. The second was approved entirely; and the third, by all except myself. I doubted the expediency of attempting to keep accounts for the benefit of the inhabitants of rebel States. The Colonization project was not much discussed.

The Secretary of War presented some letters from Genl. Hunter in which he advised the Department that the withdrawal of a large proportion of his troups to reinforce Genl. McClellan,[12] rendered it highly important that he should be immediately authorized to enlist all loyal persons without reference to complexion. Messrs. Stanton,[13] Seward[14] and myself, expressed ourselves in favor of this plan, and no one expressed himself against it. (Mr. Blair[15] was not present.) The President was not prepared to decide the question but expressed himself as averse to arming negroes. The whole matter was postponed until tomorrow. . . .

6. Diary of Salmon P. Chase, Entry for July 22, 1862.

. . . The question of arming slaves was then brought up and I advocated it warmly. The President was unwilling to adopt this measure, but proposed to issue a proclamation, on the basis of the Confiscation Bill, calling upon the States to return to their allegiance—warning the rebels the provisions of the Act would have full force at the expiration of sixty days adding on his own part, a declaration of his intention to renew, at the next session of Congress, his recommendation of compensation to States adopting the gradual abolishment of slavery and proclaiming the emancipation of all slaves within States remaining in insurrection on the first of January, 1863.

I said that I should give to such a measure my cordial support: but I should prefer that no new expression on the subject of compensation should be made, and I thought that the measure of Emancipation could be much better and more quietly accomplished by allowing Generals to organize and arm the slaves (thus avoiding depredation and massacre on the one hand, and support to the insurrection on the other) and by directing the Commanders of Departments to proclaim emancipation within their Districts

12. George McClellan (1826–1885) was commander of the Army of the Potomac in 1862. Lincoln removed him because of his excessive caution and lack of boldness.
13. Edwin Stanton (1814–1869), secretary of war.
14. William Seward (1801–1872), secretary of state.
15. Montgomery Blair (1813–1883), postmaster general.

as soon as practicable; but I regarded this as so much better than inaction on the subject, that I should give it my entire support.

The President determined to publish the first three Orders forthwith, and to leave the other for some further consideration. The impression left upon my mind by the whole discussion was, that while the President thought that the organization, equipment and arming of negroes, like other soldiers, would be productive of more evil than good, he was not willing that Commanders should, at their discretion, arm, for purely defensive purposes, slaves coming within their lines.

Mr. Stanton brought forward a proposition to draft 50,000 men. Mr. Seward proposed that the number should be 100,000. The President directed that, whatever number were drafted, should be a part of the 3,000,000 already called for. No decision was reached, however.

Source 7 from Basler, ed., *The Collected Works of Abraham Lincoln*, Vol. V, p. 338.

7. Lincoln's Memorandum on Recruiting Negroes.

[July 22, 1862?]

To recruiting free negroes, no objection.

To recruiting slaves of disloyal owners, no objection.

To recruiting slaves of loyal owners, *with their consent*, no objection.

To recruiting slaves of loyal owners *without* consent, objection, *unless the necessity is urgent.*

To conducting offensively, while recruiting, and to carrying away slaves not suitable for recruits, objection.

Source 8 from *Diary and Correspondence of Salmon P. Chase*, pp. 53–54.

8. Diary of Salmon P. Chase, Entry for August 3, 1862.

. . . There was a good deal of conversation on the connection of the Slavery question with the rebellion. I expressed my conviction for the tenth or twentieth time, that the time for the suppression of the rebellion without interference with slavery had passed; that it was possible, probably, at the outset, by striking the insurrectionists wherever found, strongly and decisively; but we had elected to act on the principles of a civil war, in which the whole population of every seceding state was engaged against the

CHAPTER 10

THE PRICE FOR
VICTORY: THE
DECISION TO
USE AFRICAN
AMERICAN
TROOPS

Federal Government, instead of treating the active secessionists as insurgents and exerting our utmost energies for their arrest and punishment;— that the bitternesses of the conflict had now substantially united the white population of the rebel states against us; that the loyal whites remaining, if they would not prefer the Union without Slavery, certainly would not prefer Slavery to the Union; that the blacks were really the only loyal population worth counting; and that, in the Gulf States at least, their right to Freedom ought to be at once recognized, while, in the Border States, the President's plan of Emancipation might be made the basis of the necessary measures for their ultimate enfranchisement;—that the practical mode of effecting this seemed to me quite simple;—that the President had already spoken of the importance of making of the freed blacks on the Mississippi, below Tennessee, a safeguard to the navigation of the river;—that Mitchell, with a few thousand soldiers, could take Vicksburgh;—assure the blacks freedom on condition of loyalty; organize the best of them in companies, regiments etc. and provide, as far as practicable for the cultivation of the plantations by the rest:—that Butler should signify to the slaveholders of Louisiana that they must recognize the freedom of their workpeople by paying them wages;—and that Hunter should do the same thing in South-Carolina.

Mr. Seward expressed himself as in favor of any measures likely to accomplish the results I contemplated, which could be carried into effect without Proclamations; and the President said he was pretty well cured of objections to any measure except want of adaptedness to put down the rebellion; but did not seem satisfied that the time had come for the adoption of such a plan as I proposed. . . .

Source 9 from Basler, ed., *The Collected Works of Abraham Lincoln*, Vol. V, pp. 356–357.

9. President Lincoln, "Remarks to Deputation of Western Gentlemen," August 4, 1862. From an article in the New York *Tribune*, August 5, 1862.

A deputation of Western gentlemen waited upon the President this morning to offer two colored regiments from the State of Indiana. Two members of Congress were of the party. The President received them courteously, but stated to them that he was not prepared to go the length of enlisting negroes as soldiers. He would employ all colored men offered as laborers, but would not promise to make soldiers of them.

The deputation came away satisfied that it is the determination of the Government not to arm negroes unless some new and more pressing emergency arises. The President argued that the nation could not afford to lose Kentucky at this crisis, and gave it as his opinion that to arm the negroes would turn 50,000 bayonets from the loyal Border States against us that were for us. . . .

Source 10 from McPherson, *The Negro's Civil War*, pp. 163–164.

10. Letter to the Editor, New York *Tribune,* August 16, 1862.[16]

I am quite sure there is not one man in ten but would feel himself degraded as a volunteer if negro equality is to be the order in the field of battle. . . . I take the liberty of warning the abettors of fraternizing with the blacks, that one negro regiment, in the present temper of things, put on equality with those who have the past year fought and suffered, will withdraw an amount of life and energy in our army equal to disbanding ten of the best regiments we can now raise.

Source 11 from William Wells Brown,[17] *The Negro in the American Rebellion: His Heroism and His Fidelity* (Boston: Lee & Shepard, 1867), pp. 101–104.

11. Reminiscence of a Black Man of the Threat to Cincinnati, September 1862.[18]

The mayor's proclamation, under ordinary circumstances, would be explicit enough. "Every man, of every age, be he citizen or alien," surely meant the colored people. . . . Seeking to test the matter, a policeman was approached, as he strutted in his new dignity of provostguard. To the question, humbly, almost trembling, put, "Does the mayor desire colored men to report for service in the city's defence?" he replied, "You know d---d well he doesn't mean you. Niggers ain't citizens."—"But he calls on all, citizens and aliens.

16. This was a letter to the editor and did not reflect the opinion of Horace Greeley, editor of the *Tribune* and supporter of racial equality for African Americans.
17. Brown was an African American who ultimately served in the Union army and recorded his experiences.
18. In early September 1862, the citizens of Cincinnati, Ohio, feared a raid on the city by Confederates. Mayor George Hatch issued a proclamation calling on "every man of every age" to take part in the defense of the city.

CHAPTER 10

THE PRICE FOR
VICTORY: THE
DECISION TO
USE AFRICAN
AMERICAN
TROOPS

If he does not mean all, he should not say so."—"The mayor knows as well as you do what to write, and all he wants is for you niggers to keep quiet." This was at nine o'clock on the morning of the second. The military authorities had determined, however, to impress the colored men for work upon the fortifications. The privilege of volunteering, extended to others, was to be denied to them. Permission to volunteer would imply some freedom, some dignity, some independent manhood. . . .

If the guard appointed to the duty of collecting the colored people had gone to their houses, and notified them to report for duty on the fortifications, the order would have been cheerfully obeyed. But the brutal ruffians who composed the regular and special police took every opportunity to inflict abuse and insult upon the men whom they arrested. . . .

The captain of these conscripting squads was one William Homer, and in him organized ruffianism had its fitting head. He exhibited the brutal malignity of his nature in a continued series of petty tyrannies. Among the first squads marched into the yard was one which had to wait several hours before being ordered across the river. Seeking to make themselves as comfortable as possible, they had collected blocks of wood, and piled up bricks, upon which they seated themselves on the shaded side of the yard. Coming into the yard, he ordered all to rise, marched them to another part, then issued the order, "D--n you, squat." Turning to the guard, he added, "Shoot the first one who rises." Reaching the opposite side of the river, the same squad were marched from the sidewalk into the middle of the dusty road, and again the order, "D--n you, squat," and the command to shoot the first one who should rise. . . .

Calling up his men, he would address them thus: "Now, you fellows, hold up your heads. Pat, hold your musket straight; don't put your tongue out so far; keep your eyes open: I believe you are drunk. Now, then, I want you fellows to go out of this pen, and bring all the niggers you can catch. Don't come back here without niggers: if you do, you shall not have a bit of grog. Now be off, you shabby cusses, and come back in forty minutes, and bring me niggers; that's what I want." This barbarous and inhuman treatment of the colored citizens of Cincinnati continued for four days, without a single word of remonstrance, except from the "Gazette."

Source 12 from John G. Nicolay and John Hay, eds., *Abraham Lincoln—Complete Works* (New York: The Century Co., 1894), Vol. II, pp. 234–235, 242–243.

12. Lincoln's Reply to a Committee from the Religious Denominations of Chicago, Asking the President to Issue a Proclamation of Emancipation, September 13, 1862.

The subject presented in the memorial is one upon which I have thought much for weeks past, and I may even say for months. I am approached with the most opposite opinions and advice, and that by religious men who are equally certain that they represent the divine will. I am sure that either the one or the other class is mistaken in that belief, and perhaps in some respects both. I hope it will not be irreverent for me to say that if it is probable that God would reveal his will to others on a point so connected with my duty, it might be supposed he would reveal it directly to me; for, unless I am more deceived in myself than I often am, it is my earnest desire to know the will of Providence in this matter. And if I can learn what it is, I will do it. These are not, however, the days of miracles, and I suppose it will be granted that I am not to expect a direct revelation. I must study the plain physical facts of the case, ascertain what is possible, and learn what appears to be wise and right. . . .

I admit that slavery is the root of the rebellion, or at least its *sine qua non*.[19] The ambition of politicians may have instigated them to act, but they would have been impotent without slavery as their instrument. I will also concede that emancipation would help us in Europe, and convince them that we are incited by something more than ambition. I grant, further, that it would help somewhat at the North, though not so much, I fear, as you and those you represent imagine. Still, some additional strength would be added in that way to the war, and then, unquestionably, it would weaken the rebels by drawing off their laborers, which is of great importance; but I am not so sure we could do much with the blacks. If we were to arm them, I fear that in a few weeks the arms would be in the hands of the rebels; and, indeed, thus far we have not had arms enough to equip our white troops. I will mention another thing, though it meet only your scorn and contempt. There are fifty thousand bayonets in the Union armies from the border slave States. It would be a serious matter if, in consequence of a proclamation such as you desire, they should go over to the rebels. I do not think they all would—not so many, indeed, as a year ago, or as six months

19. An essential element or condition; a necessary ingredient.

CHAPTER 10

THE PRICE FOR
VICTORY: THE
DECISION TO
USE AFRICAN
AMERICAN
TROOPS

ago—not so many to-day as yesterday. Every day increases their Union feeling. They are also getting their pride enlisted, and want to beat the rebels.

Sources 13 through 15 from Basler, ed., *The Collected Works of Abraham Lincoln*, Vol. V, pp. 444, 509, 28–30.

13. Lincoln to Vice President Hannibal Hamlin.

(Strictly private.)   Executive Mansion,
Washington, September 28, 1862.

My Dear Sir:

Your kind letter of the 25th is just received. It is known to some that while I hope something from the proclamation,[20] my expectations are not as sanguine as are those of some friends. The time for its effect southward has not come; but northward the effect should be instantaneous.

It is six days old, and while commendation in newspapers and by distinguished individuals is all that a vain man could wish, the stocks have declined, and troops came forward more slowly than ever. This, looked soberly in the face, is not very satisfactory. We have fewer troops in the field at the end of six days than we had at the beginning—the attrition among the old outnumbering the addition of the new. The North responds to the proclamation sufficiently in breath; but breath alone kills no rebels.

I wish I could write more cheerfully; nor do I thank you the less for the kindness of your letter. Yours very truly,

                                                             A. LINCOLN

14. Lincoln to Carl Schurz.

Gen. Carl Schurz   Executive Mansion,
Washington, Nov. 24, 1862.

My dear Sir

I have just received, and read your letter of the 20th. The purport of it is that we lost the late elections,[21] and the administration is failing, because

20. Lincoln was referring to his preliminary Emancipation Proclamation, which he issued on September 22, 1862. Lincoln's hope was that the threat of emancipation would cause the South to surrender so as to keep slavery intact. See again Lincoln's letter to Horace Greeley, August 22, 1862.
21. In the congressional elections of 1862, the Republicans lost three seats in the House of

the war is unsuccessful; and that I must not flatter myself that I am not justly to blame for it. I certainly know that if the war fails, the administration fails, and that I *will* be blamed for it, whether I deserve it or not. And I ought to be blamed, if I could do better. You think I could do better; therefore you blame me already. I think I could not do better; therefore I blame you for blaming me. . . .

15. The Emancipation Proclamation.

January 1, 1863

By the President of the United States of America:

A Proclamation. . . .

Now, therefore I, Abraham Lincoln, President of the United States, by virtue of the power in me vested as Commander-in-Chief, of the Army and Navy of the United States in time of actual armed rebellion against authority and government of the United States, and as a fit and necessary war measure for suppressing said rebellion, do, on this first day of January, in the year of our Lord one thousand eight hundred and sixty three, and in accordance with my purpose so to do publicly proclaimed for the full period of one hundred days, from the day first above mentioned, order and designate as the States and parts of States wherein the people thereof respectively, are this day in rebellion against the United States, the following, to wit: . . .

[*Here Lincoln identified the geographic areas of the South still under the control of the Confederacy.*]

And by virtue of the power, and for the purpose aforesaid, I do order and declare that all persons held as slaves within said designated States, and parts of States, are, and henceforward shall be free; and that the Executive government of the United States, including the military and naval authorities thereof, will recognize and maintain the freedom of said persons.

And I hereby enjoin upon the people so declared to be free to abstain from all violence, unless in necessary self-defence; and I recommend to them that, in all cases when allowed, they labor faithfully for reasonable wages.

And I further declare and make known, that such persons of suitable condition, will be received into the armed services of the United States to

---

Representatives, although they were still the majority party. Senators were not elected by the people until the Seventeenth Amendment to the Constitution was ratified in 1913.

CHAPTER 10

THE PRICE FOR
VICTORY: THE
DECISION TO
USE AFRICAN
AMERICAN
TROOPS

garrison forts, positions, stations, and other places, and to man vessels of all sorts in said service.[22]

And upon this act, sincerely believed to be an act of justice, warranted by the Constitution, upon military necessity, I invoke the considerate judgment of mankind, and the gracious favor of Almighty God.

In witness whereof, I have hereunto set my hand and caused the seal of the United States to be affixed.

Done at the City of Washington, this first day of January, in the year of our Lord one thousand eight hundred and sixty three, and of the Independence of the United States of America the eighty-seventh.

By the President: ABRAHAM LINCOLN

Source 16 from George Washington Williams, *A History of the Negro Troops in the War of the Rebellion, 1861–65* (New York: Harper and Brothers, 1888), pp. 66–67, 90–91.

16. Reminiscence of a Former Black Soldier in the Union Army.

At first the faintest intimation that Negroes should be employed as soldiers in the Union Army was met with derision. By many it was regarded as a joke. The idea of arming the ex-slaves seemed ridiculous to most civil and military officers. . . .

Most observing and thoughtful people concluded that centuries of servitude had rendered the Negro slave incapable of any civil or military service. . . . Some officers talked of resigning if Negroes were to be called upon to fight the battles of a free republic. The privates in regiments from large cities and border States were bitter and demonstrative in their opposition. The Negro volunteers themselves were subjected to indignities from rebel civilians within the Union lines, and obtained no protection from the white troops. . . .

22. This paragraph was not part of the preliminary proclamation issued by Lincoln on September 22, 1862. See Basler, ed., *The Collected Works of Abraham Lincoln*, Vol. V, pp. 433–436.

Source 17 from Lawrence Frederick Kohl and Margaret Cosse Richard, eds., *Irish Green and Union Blue: The Civil War Letters of Peter Welsh, Color Sergeant, 28th Regiment, Massachusetts Volunteers* (New York: Fordham University Press, 1986), p. 62.

17. Fragment of a Letter from a Union Soldier, Early 1863.

I see by late papers that the governor of Massachusetts has been autheured to raise nigar regiments. i hope he may succeed but i doubt it very much if they can raise a few thousand and sent them out here i can assure you that whether they have the grit to go into battle or not if they are placed in front and any brigade of this army behind them they will have to go in or they will meet as hot a reception in their retreat as in their advance[.] The feeling against nigars is intensly strong in this army as is plainly to be seen wherever and whenever they meet them[.] They are looked upon as the principal cause of this war and this feeling is especially strong in the Irish regiments[.]

Source 18 from *The War of the Rebellion*, Series III, Vol. III, p. 16.

18. L. Thomas to Governor of Rhode Island, January 15, 1863.

ADJUTANT-GENERAL'S OFFICE,
Washington, D.C., January 15, 1863.

GOVERNOR OF RHODE ISLAND,
     Providence, R. I.:
   SIR: I am directed to say that the President will accept into the service of the United States an infantry regiment of volunteers of African descent, if offered by your State and organized according to the rules and regulations of the service.
   I am, very respectfully,

L. THOMAS,
Adjutant-General.

CHAPTER 10

THE PRICE FOR
VICTORY: THE
DECISION TO
USE AFRICAN
AMERICAN
TROOPS

Source 19 from Glenn W. Sunderland, *Five Days to Glory* (South Brunswick, N.J.:
A. S. Barnes & Co., 1970), pp. 97–98.

19. Letter from Tighlman Jones (a Union Soldier) to Brother Zillman Jones, October 6, 1863.

You have heard of Negroes being enlisted to fight for Uncle Sam. If you
would like to know what the soldiers think about the idea I can almost tell
you. Why, that is just what they desire. There is some soldiers who curse
and blow and make a great noise about it but we set him as a convalescent
who is like a man who is afraid of the smallpox who curses the works of a
power he can in no way avoid, but will kick and rail and act the part of a
fool, but of no avail, nature will have its own course, or to say that this
war will free the Negroes and that they will enlist and fight to sustain the
Government. I think more of a Negro Union soldier than I do of all the
cowardly Copperhead trash of the north[23] and there is no soldier but what
approves of the course of the present administration and will fight till the
Rebels unconditionally surrender and return to their allegiance.

Source 20 from Dudley Cornish, *The Sable Arm: Negro Troops in the Union
Army, 1861–1865* (New York: W. W. Norton, 1966), pp. ix–x.

20. Editorial, *New York Times*, March 7, 1864.

There has been no more striking manifestation of the marvelous times that
are upon us than the scene in our streets at the departure of the first of
our colored regiments. Had any man predicted it last year he would have
been thought a fool, even by the wisest and most discerning. History
abounds with strange contrasts. It always has been an ever-shifting melo-
drama. But never, in this land at least, has it presented a transition so
extreme and yet so speedy as what our eyes have just beheld.

Eight months ago the African race in this City were literally hunted
down like wild beasts.[24] They fled for their lives. When caught, they were
shot down in cold blood, or stoned to death, or hung to the trees or the
lamp-posts. Their homes were pillaged; the asylum which Christian charity

23. Copperheads were northerners who opposed the war and advocated peace at any price.
24. In mid-1863, demonstrations against conscription in New York City turned into an ugly
mob action against African Americans, partly because of their connection, through the Emancipation Proclamation of January 1, 1863, to the war and partly because of economic competition with the poorer whites who constituted most of the rioters.

had provided for their orphaned children was burned; and there was no limit to the persecution but in the physical impossibility of finding further material on which the mob could wreak its ruthless hate. Nor was it solely the raging horde in the streets that visited upon the black man the nefarious wrong. Thousands and tens of thousands of men of higher social grade, of better education, cherished precisely the same spirit. . . .

How astonishingly has all this been changed. The same men who could not have shown themselves in the most obscure street in the City without peril of instant death, even though in the most suppliant attitude, now march in solid platoons, with shouldered muskets, slung knapsacks, and buckled cartridge boxes down through our gayest avenues and our busiest thoroughfares to the pealing strains of martial music and are everywhere saluted with waving handkerchiefs, with descending flowers, and with the acclamations and plaudits of countless beholders. They are halted at our most beautiful square, and amid an admiring crowd, in the presence of many of our most prominent citizens, are addressed in an eloquent and most complimentary speech by the President of our chief literary institution, and are presented with a gorgeous stand of colors in the names of a large number of the first ladies of the City, who attest on parchment, signed by their own fair hands, that they "will anxiously watch your career, glorifying in your heroism, ministering to you when wounded and ill, and honoring your martyrdom with benedictions and with tears."

It is only by such occasions that we can at all realize the prodigious revolution which the public mind everywhere is experiencing. Such developments are infallible tokens of a new epoch.

SOUTH

Sources 21 and 22 from *The War of the Rebellion*, Series IV, Vol. I, pp. 482, 529.

21. Correspondence Between W. S. Turner and the Confederate War Department, July 17, 1861.

HELENA, ARK., *July 17, 1861*.

Hon. L. P. WALKER:[25]

DEAR SIR: I wrote you a few days since for myself and many others in this district to ascertain if we could get negro regiments received for Confederate

25. Walker was the Confederate secretary of war from February to September 1861.

CHAPTER 10

THE PRICE FOR
VICTORY: THE
DECISION TO
USE AFRICAN
AMERICAN
TROOPS

service, officered, of course, by white men. All we ask is arms, clothing, and provisions, and usual pay for officers and not one cent pay for negroes. Our negroes are too good to fight Lincoln hirelings, but as they pretend to love negroes so much we want to show them how much the true Southern cotton-patch negro loves them in return. The North cannot complain at this. They proclaim negro equality from the Senate Chamber to the pulpit, teach it in their schools, and are doing all they can to turn the slaves upon master, mistress, and children. And now, sir, if you can receive the negroes that can be raised we will soon give the Northern thieves a gorge of the negroes' love for them that will never be forgotten. As you well know, I have had long experience with negro character. I am satisfied they are easy disciplined and less trouble than whites in camp, and will fight desperately as long as they have a single white officer living. I know one man that will furnish and arm 100 of his own and his son for their captain. The sooner we bring a strong negro force against the hirelings the sooner we shall have peace, in my humble judgment. Let me hear from you.

Your old friend,

W. S. TURNER

22. Correspondence Between W. S. Turner and the Confederate War Department, August 2, 1861.

CONFEDERATE STATES OF AMERICA, WAR DEPARTMENT,
Richmond, August 2, 1861.

W. S. TURNER,
Helena, Ark.:

SIR: In reply to your letter of the 17th of July I am directed by the Secretary of War to say that this Department is not prepared to accept the negro regiment tendered by you, and yet it is not doubted that almost every slave would cheerfully aid his master in the work of hurling back the fanatical invader. Moreover, if the necessity were apparent there is high authority for the employment of such forces. Washington himself recommended the enlistment of two negro regiments in Georgia, and the Congress sanctioned the measure. But now there is a superabundance of our own color tendering their services to the Government in its day of peril and ruthless invasion, a superabundance of men when we are bound to admit the inadequate supply of arms at present at the disposal of the Government.

Respectfully,

A. T. BLEDSOE
Chief of Bureau of War.

Sources 23 through 26 from Robert F. Durden, *The Gray and the Black: The Confederate Debate on Emancipation* (Baton Rouge: Louisiana State University Press, 1972), pp. 30–31, 54–58, 61, 66–67.

23. *Montgomery* (Ala.) *Weekly Mail*, "Employment of Negroes in the Army," September 9, 1863.

. . . We must either employ the negroes ourselves, or the enemy will employ them against us. While the enemy retains so much of our territory, they are, in their present avocation and status, a dangerous element, a source of weakness. They are no longer negative characters, but subjects of volition as other people. They must be taught to know that this is peculiarly the country of the black man—that in no other is the climate and soil so well adapted to his nature and capacity. He must further be taught that it is his duty, as well as the white man's, to defend his home with arms, if need be.

We are aware that there are persons who shudder at the idea of placing arms in the hands of negroes, and who are not willing to trust them under any circumstances. The negro, however, is proverbial for his faithfulness under kind treatment. He is an affectionate, grateful being, and we are persuaded that the fears of such persons are groundless.

There are in the slaveholding States four millions of negroes, and out of this number at least six hundred thousand able-bodied men capable of bearing arms can be found. Lincoln proposes to free and arm them against us. There are already fifty thousand of them in the Federal ranks. Lincoln's scheme has worked well so far, and if no[t] checkmated, will most assuredly be carried out. The Confederate Government must adopt a counter policy. It must thwart the enemy in this gigantic scheme, at all hazards, and if nothing else will do it—if the negroes cannot be made effective and trustworthy to the Southern cause in no other way, we solemnly believe it is the duty of this Government to forestall Lincoln and proceed at once to take steps for the emancipation or liberation of the negroes itself. Let them be declared free, placed in the ranks, and told to fight for their homes and country. . . .

Such action on the part of our Government would place our people in a purer and better light before the world. It would disabuse the European mind of a grave error in regard to the cause of our separation. It would prove to them that there were higher and holier motives which actuated our people than the mere love of property. It would show that, although slavery is one of the principles that we started to fight for, yet it falls far short of being the chief one; that, for the sake of our liberty, we are capable of any personal sacrifice; that we regard the emancipation of slaves, and the consequent loss of property as an evil infinitely less than the subjuga-

CHAPTER 10
THE PRICE FOR
VICTORY: THE
DECISION TO
USE AFRICAN
AMERICAN
TROOPS

tion and enslavement of ourselves; that it is not a war exclusively for the privilege of holding negroes in bondage. It would prove to our soldiers, three-fourths of whom never owned a negro, that it is not "the rich man's war and the poor man's fight," but a war for the most sacred of all principles, for the dearest of all rights—the right to govern ourselves. It would show them that the rich man who owned slaves was not willing to jeopardize the precious liberty of the country by his eagerness to hold on to his slaves, but that he was ready to give them up and sacrifice his interest in them whenever the cause demanded it. It would lend a new impetus, a new enthusiasm, a new and powerful strength to the cause, and place our success beyond a peradventure. It would at once remove all the odium which attached to us on account of slavery, and bring us speedy recognition, and, if necessary, intervention.

24. General Patrick Cleburne to General Joseph Johnston, January 2, 1864.

We have now been fighting for nearly three years, have spilled much of our best blood, and lost, consumed, or thrown to the flames an amount of property equal in value to the specie currency of the world. . . . Our soldiers can see no end to this state of affairs except in our own exhaustion; hence, instead of rising to the occasion, they are sinking into a fatal apathy, growing weary of hardships and slaughters which promise no results. In this state of things it is easy to understand why there is a growing belief that some black catastrophe is not far ahead of us, and that unless some extraordinary change is soon made in our condition we must overtake it. . . .

In view of the state of affairs what does our country propose to do? In the words of President Davis "no effort must be spared to add largely to our effective force as promptly as possible. The sources of supply are to be found in restoring to the army all who are improperly absent, putting an end to substitution, modifying the exemption law, restricting details, and placing in the ranks such of the able-bodied men now employed as wagoners, nurses, cooks, and other employees, as are doing service for which the negroes may be found competent." . . . [W]e propose, in addition to a modification of the President's plans, that we retain in service for the war all troops now in service, and that we immediately commence training a large reserve of the most courageous of our slaves, and further that we guarantee freedom within a reasonable time to every slave in the South who shall remain true to the Confederacy in this war. As between the loss of independence and the loss of slavery, we assume that every patriot will freely give up the latter—give up the negro slave rather than be a slave himself. If we are correct in this assumption it only remains to show how this great national sacrifice is, in all human probabilities, to change the current of success and sweep the invader from our country.

Our country has already some friends in England and France, and there are strong motives to induce these nations to recognize and assist us, but they cannot assist us without helping slavery, and to do this would be in conflict with their policy for the last quarter of a century. . . . But this barrier once removed, the sympathy and the interests of these and other nations will accord with their own, and we may expect from them both moral support and material aid. . . .

Will the slaves fight? . . . The negro slaves of Saint Domingo, fighting for freedom, defeated their white masters and the French troops sent against them.[26] The negro slaves of Jamaica revolted, and under the name of Maroons held the mountains against their masters for 150 years; and the experience of this war has been so far that half-trained negroes have fought as bravely as many other half-trained Yankees. If, contrary to the training of a lifetime, they can be made to face and fight bravely against their former masters, how much more probable is it that with the allurement of a higher reward, and led by those masters, they would submit to discipline and face dangers.

25. President Jefferson Davis to General Walker, January 13, 1864— Reaction to Cleburne's Proposal.

I have received your letter, with its inclosure, informing me of the propositions [Cleburne's proposal] submitted to a meeting of the general officers on the 2d instant, and thank you for the information. Deeming it to be injurious to the public service that such a subject should be mooted, or even known to be entertained by persons possessed of the confidence and respect of the people, I have concluded that the best policy under the circumstances will be to avoid all publicity, and the Secretary of War has therefore written

26. On August 23, 1791, thousands of slaves in the French colony of Saint Dominigue (in Spanish, Santo Domingo, now Haiti) revolted against their white masters. Ultimately led by Toussaint Louverture (often spelled L'Ouverture), the slaves overthrew their masters, beat back invasions from both Britain and France, and declared Haiti an independent republic in 1804. Whites who fled from Haiti to the United States reported atrocities that filled white southerners with alarm for years after. See especially Alfred N. Hunt, *Haiti's Influence on Antebellum America* (Baton Rouge: Louisiana State University Press, 1988).

CHAPTER 10

THE PRICE FOR
VICTORY: THE
DECISION TO
USE AFRICAN
AMERICAN
TROOPS

to General Johnston requesting him to convey to those concerned my desire that it should be kept private. If it be kept out of public journals its ill effect will be much lessened.

26. General Joseph Johnston to General Hardee et al., January 31, 1864—Reaction to Cleburne's Proposal.

Lieutenant-General Hardee, Major-Generals Cheatham, Hindman, Cleburne, Stewart, Walker, Brigadier-Generals Bate and P. Anderson:

GENERAL:

I have just received a letter from the Secretary of War in reference to Major-General Cleburne's memoir read in my quarters about the 2d instant. In this letter the Honorable Secretary expresses the earnest conviction of the President "that the dissemination or even promulgation of such opinions under the present circumstances of the Confederacy, whether in the Army or among the people, can be productive only of discouragement, distraction, and dissension." The agitation and controversy which must spring from the presentation of such views by officers high in the public confidence are to be deeply deprecated, and while no doubt or mistrust is for a moment entertained of the patriotic intents of the gallant author of the memorial, and such of his brother officers as may have favored his opinions, it is requested that you communicate to them, as well as all others present on the occasion, the opinions, as herein expressed, of the President, and urge on them the suppression, not only of the memorial itself, but likewise of all discussion and controversy respecting or growing out of it. . . .

Source 27 from Bell Irvin Wiley, ed., *Letters of Warren Akin, Confederate Congressman* (Athens: University of Georgia Press, 1959), pp. 32–33.

27. Letter from Warren Akin to Nathan Land, October 31, 1864.

As to calling out the negro men and placing them in the army, with the promise that they shall be free at the end of the war, I can only say it is a question of fearful magnitude. Can we prevent subjugation, confiscation, degradation and slavery without it? If not, will our condition or that of the negro, be any worse by calling them into service?

On the other hand: Can we feed our soldiers and their families if the negro men are taken from the plantations? Will our soldiers submit to having our negroes along side them in the ditches, or in line of battle? When the negro is taught the use of arms and the art of war, can we live in safety with them afterwards? Or if it be contemplated to send them off to another country, when peace is made, will it be right to force them to a new, distant and strange land, after they have fought for and won the independence of this? Would they go without having another war? Involving, perhaps a general insurrection of all the negroes? To call forth the negroes into the army, with the promise of freedom, will it not be giving up the great question involved by doing the very thing Lincoln is now doing? The Confederate States may take private property for public use, by paying for it; but can we ever pay for 300,000 negro men at present prices, in addition to our other indebtedness? The Confederate Government may buy the private negro property of the Citizens, but can it set them free among us, to corrupt our slaves, and place in peril our existence? These are some of the thoughts that have passed th[r]ough my mind on the subject. But I can not say that I have a definite and fixed opinion. If I were convinced that we will be subjugated, with the long train of horrors that will follow it, unless the negroes be placed in the army, I would not hesitate to enrol our slaves and put them to fighting. Subjugation will give us free negroes in abundance—enemies at that—while white slaves will be more numerous than free negroes. We and our children will be slaves, while our freed negroes will lord it over us. It is impossible for the evils resulting from placing our slaves in the army to be greater than those that will follow subjugation. We may (if necessary) put our slaves in the army, win our independence, and have liberty and homes for ourselves and children. But subjugation will deprive us of our homes, houses, property, liberty, honor, and every thing worth living for, leaving for us and our posterity only the chains of slavery, tenfold more galling and degrading than that now felt by our negroes. But I will not enlarge, I have made suggestions merely for your reflection.

Source 28 from McPherson, *The Negro's Civil War*, pp. 243–244.

28. Judah P. Benjamin (Secretary of War, Confederacy) to Fred A. Porcher (an Old Friend and Former Classmate), December 21, 1864.

For a year past I have seen that the period was fast approaching when we should be compelled to use every resource of our command for the defense of our liberties. . . . The negroes will certainly be made to fight against us if not armed for our defense. The drain of that source of our strength is

CHAPTER 10

THE PRICE FOR
VICTORY: THE
DECISION TO
USE AFRICAN
AMERICAN
TROOPS

steadily fatal, and irreversible by any other expedient than that of arming the slaves as an auxiliary force.

I further agree with you that if they are to fight for our freedom they are entitled to their own. Public opinion is fast ripening on the subject, and ere the close of the winter the conviction on this point will become so wide-spread that the Government will have no difficulty in inaugurating the policy [of recruiting Negro soldiers].

. . . It is well known that General Lee, who commands so largely the con-fidence of the people, is strongly in favor of our using the negroes for de-fense, and emancipating them, if necessary, for that purpose. Can you not yourself write a series of articles in your papers, always urging this point as the true issue, viz, is it better for the negro to fight for us or against us?

Source 29 from Durden, *The Gray and the Black*, pp. 89–91.

29. *Richmond Enquirer*, November 4, 1864, Letter to the Editor in Reply to the Editorial of October 6, 1864.

Can it be possible that you are serious and earnest in proposing such a step to be taken by our Government? Or were you merely discussing the matter as a something which might be done? An element of power which might be used—meaning thereby to intimidate or threaten our enemy with it as a weapon of offence which they may drive us to use? Can it be possible that a Southern man—editor of a Southern journal—recognizing the right of property in slaves, admitting their inferiority in the scale of being and also their social inferiority, would recommend the passage of a law which at one blow levels all distinctions, deprives the master of a right to his property, and elevates the negro to an equality with the white man?—for, disguise it as you may, those who fight together in a common cause, and by success win the *same* freedom, enjoy equal rights and equal position, and in this case, are distinguished only by color. Are we prepared for this? Is it for this we are contending? Is it for this we would seek the aid of our slaves? . . .
When President Davis said: "We are not fighting for slavery, but indepen-dence," he meant that the question and subject of slavery was a matter settled amongst ourselves and one that admitted of no dispute—that he intended to be independent of all foreign influences on this as well as on other matters—free to own slaves if he pleased—free to lay our own taxes—free to govern ourselves. He never intended to ignore the question of slavery or to do aught else but express the determination to be *independent* in this as well as in all other matters. What has embittered the feelings of the two

sections of the old Union? What has gradually driven them to the final separation? What is it that has made two nationalities of them, if it is not slavery?

The Yankee *steals* my slave, and makes a soldier and freeman of him to *destroy* me. You *take* my slave, and make a soldier and freeman of him to *defend* me. The difference in your intention is very great; but is not the practice of both equally pernicious to the slave and destruction to the country? And at the expiration of ten years after peace what would be the relative difference between my negro *stolen* and freed by the Yankee and my negro taken and freed by you? Would they not be equally worthless and vicious? How would you distinguish between them? How prevent the return of him whose hand is red with his master's blood, and his enjoyment of those privileges which you so lavishly bestow upon the faithful freedman?

Have you thought of the influence to be exerted by these half or quarter million of free negroes in the midst of slaves as you propose to leave them at the end of the war; these men constitute the bone and sinew of our slaves, the able-bodied between 18 and 45. They will be men who know the value and power of combination; they will be well disciplined, trained to the use of arms, with the power and ability of command; at the same time they will be grossly and miserably ignorant, without any fixed principle of life or the ability of acquiring one. . . .

Sources 30 and 31 from McPherson, *The Negro's Civil War*, p. 244.

30. Howell Cobb, Speech in the Confederate Senate, 1864.

. . . if slaves will make good soldiers our whole theory of slavery is wrong. . . . The day you make soldiers of them is the beginning of the end of the revolution.

31. Robert Toombs, Speech in the Confederate Senate, 1864.

. . . the worst calamity that could befall us would be to gain our independence by the valor of our slaves. . . . The day that the army of Virginia allows a negro regiment to enter their lines as soldiers they will be degraded, ruined, and disgraced.

CHAPTER 10

THE PRICE FOR
VICTORY: THE
DECISION TO
USE AFRICAN
AMERICAN
TROOPS

Source 32 from Durden, *The Gray and the Black*, pp. 93–94.

32. *Lynchburg* (Va.) *Republican*, November 2, 1864.

The proposition is so strange—so unconstitutional—so directly in conflict with all of our former practices and teachings—so entirely subversive of our social and political institutions—and so completely destructive of our liberties, that we stand completely appalled [and] dumfounded [sic] at its promulgation.

They propose that Congress shall conscribe two hundred and fifty thousand slaves, arm, equip and fight them in the field. As an inducement of them to be faithful, it is proposed that, at the end of the war, they shall have their freedom and live amongst us. "The conscription of negroes," says the *Enquirer*, "should be accompanied with freedom and the privilege of remaining in the States." This is the monstrous proposition. The South went to war to defeat the designs of the abolitionists, and behold! in the midst of the war, we turn abolitionists ourselves! We went to war because the Federal Congress kept eternally meddling with our domestic institutions, with which we contended they had nothing to do, and now we propose to end the war by asking the Confederate Congress to do precisely what Lincoln proposes to do—free our negroes and make them the equals of the white man! We have always been taught to believe that slaves are property, and under the exclusive control of the States and the courts. This new doctrine teaches us that Congress has a right to free our negroes and make them the equals of their masters. . . .

Source 33 from Wiley, ed., *Letters of Warren Akin*, p. 117.

33. Mary V. Akin to Warren Akin, January 8, 1865.

. . . Every one I talk to is in favor of putting negros in the army and that *immediately*. Major Jones speaks very strongly in favor of it. I think slavery is now gone and what little there is left of it should be rendered as serviceable as possible and for that reason the negro men ought to be put to fighting and where some of them will be killed, if it is not done there will soon be more negroes than whites in the country and they will be the free race. I want to see them *got rid of soon*. . . .

Sources 34 through 36 from Durden, *The Gray and the Black*, pp. 163, 195, 202–203.

34. *Macon* (Ga.) *Telegraph and Confederate*, January 11, 1865.

Mr. Editor:

A lady's opinion may not be worth much in such an hour as this, but I cannot resist the temptation of expressing my approbation of "The crisis—the Remedy," copied from the Mobile Register. Would to God our Government would act upon its suggestions at once. The women of the South are not so in love with their negro property, as to wish to see husbands, fathers, sons, brothers, slain to protect it; nor would they submit to Yankee rule, could it secure to them a thousand waiting maids, whence now they possess one. . . .

35. *Richmond Whig*, February 28, 1865.

Mobile, Feb. 14—One of the largest meetings ever assembled in Mobile was held at the Theatre last night, which was presided over by Hon. Judge Forsyth.

Resolutions were unanimously adopted declaring our unalterable purpose to sustain the civil and military authorities to achieve independence—that our battle-cry henceforth should be—"Victory or Death"—that there is now no middle-ground between treachery and patriotism—that we still have an abiding confidence in our ability to achieve our independence—that the Government should immediately place one hundred thousand negroes in the field—that reconstruction is no longer an open question.

36. Confederate Congress, "An Act to Increase the Military Force of the Confederate States," March 13, 1865.

The Congress of the Confederate States of America do enact, That in order to provide additional forces to repel invasion, maintain the rightful possession of the Confederate States, secure their independence, and preserve their institutions, the President be, and he is hereby, authorized to ask for and accept from the owners of slaves, the services of such number of able-

CHAPTER 10

THE PRICE FOR
VICTORY: THE
DECISION TO
USE AFRICAN
AMERICAN
TROOPS

bodied negro men as he may deem expedient, for and during the war, to perform military service in whatever capacity he may direct.

Sec. 2. That the General-in-Chief be authorized to organize the said slaves into companies, battalions, regiments and brigades, under such rules and regulations as the Secretary of War may prescribe, and to be commanded by such officers as the President may appoint.

Sec. 3. That while employed in the service the said troops shall receive the same rations, clothing and compensation as are allowed to other troops in the same branch of the service.

Sec. 4. That if, under the previous sections of this act, the President shall not be able to raise a sufficient number of troops to prosecute the war successfully and maintain the sovereignty of the States and the independence of the Confederate States, then he is hereby authorized to call on each State, whenever he thinks it expedient, for her quota of 300,000 troops, in addition to those subject to military service under existing laws, or so many thereof as the President may deem necessary to be raised from such classes of the population, irrespective of color, in each State, as the proper authorites thereof may determine: *Provided*, that no more than twenty-five per cent of the male slaves between the ages of eighteen and forty-five, in any State, shall be called for under the provisions of this act.

Sec. 5. That nothing in this act shall be construed to authorize a change in the relation which the said slaves shall bear toward their owners, except by consent of the owners and of the States in which they may reside, and in pursuance of the laws thereof.

Approved March 13, 1865.

∽ QUESTIONS TO CONSIDER ∾

Begin by examining the evidence from the North. For each piece of evidence, answer the following questions:

1. Is the writer for or against using African Americans as soldiers?
2. What are the principal reasons for taking this position? (A piece of evidence may have more than one reason, as does Lincoln's September

13, 1862, reply to a delegation of Chicago Christians.)

At this point, you will confront your first problem. Some pieces of evidence do not speak directly to the issue of enlisting African Americans as soldiers (two such examples are A. Davenport's letter and William Wells Brown's recollections, Sources 2 and 11). Yet are there implied reasons for or against arming African Americans? Included in these reasons may be unstated racial feelings (look again at Lincoln's September 13, 1862, remarks in Source 12), casualty figures (note when the casualties were suffered and consult the evidence for any shifts in the argument at that time), or political considerations.

The central figure in the decision of whether or not the United States should arm African Americans was Abraham Lincoln. In July 1862, Congress gave the president the authority to do so, yet Lincoln hesitated. How did members of Lincoln's cabinet attempt to influence his opinion in July–August 1862? What was Lincoln's reply?

President Lincoln's memorandum (Source 7), probably written after the July 22 cabinet meeting, appears to show a shift in his opinion. How does this compare with his remarks on August 3 and 4, 1862 (Sources 8 and 9), and September 13, 1862? How would you explain this shift?

By January 1, 1863, the president had changed his public stance completely and was on record as favoring taking African Americans into the United States Army (Source 15). Because President Lincoln did not live to write his memoirs and kept no diary, we are not sure what arguments or circumstances were responsible for the shift in his position. Yet a close examination of the evidence and some educated guesswork will allow you to come very close to the truth. Do Lincoln's letters to Hamlin and Schurz (Sources 13 and 14) provide any clues?

The remaining evidence from the North deals with northern reactions to Lincoln's decision (Sources 16 through 20). Was the decision a popular one in the army? Among private citizens? Can you detect a shift in northern white public opinion? Can you explain this shift?

Now repeat the same steps for the South (Sources 21 through 36). In what ways was the debate in the South similar to that in the North? In what ways was it different? Which reasons do you think were most influential in the Confederacy's change of mind about arming African Americans? How would you prove this?

∽ EPILOGUE ∾

Even after northern leaders adopted the policy that blacks would be recruited as soldiers in the Union army, many white northerners still doubted whether blacks would volunteer and, if they did, whether they would fight. Yet the evidence overwhelmingly demonstrates that African Americans rushed to the colors and were an effective part of the Union war effort. By the end of the Civil War, approximately 190,000 African American men had served in the United States Army and Navy, a figure that represents roughly 10 percent of all the North's fighting men throughout the

CHAPTER 10

THE PRICE FOR
VICTORY: THE
DECISION TO
USE AFRICAN
AMERICAN
TROOPS

war. Former slaves who had come within the Union lines during the war made up the majority of African American soldiers, and Louisiana, Kentucky, and Tennessee contributed the most African American soldiers to the Union cause (approximately 37 percent of the total), probably because these states had been occupied the longest by United States troops.

Although, as we have seen, Lincoln initially opposed the use of black soldiers, once he changed his mind, he pursued the new policy with vigor. Moreover, the president was determined to be fair to those African Americans who had volunteered to serve the Union. In an August 19, 1864, interview, Lincoln said, "There have been men who have proposed to me to return to slavery the black warriors . . . to their masters to conciliate the South. I should be damned in time & in eternity for so doing. The world shall know that I will keep my faith. . . ."[27]

Black soldiers were employed by the Union largely in noncombat roles (to garrison forts, protect supply dumps and wagons, load and unload equipment and supplies, guard prison camps, and so on). Nevertheless, a number of black regiments saw combat, participating in approximately four hundred engagements, including thirty-nine major battles. One of the most famous battles was the ill-fated assault on Fort Wagner (near Charleston, South Carolina), led by the 54th Massachusetts Infantry, the first black regiment recruited in the North. Al-

most half the regiment, including its commander, Colonel Robert Gould Shaw, was lost in the frontal attack, but the troops fought valiantly in the losing effort. The *Atlantic Monthly* reported, "Through the cannon smoke of that dark night, the manhood of the colored race shines before many eyes. . . ." Over a century later, the regiment was immortalized in the film *Glory*.[28]

Overall, African American casualties were high: more than one-third of the African American soldiers were killed or wounded, although the majority of deaths, as with white soldiers, came from disease rather than battle wounds. The percentage of desertions among African Americans was lower than for the army as a whole. Moreover, twenty-one black soldiers and sailors were awarded the Congressional Medal of Honor, the nation's most distinguished award to military personnel.

Yet there is another side to the story of African American service in the Union army and navy. African American volunteers were rigidly segregated, serving in all-black regiments, usually under white officers. At first, black troops received less pay than their white counterparts. However, after many petitions and protests by African American soldiers, Congress at last established the principle of equal pay for African American soldiers in June 1864. Unfortunately, racial incidents within the Union army and navy were common.

27. Basler, ed., *The Collected Works of Abraham Lincoln,* Vol. VII, pp. 506–508.

28. The Confederates refused to return Shaw's body to his parents for burial, saying, "We have buried him with his niggers."

Confederate reaction to the Union's recruitment of African American troops was predictably harsh. The Confederate government announced that any blacks taken as prisoners of war would be either shot on the spot or returned to slavery. In retaliation, Lincoln stated that he would order a Confederate prisoner of war executed for every African American prisoner shot by the South and would order a southern prisoner to do hard labor for every African American prisoner returned to slavery. Most Confederates treated black prisoners of war the same as they did whites. Nevertheless, in several instances, surrendering African Americans were murdered, the most notable instance occurring at Fort Pillow, Tennessee, where apparently several dozen African American prisoners of war and their white commander, Major William Bradford, were shot "while attempting to escape." After another engagement, one Confederate colonel bragged, "I then ordered every one shot, and with my Six Shooter I assisted in the execution of the order." Yet in spite of his warning, Lincoln did not retaliate, even though a United States Senate investigating committee charged that about three hundred African American Union soldiers had been murdered.

The president probably felt that any action on his part would only further inflame the Confederates.

Within the Confederacy, the adoption of the policy to recruit African American soldiers came too late, the last gasp of a dying nation that had debated too long between principle and survival. In the month between the approval of the policy and the end of the war at Appomatox Court House, some black companies were organized, but there is no record that they ever saw action. For a conflict that had raged for four agonizingly long years, the end came relatively quickly.

The debate over the use of African American troops points out what many abolitionists had maintained for years: although slavery was a moral concern that consumed all who touched it, the institution of slavery was but part of the problem facing black—and white—Americans. More insidious and less easily eradicated was racism, a set of assumptions, feelings, and emotions that has survived long after slavery was destroyed. The debate in both the North and the South over the use of African American troops clearly demonstrates that the true problem confronting many people of the Civil War era was their own feelings, anxieties, and fears.

CHAPTER 11

RECONSTRUCTING RECONSTRUCTION: THE POLITICAL CARTOONIST AND THE NATIONAL MOOD

∽ **THE PROBLEM** ∽

The Civil War took a tremendous toll on North and South alike. In the defeated South, more than one-fourth of all men who had borne arms for the Confederacy died, and an additional 15 percent were permanently disabled. Indeed, in 1865 Mississippi spent one-fifth of the state's total revenue on artificial arms and legs for Confederate veterans. Combined with the damage to agriculture, industry, and railroads, the human cost of the Civil War to the South was nearly catastrophic. For its part, the North had suffered frightful human losses as well, although proportionately less than those of the South.

And yet the Civil War, although appalling in its human, physical, and psychological costs, did settle some important issues that had plagued the

nation for decades before that bloody conflict. First, the triumph of Union arms had established the United States as "one nation indivisible," from which no state could secede.[1] No less important, the "peculiar institution" of slavery was eradicated, and African Americans at last were free. In truth, although the Civil War had been costly, the issues it settled were momentous.

1. In response to President Benjamin Harrison's 1892 appeal for schoolchildren to mark the four hundredth anniversary of Columbus's discovery with patriotic exercises, Bostonian Francis Bellamy composed the pledge of allegiance to the American flag, from which the phrase "one nation indivisible" comes. In 1942, Congress made it the official pledge to the flag, and in 1954 Congress added the words "under God" in the middle of Bellamy's phrase.

The victory of the United States, however, raised at least as many questions as it settled. There was the question of what should happen to the defeated South. Should the states of the former Confederacy be permitted to take their natural place in the Union as quickly and smoothly as possible, with minimum concessions to their northern conquerors? Or should the North insist on a thorough reconstruction of the South, with new economic and social institutions to replace the old? Tied to this issue was the thorny constitutional question of whether the South actually had left the Union at all in 1861. If so, then the southern states in 1865 were territories, to be governed and administered by Congress. If not, then the Civil War had been an internal insurrection and the president, as commander in chief, would administer the South's re-entry into the Union.

Perhaps the most difficult question the Union's victory raised was the status of the former slaves. To be sure, they were no longer in bondage. But should they possess all the rights that whites had? Should they be assisted in becoming landowners; if not, how would they earn a living? Should they be allowed to vote and run for elective office? Indeed, no more complex and difficult issue confronted the country than the "place" of the newly freed slaves in the nation.

In all these questions, public opinion in the victorious North was a critical factor in shaping or altering the policies designed to reconstruct the South. Earlier democratic reforms made it unlikely that either the president or Congress could defy public opinion successfully. Yet public opinion can shift with remarkable speed, and political figures forever must be sensitive to its sometimes fickle winds.

Among the many influences on public opinion in the second half of the nineteenth century were writers and artists who worked for newspapers and magazines. In this chapter, you will be examining and analyzing the work of one man who attempted to shape public opinion in the North: editorial cartoonist Thomas Nast (1840–1902). Nast was not the only person who attempted to influence public opinion in the North, but at the peak of his career, he and his cartoons were well-known and widely appreciated. What were Nast's views on the controversial issues of the Reconstruction era, and how did he try to influence public opinion?

⊘ BACKGROUND ⊘

By early 1865, it was evident to most northerners and southerners that the Civil War was nearly over. While Grant was hammering at Lee's depleted forces in Virginia, Union general William Tecumseh Sherman broke the back of the Confederacy with his devastating march through Georgia and then northward into the Carolinas. Atlanta fell to Sherman's

CHAPTER 11

RECONSTRUCTING
RECONSTRUCTION:
THE POLITICAL
CARTOONIST
AND THE
NATIONAL MOOD

troops in September 1864, Savannah in December, and Charleston and Columbia, South Carolina, in February 1865. Two-thirds of Columbia lay in ashes. Meanwhile, General Philip Sheridan had driven the Confederates out of the Shenandoah Valley of Virginia, thus blocking any escape attempts by Lee and further cutting southern supply routes. The Union naval blockade of the South was taking its fearful toll, as parts of the dying Confederacy were facing real privation. Hence, although northern armies had suffered terrible losses, by 1865 they stood poised on the brink of victory.

In the South, all but the extreme die-hards recognized that defeat was inevitable. The Confederacy was suffering in more ways than militarily. The Confederate economy had almost completely collapsed, and Confederate paper money was nearly worthless. Slaves were abandoning their masters and mistresses in great numbers, running away to Union armies or roaming through the South in search of better opportunities. In many areas, civilian morale had almost totally deteriorated, and one Georgian wrote, "The people are soul-sick and heartily tired of the hateful, hopeless strife. . . . We have had enough of want and woe, of cruelty and carnage, enough of cripples and corpses."[2] As the Confederate government made secret plans to evacuate Richmond, most southerners knew that the end was very near.

Yet even with victory almost in hand, many northerners had given little thought to what should happen after the war. Would southerners accept the changes that defeat would almost inevitably force on them (especially the end of slavery)? What demands should the victors make on the vanquished? Should the North assist the South in rebuilding after the devastation of war? If so, should the North dictate how that rebuilding, or reconstruction, should take place? What efforts should the North make to ensure that the former slaves were receiving the rights of free men and women? During the war, few northerners had seriously considered these questions. Now that victory was within their grasp, they could not avoid them.

One person who had been wrestling with these questions was Abraham Lincoln. In December 1863, the president announced his own plan for reconstructing the South, a plan in keeping with his later hope, as expressed in his second inaugural address, for "malice toward none; with charity for all; . . . Let us . . . bind up the nation's wounds."[3] In Lincoln's plan, a southern state could resume its normal activities in the Union as soon as 10 percent of the voters of 1860 had taken an oath of loyalty to the United States. High-ranking Confederate leaders would be excluded, and some blacks might gain the right to vote. No men-

2. The letter probably was written by Georgian Herschel V. Walker. See Allan Nevins, *The Organized War to Victory, 1864–1865,* Vol. IV of *The War for the Union* (New York: Charles Scribner's Sons, 1971), p. 221.

3. The full text of Lincoln's second inaugural address, delivered on March 4, 1865, can be found in Roy P. Basler, ed., *The Collected Works of Abraham Lincoln,* Vol. VIII (New Brunswick, N.J.: Rutgers University Press, 1953), pp. 332–333.

tion was made of protecting the civil rights of former slaves; it was presumed that this matter would be left to the slaves' former masters and mistresses.

To many northerners, later known as Radical Republicans, Lincoln's plan was much too lenient. In the opinion of these people, a number of whom had been abolitionists, the South, when conquered, should not be allowed to return to its former ways. Not only should slavery be eradicated, they claimed, but freed blacks should be assisted in their efforts to attain economic, social, and political equity. Most of the Radical Republicans favored education for African Americans, and some advocated carving the South's plantations into small parcels to be given to the freedmen. To implement these reforms, Radical Republicans wanted detachments of the United States Army to remain in the South and favored the appointment of provisional governors to oversee the transitional governments in the southern states. Lincoln approved plans for the Army to stay and supported the idea of provisional governors. But he opposed the more far-reaching reform notions of the Radical Republicans, and as president he was able to block them.

In addition to having diametrically opposed views of Reconstruction, Lincoln and the Radical Republicans differed over the constitutional question of which branch of the federal government would be responsible for the reconstruction of the South. The Constitution made no mention of secession, reunion, or reconstruction. But Radical Republicans, citing passages in the Constitution giving Congress the power to guarantee each state a republican government, insisted that the reconstruction of the South should be carried out by Congress.[4] For his part, however, Lincoln maintained that as chief enforcer of the law and as commander in chief, the president was the appropriate person to be in charge of Reconstruction. Clearly, a stalemate was in the making, with Radical Republicans calling for a more reform-minded Reconstruction policy and Lincoln continuing to block them.

President Lincoln's death on April 15, 1865 (one week after Lee's surrender at Appomattox Court House),[5] brought Vice President Andrew Johnson to the nation's highest office. At first, Radical Republicans had reason to hope that the new president would follow policies more to their liking. A Tennessean, Johnson had risen to political prominence from humble circumstances, had become a spokesperson for the common white men and women of the South, and had opposed the planter aristocracy. Upon becoming president, he excluded from amnesty all former Confederate political and military leaders as well as all southerners who owned taxable property worth more than $20,000 (an obvious slap at his old planter-aristocrat foes). Moreover, Johnson issued a proclamation setting up provisional mil-

4. See Article IV, Section 4, of the Constitution. Later Radical Republicans also justified their position using the Thirteenth Amendment, adopted in 1865, which gave Congress the power to enforce the amendment ending slavery in the South.
5. The last Confederate army to give up, commanded by General Joseph Johnston, surrendered to Sherman at Durham Station, North Carolina, on April 18, 1865.

CHAPTER 11

RECONSTRUCTING
RECONSTRUCTION:
THE POLITICAL
CARTOONIST
AND THE
NATIONAL MOOD

itary governments in the conquered South and told his cabinet he favored black suffrage, although as a states' rightist he insisted that states adopt the measure voluntarily. At the outset, then, Johnson appeared to be all the Radical Republicans wanted, preferable to the more moderate Lincoln.

Yet it did not take Radical Republicans long to realize that President Johnson was not one of them. Although he spoke harshly, he pardoned hundreds of former Confederates, who quickly captured control of southern state governments and congressional delegations. Many northerners were shocked to see former Confederate generals and officials, and even former Confederate vice president Alexander Stephens, returned to Washington. The new southern state legislatures passed a series of laws, known collectively as black codes, that so severely restricted the rights of former slaves that they were all but slaves again. Moreover, Johnson privately told southerners that he opposed the Fourteenth Amendment to the Constitution, which was intended to confer full civil rights on the newly freed slaves. He also used his veto power to block Radical Republican Reconstruction measures in Congress and seemed to do little to combat the general defiance of the former Confederacy (exhibited in many forms, including insults thrown at Union occupation soldiers, the desecration of the United States flag, and the formation of organized resistance groups such as the Ku Klux Klan).

To an increasing number of northerners, the unrepentant spirit of the South and Johnson's acquiescence to it were nothing short of appalling. Had the Civil War been fought for nothing? Had more than 364,000 federal soldiers died in vain? White southerners were openly defiant, African Americans were being subjugated by white southerners and virtually ignored by President Johnson, and former Confederates were returning to positions of power and prominence. Radical Republicans had sufficient power in Congress to pass harsher measures, but Johnson kept vetoing them, and the Radicals lacked the votes to override his vetoes.[6] Indeed, the impasse that had existed before Lincoln's death continued.

In such an atmosphere, the congressional elections of 1866 were bitterly fought campaigns, especially in the northern states. President Johnson traveled throughout the North, defending his moderate plan of Reconstruction and viciously attacking his political enemies. However, the Radical Republicans were even more effective. Stirring up the hostilities of wartime, they "waved the bloody shirt" and excited northern voters by charging that the South had never accepted its defeat and that the 364,000 Union dead and 275,000 wounded would be for nothing if the South was permitted to continue its arrogant and stubborn behavior. Increasingly, Johnson was greeted by hostile audiences as the North underwent a major shift in public opinion.

The Radical Republicans won a stunning victory in the congressional

6. Congress was able to override Johnson's vetoes of the Civil Rights Act and a revised Freedmen's Bureau bill.

elections of 1866 and thus broke the stalemate between Congress and the president. Armed with enough votes to override Johnson's vetoes almost at will, the new Congress proceeded rapidly to implement the Radical Republican vision of Reconstruction. The South was divided into five military districts to be ruled by martial law. Southern states had to ratify the Fourteenth Amendment and institute black suffrage before being allowed to take their formal places in the Union. The Freedmen's Bureau, founded earlier, was given additional federal support to set up schools for African Americans, negotiate labor contracts, and, with the military, help monitor elections. Only the proposal to give land to blacks was not adopted, being seen as too extreme even by some Radical Republicans. Congressional Reconstruction had begun.

President Johnson, however, had not been left completely powerless. Determined to undercut the Radical Republicans' Reconstruction policies, he issued orders increasing the powers of civil governments in the South and removed military officers who were enforcing Congress's will, replacing them with commanders less determined to protect black voting rights and more willing to turn the other way when disqualified white southerners voted. Opposed most vigorously by his own secretary of war, Edwin Stanton, Johnson tried to discharge Stanton. To an increasing number of Radicals, it became clear that the president would have to be removed from office.

In 1868, the House of Representatives voted to impeach Andrew Johnson. Charged with violating the Ten-ure of Office Act and the Command of the Army Act (both of which had been passed over Johnson's vetoes), the president was tried in the Senate, where two-thirds of the senators would have to vote against Johnson for him to be removed.[7] The vast majority of senators disagreed with the president's Reconstruction policies, but they feared that impeachment had become a political tool that, if successful, threatened to destroy the balance of power between the branches of the federal government. The vote on removal fell one short of the necessary two-thirds, and Johnson was spared the indignity of removal. Nevertheless, the Republican nomination of General Ulysses Grant and his subsequent landslide victory (running as a military hero, Grant carried twenty-six out of thirty-four states) gave Radical Republicans a malleable president, one who, although not a Radical himself, could ensure the continuation of their version of Reconstruction.[8]

The Democratic party, however, was not dead, even though the Republican party dominated national politics in the immediate aftermath of the Civil War. In addition to white farmers and planters in the South and border states, the Democratic party contained many northerners who favored conservative ("sound money") policies, voters who opposed Radical Reconstruction,

7. See Article I, Sections 2 and 3, of the Constitution.
8. In 1868, southern states, where the Democratic party had been strong, either were not in the Union or were under the control of Radical Reconstruction governments. Grant's victory, therefore, was not as sweeping as it may first appear.

CHAPTER 11

RECONSTRUCTING
RECONSTRUCTION:
THE POLITICAL
CARTOONIST
AND THE
NATIONAL MOOD

and first- and second-generation Irish immigrants who had settled in urban areas and had established powerful political machines such as Tammany Hall in New York City.

By 1872, a renewed Democratic party believed it had a chance to oust Grant and the Republicans. The Grant administration had been rocked by a series of scandals, some involving men quite close to the president. Although honest himself, Grant had lost a good deal of popularity by defending the culprits and naively aiding in a cover-up of the corruption. These actions, along with some of his other policies, triggered a revolt within the Republican party, in which a group calling themselves Liberal Republicans bolted the party ranks and nominated well-known editor and reformer Horace Greeley to oppose Grant for the presidency.[9] Hoping for a coalition to defeat Grant, the Democrats also nominated the controversial Greeley.

Greeley's platform was designed to attract as many different groups of voters as possible to the Liberal Republican-Democratic fold. He favored civil service reform, the return to a "hard money" fiscal policy, and the reservation of western lands for settlers rather than for large land companies. He vowed an end to corruption in government. But the most dramatic part of Greeley's message was his call for an end to the bitterness of the Civil War, a thinly veiled promise to bring an end to Radical Reconstruction in the South. "Let us," he said, "clasp hands over the bloody chasm."

For their part, Radical Republicans attacked Greeley as the tool of die-hard southerners and labeled him as the candidate of white southern bigots and northern Irish immigrants manipulated by political machines. By contrast, Grant was labeled as a great war hero and a friend of blacks and whites alike. The incumbent Grant won easily, capturing 55 percent of the popular vote. Greeley died soon after the exhausting campaign.

Gradually, however, the zeal of Radical Republicanism began to fade. An increasing number of northerners grew tired of the issue. Their commitment to full civil rights for African Americans had never been strong, and they had voted for Radical Republicans more out of anger at southern intransigence than out of any lofty notions of black equality. Thus northerners did not protest when, one by one, southern Democrats returned to power in the states of the former Confederacy.[10] As an indication of how little their own attitudes had changed, white southerners labeled these native Democrats "Redeemers."

Although much that was fruitful and beneficial was accomplished in the South during the Reconstruction period (most notably black suffrage and public education), some of this was to

9. See Volume I, Chapter 10, for a discussion of Greeley's position on the emancipation of slaves in 1862.

10. Southerners regained control of the state governments in Tennessee and Virginia 1869, North Carolina in 1870, Georgia in 1871, Arkansas and Alabama in 1874, and Mississippi in early 1876. By the presidential election of 1876, only South Carolina, Louisiana, and Florida were still controlled by Reconstruction governments.

be temporary, and many opportunities for progress were lost. By the presidential election of 1876, both candidates (Rutherford B. Hayes and Samuel Tilden) promised an end to Reconstruction, and the Radical Republican experiment, for all intents and purposes, was over.

It is clear that northern public opinion from 1865 to 1876 was not static but was almost constantly shifting. This public opinion was influenced by a number of factors, among them speeches, newspapers, and word of mouth. Especially influential were editorial cartoons, which captured the issues visually, often simplifying them so that virtually everyone could understand them. Perhaps the master of this style was Thomas Nast, a political cartoonist whose career, principally with *Harper's Weekly,* spanned the tumultuous years of the Civil War and Reconstruction. Throughout his career, Nast produced more than three thousand cartoons, illustrations for books, and paintings. He is credited with originating the modern depiction of Santa Claus, the Republican elephant, and the Democratic donkey. Congratulating themselves for having hired Nast, the editors of *Harper's Weekly* once exclaimed that each of Nast's drawings was at once "a poem and a speech."

Apparently, Thomas Nast developed his talents early in life. Born in the German Palatinate (one of the German states) in 1840, Nast was the son of a musician in the Ninth Regiment Bavarian Band. The family moved to New York City in 1846, at which time young Thomas was enrolled in school. It seems that art was his only interest.

One teacher admonished him, "Go finish your picture. You will never learn to read or figure." After unsuccessfully trying to interest their son in music, his parents eventually encouraged the development of his artistic talent. By the age of fifteen, Thomas Nast was drawing illustrations for *Frank Leslie's Illustrated Newspaper.* He joined *Harper's Weekly* in 1862 (at the age of twenty-two), where he developed the cartoon style that was to win him a national reputation, as well as enemies. He received praise from Abraham Lincoln, Ulysses Grant, and Samuel Clemens (also known as Mark Twain, who in 1872 asked Nast to do the illustrations for one of his books so that "then I will have good pictures"). In contrast, one of Nast's favorite targets, political boss William Marcy Tweed of New York's Tammany Hall, once shouted, "Let's stop these damn pictures. I don't care so much what the papers say about me—my constituents can't read; but damn it, they can see pictures!"

It is obvious from his work that Nast was a man of strong feelings and emotions. In his eyes, those people whom he admired possessed no flaws. Conversely, those whom he opposed were, to him, capable of every conceivable villainy. As a result, his characterizations often were terribly unfair, gross distortions of reality and more than occasionally libelous. In his view, however, his central purpose was not to entertain but to move his audience, to make them scream out in outrage or anger, to prod them to action. The selection of Nast's cartoons in this chapter is typical of the body of his work for *Harper's Weekly:* artistically

CHAPTER 11

RECONSTRUCTING
RECONSTRUCTION:
THE POLITICAL
CARTOONIST
AND THE
NATIONAL MOOD

inventive and polished, blatantly slanted, and brimming with indignation and emotion.

Your tasks in this chapter are (1) to identify the principal issues and events of the Reconstruction era, (2) to analyze Nast's cartoons to determine what he thought about each issue or event, and (3) to trace any changes in Nast's beliefs between 1865 (Source 1) and the end of Reconstruction in 1876 (Source 13).

∽ THE METHOD ∾

Although Thomas Nast developed the political cartoon into a true art form, cartoons and caricatures had a long tradition in both Europe and America before Nast. English artists helped bring forth the cartoon style that eventually made *Punch* (founded in 1841) one of the liveliest illustrated periodicals on both sides of the Atlantic. In America, Benjamin Franklin is traditionally credited with publishing the first newspaper cartoon in 1754— the multidivided snake (each part of the snake representing one colony) with the ominous warning "Join or Die." By the time Andrew Jackson sought the presidency, the political cartoon had become a regular and popular feature of American political life. Crude by modern standards, these cartoons influenced some people far more than did the printed word.

As we noted, the political cartoon, like the newspaper editorial, is intended to do more than objectively report events. It is meant to express an opinion, a point of view, approval or disapproval. Political cartoonists want to move people, to make them laugh, to anger them, or to move them to action. In short, political cartoons do not depict exactly what is happening; rather, they portray popular reaction to what is happening and try to persuade people to react in a particular way.

How do you analyze political cartoons? First, using your text and the Problem and Background sections of this chapter, make a list of the most important issues and events (including elections) of the period between 1865 and 1876. As you examine the cartoons in this chapter, try to determine what event or issue is being portrayed. Often a cartoon's caption, dialogue, or date will help you discover its focus.

Next, look closely at each cartoon for clues that will help you understand the message that Nast was trying to convey. People who saw these cartoons more than one hundred years ago did not have to study them so carefully, of course. The individuals and events shown in each cartoon were immediately familiar to them, and the message was obvious. But you are historians, using these cartoons as evidence to help you understand how people were reacting to important events many years ago.

[272]

As you can see, Nast was a talented artist. Like many political cartoonists, he often explored the differences between what he believed was the ideal (justice, fairness) and the reality (his view of what was actually happening). To "read" Nast's cartoons, you should identify the issue or event on which the cartoon is based. Then look at the *imagery* Nast used: the situation, the setting, the clothes people are wearing, and the objects in the picture. It is especially important to note how people are portrayed: Do they look handsome and noble, or do they look like animals? Are they happy or sad? Intelligent or stupid?

Political cartoonists often use *symbolism* to make their point, sometimes in the form of an *allegory*. In an allegory, familiar figures are shown in a situation or setting that everyone knows—for example, a setting from the Bible, a fairy tale, or another well-known source. For instance, a cartoon showing a tiny president of the United States holding a slingshot, dressed in sandals and rags, and fighting a giant, muscular man labeled "Congress" would remind viewers of the story of David and Goliath. In that story, the small man won. The message of the cartoon is that the president will win in his struggle with Congress.

Other, less complicated symbolism is often used in political cartoons. In Nast's time, as today, the American flag was an important symbol of the ideals of our democratic country, and an olive branch or dove represented the desire for peace. Some symbols have changed, however. Today, the tall, skinny figure we call Uncle Sam represents the United States. In Nast's time, Columbia, a tall woman wearing a long classical dress, represented the United States. Also in Nast's time, an hourglass, rather than a clock, symbolized that time was running out. And military uniforms, regardless of the fact that the Civil War had ended in 1865, were used to indicate whether a person had supported the Union (and, by implication, was a Republican) or the Confederacy (by implication, a Democrat).

As you can see, a political cartoon must be analyzed in detail to get the full meaning the cartoonist was trying to convey. From that analysis, one can discover the message of the cartoon, along with the cartoonist's views on the subject and the ways in which the cartoonist was trying to influence public opinion. Now you are ready to begin your analysis of the Reconstruction era through the cartoons of Thomas Nast.

⨝ THE EVIDENCE ⨝

Sources 1 through 12 from Morton Keller, *The Art and Politics of Thomas Nast* (New York: Oxford University Press, 1968), plates 55 and 56, 22, 17, 27, 32, 47, 50, 38, 196, 197, 155, 209. Courtesy of the publisher.

1.

August 5, 1865.

FRANCHISE.

"And Not This Man?"

[55]

Columbia.—"Shall I Trust These Men,

THE CONTRAST OF SUFFERING: ANDERSONVILLE & FORTRESS MONROE.

TREASON MUST BE MADE ODIOUS.

June 30, 1866

3.

4.

September 5, 1868

"This Is a White Man's Government."

"We regard the Reconstruction Acts (so called) of Congress as usurpations, and unconstitutional, revolutionary, and void."—*Democratic Platform.*

October 3, 1868

The Modern Samson.

5.

August 3, 1872

Baltimore 1861–1872.

"Let Us Clasp Hands over the Bloody Chasm."

CHAPTER 11

RECONSTRUCTING
RECONSTRUCTION:
THE POLITICAL
CARTOONIST
AND THE
NATIONAL MOOD

7.

This is a white man's government.

Auction block.

Hunting down with blood-hounds.

A negro has no rights which a white man is bound to respect.

Slavery.

Whipping-post.

New York riots.

Negroes hung at lamp-posts.

Attempt to introduce pestilence in the North.

Attempt to burn Northern cities.

Burning of colored orphan asylum.

New Orleans and Memphis massacres.

Belle Isle and Andersonville atrocities.

Assassination of Lincoln.

Ku-klux outrages to Unionists, white and black.

Burning of Freedmen's schools.

Whipping and shooting of teachers.

Repudiation.

Fort Pillow massacre, approved by Congress of Confederate States of America.

KU-KLUX.

THE RULE OF TAMMANY RING.
WHOLESALE FRAUD.
CORRUPTION.
NO CITIZEN HAD ANY RIGHTS THAT A TAMMANY ROUGH
WAS BOUND TO RESPECT.
CORRUPT JUDICIARY—CARDOZO, BARNARD, AND M'CUNN.
FRAUDULENT AND ILLEGAL VOTING.
BRIBERY.
COUNTING OUT THE VOTES OF CITIZENS.
RIOT AND BLOODSHED.

NAMES NOT TO BE FORGOTTEN:
TWEED, SWEENY, CONNOLLY, and HALL.

SLAVERY

September 7, 1872

The Whited Sepulchre.
Covering the monument of infamy with his white hat and coat.

[280]

April 13, 1872

The Republic Is Not Ungrateful.

"It is not what is *charged* but what is *proved* that damages the party defendant. Any one may be accused of the most heinous offenses; the Saviour of mankind was not only arraigned but convicted; but what of it? Facts alone are decisive."—*New York Tribune*, March 13, 1872.

CHAPTER 11   9.

RECONSTRUCTING
RECONSTRUCTION:
THE POLITICAL
CARTOONIST
AND THE
NATIONAL MOOD

March 14, 1874

Colored Rule in a Reconstructed (?) State.

(THE MEMBERS CALL EACH OTHER THIEVES, LIARS, RASCALS, AND COWARDS.)

COLUMBIA. "You are aping the lowest whites. If you disgrace your race in this way you had better take back seats."

September 26, 1874

The Commandments in South Carolina.

"We've pretty well smashed that; but I suppose, Massa Moses, you can get another one."

CHAPTER 11

RECONSTRUCTING
RECONSTRUCTION:
THE POLITICAL
CARTOONIST
AND THE
NATIONAL MOOD

11.

December 9, 1876

The Ignorant Vote—Honors Are Easy.

12.

October 24, 1874

A Burden He Has To Shoulder.
And they say, "He wants a third term."

Source 13 from J. Chal Vinson, *Thomas Nast, Political Cartoonist* (Athens: University of Georgia Press, 1967), Plate 103.

13.

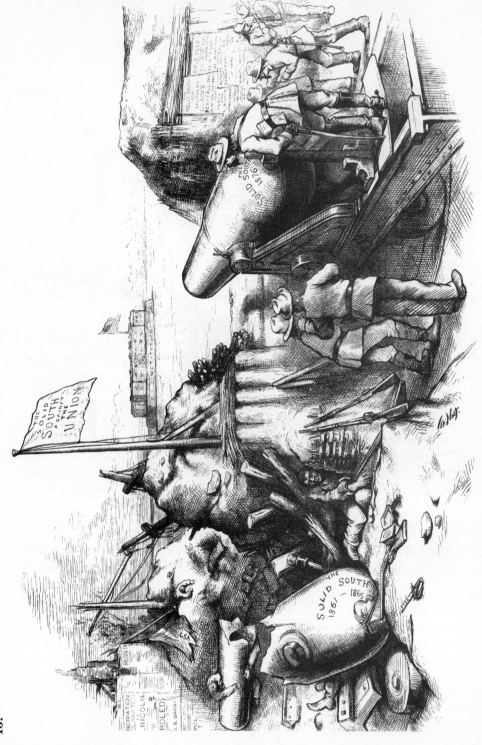

⟨∽ QUESTIONS TO CONSIDER ∽⟩

Begin by reviewing your list of the important issues and events of the Reconstruction era. Then systematically examine the cartoons, answering the following questions for each one:

1. What issue or event is represented by this cartoon?
2. Who are the principal figures, and how are they portrayed?
3. What *imagery* is used?
4. Is this cartoon an *allegory?* if so, what is the basis of the allegory?
5. What *symbols* are used?
6. How was Nast trying to influence public opinion through this cartoon?

You may find that making a chart is the easiest way to do this.

Sources 1 through 3 represent Nast's views of Reconstruction under President Andrew Johnson. Sources 4 and 5 deal with an issue crucial to Radical Republicans. Sources 6 and 7 focus on the presidential election of 1872, and Sources 8 through 12 evaluate Radical Reconstruction in its later years. The cartoons are roughly in chronological order, and you should watch for any changes in Nast's portrayal of the major issues between the end of the Civil War in 1865 and the end of Radical Reconstruction after the election of 1876.

Who is the woman in Source 1? What emotions do her two different poses suggest? Who are the people asking for pardon in the first frame? Look carefully at the black man in the second frame. Who does he represent? Can you formulate one sentence that summarizes the message of both parts of Source 1?

Source 2 is more complex: two drawings within two other drawings. If you do not already know what purpose Andersonville and Fortress Monroe served, consult a text on this time period, an encyclopedia, or a good Civil War history book. Then look at the upper left and upper right outside drawings. Contrast the appearance of the man entering with the man leaving. Now examine the lower left and lower right outside drawings the same way. What was Nast trying to tell? The larger inside drawings explain the contrast. What were the conditions like at Andersonville? At Fortress Monroe? What did the cartoonist think were the physical and psychological results?

On July 30, 1866, several blacks attending a Radical Republican convention in New Orleans were shot and killed by white policemen. Who is the emperor in Source 3, and how is he portrayed? What kind of setting is used in this cartoon? Who is the person in the lower left intended to represent? What did Nast think caused this event? What was his own reaction to it?

Each of the three people standing in Source 4 represents part of the Democratic party coalition, and each has something to contribute to the party. Can you identify the groups that the man on the right and the man in the center represent? What do they offer the party? Notice the facial features of the man on the left as well as his

CHAPTER 11

RECONSTRUCTING
RECONSTRUCTION:
THE POLITICAL
CARTOONIST
AND THE
NATIONAL MOOD

dress, particularly the hatband from Five Points (a notorious slum section of New York City). Who is this man supposed to represent, and what does he give the party? Notice what the black man lying on the ground has dropped. What does he represent? What is he reaching for? What is happening in the background of the cartoon?

What issue does Source 5 explore? What story are people supposed to remember when they see this cartoon? Who is the woman, and what has she done? Who are her supporters at the left? What other things do they advocate? Who is the figure in the upper right-hand corner? What has he promised African Americans? What has he done?

Sources 6 and 7 were published just before the presidential election of 1872. Who is the plump little man with the white beard and glasses who appears in both cartoons? What part of this man's campaign did Nast find especially objectionable? Why? What is wrong with what the character is trying to do? Who is portrayed in Source 8? Why is the woman protecting him from attack?

Sources 9 through 12 reflect Nast's thinking in the later years of Reconstruction. Sources 9 and 10 portray his opinion of Reconstruction in South Carolina, presided over by Radical Republican governor Franklin J. Moses (caricatured in Source 10). How are African Americans pictured (compare to Sources 1, 4, and 5)? To whom are African Americans compared in Source 11? What does this say about Nast's opinion of Reconstruction? Source 12 portrays President Ulysses Grant (compare to Sources 3 and 8). How is he pictured?

The last cartoon (Source 13) shows Nast's opinion of the South in 1876, near the end of Reconstruction. What scene was Nast re-creating? What is the significance of this scene? How is the black man depicted? What was Nast trying to show? How would you compare or contrast this cartoon with Sources 9 through 12? How did Nast's views change? In the final analysis, what did he think had been accomplished by more than a decade of Reconstruction?

Now return to the central questions asked earlier. What significant events took place during Reconstruction? How did Nast try to influence public opinion on the important issues of the era? How did Nast's own views change between 1865 and 1876? Why did Reconstruction finally end?

∽ EPILOGUE ∽

Undoubtedly, Nast's work had an important impact on northern opinion of Reconstruction, the Democratic party,

Horace Greeley, the Irish Americans, and other issues. Yet gradually, northern ardor began to decline as other issues and concerns eased Reconstruction out of the limelight and as it appeared that the crusade to reconstruct the South would be an endless one. Radical Republicans, who insisted on equality for the freed slaves, received less and less attention, and southern Democrats, who regained control of southern state governments, were essentially allowed a free hand as long as they did not obviously violate the Constitution and federal law. By 1877, the South was once again in the hands of white Democrats.

As long as African Americans did not insist on their rights, white southern leaders allowed them to retain, in principle, all that the Civil War and Reconstruction had won. In other words, as long as black voters did not challenge the "Redeemers," they were allowed to retain their political rights. Economically, many African Americans gradually slipped into the status of tenant farmer, sharecropper, or even peon. The political structure, local courts, and law-enforcement agencies tended to support this arrangement. For his part, African American leader Booker T. Washington was praised by white southerners for urging that blacks seek education and economic opportunities but not "rock the boat" politically in the white-controlled South. Finally, in the late 1880s, when white southerners realized that the Reconstruction spirit had waned in the North, southern state legislatures began instituting rigid segregation of schools, public transportation and accommodations, parks, restaurants and theaters, elevators, drinking fountains, and so on. Not until the 1950s did those chains begin to be broken.

As the reform spirit waned in the later years of Reconstruction, Nast's popularity suffered. The public appeared to tire of his anger, his self-righteousness, his relentless crusades. The new publisher of *Harper's Weekly* sought to make the magazine less political, and in that atmosphere there was no place for Nast. He resigned in 1886.

Nast continued to free-lance for a number of magazines and tried unsuccessfully to start his own periodical, *Nast's Weekly*. Financially struggling, he appealed to friends, who influenced President Theodore Roosevelt to appoint Nast to a minor consular post in Ecuador. He died there of yellow fever in 1902.

Thomas Nast was a pioneer of a tradition and a political art form. His successors, people such as Herbert Block (Herblock), Bill Mauldin, Oliphant, and even Garry Trudeau ("Doonesbury"), have continued to prick the American conscience, fret and irritate newspaper readers, and assert through their art the proposition that no evildoer can escape the scrutiny and ultimate justice of the popular will. Sometimes these successors are effective, sometimes not.

Acknowledgments continued from p. ii.

Source 7: German engraving, 1591. Metropolitan Museum of Art.

Source 8: French engraving, 1575. New York Historical Society.

Source 9: French engraving, 1579–1600 (America personified). New York Historical Society.

Source 10: From *The Broken Spears* by Miguel Leon-Portilla. Copyright © 1962, 1990 by Beacon Press. Reprinted by permission of Beacon Press.

Sources 11–14: Illustrations, adapted from original codices paintings, by Alberto Beltran.

CHAPTER TWO

Source 1: Reprinted by permission of the publishers from *The History of the Colony and Province of Massachusetts Bay*, Volume II. Cambridge, Mass.: Harvard University Press. Copyright © 1936, 1963 by the President and Fellows of Harvard College.

CHAPTER THREE

Map of Massachusetts. Courtesy of the John Carter Brown Library at Brown University.

Sources 2, 4–6, 12, 15–17: Adapted from Philip J. Greven: *Four Generations: Population, Land, and Family in Colonial Andover, Massachusetts*. Copyright © 1970 by Cornell University. Used by permission of the publisher, Cornell University Press.

Sources 7, 11, 13: Data from *The Evolution of American Society, 1700–1815* by James A. Henretta. Copyright © 1973 by D. C. Heath and Company. Reprinted by permission of the publisher.

Sources 18, 20–22: Reprinted from *The Journal of Interdisciplinary History*, VI (1976), 549, 557, 564, with permission of the editors of *The Journal of Interdisciplinary History* and The MIT Press, Cambridge, Massachusetts. © 1976 by the Massachusetts Institute of Technology and the editors of *The Journal of Interdisciplinary History*.

CHAPTER FOUR

Source 3: Reprinted by permission of the publishers from *The Legal Papers of John Adams*, Volume III. Cambridge, Mass.: The Belknap Press of Harvard University Press. Copyright © 1965 by the President and Fellows of Harvard College.

Sources 4–5: Illustrations. Courtesy of Museum Restoration Service, © 1970, 1981.

Source 6: Paul Revere's engraving of the Boston Massacre. American Antiquarian Society.

CHAPTER FIVE

Sources 8–9: Adapted from material in Billy G. Smith: *The "Lower Sort": Philadelphia's Laboring People, 1750–1800*. Copyright © 1990 by Cornell University. Used with permission of the publisher, Cornell University Press.

Sources 13–14: Excerpts from *Letters of Benjamin Rush*, Vol. II, edited by L. H. Butterfield, American Philosophical Society, 1951, pp. 644–645, 657–658. Reprinted by permission.

CHAPTER SEVEN

Source 3: Courtesy of Museum of American Textile History.

Sources 5, 12, 15: Courtesy of Merrimack Valley Textile Museum.

Source 14: Courtesy of Mildred Tunis Tracey Memorial Library, New London, N.H.

ACKNOWL-
EDGMENTS

CHAPTER EIGHT

Sources 1–16: From *Lay My Burden Down: A Folk History of Slavery* from Federal Writer's Project, by B. A. Botkin. Copyright 1945. Reprinted by permission.

Sources 22–23: Songs from S. Stuckey, "Through the Prism of Folklore," *Massachusetts Review*, 1968, reprinted by permission of the Editors of *Massachusetts Review*.

Source 24: From *Narrative of the Life of Frederick Douglass* by Frederick Douglass, pp. 1–3, 13–15, 36–37, 40–41, 44–46, and 74–75. Copyright 1963 by Doubleday. Reprinted by permission of Doubleday, a division of Bantam, Doubleday, Dell Publishing Group, Inc.

CHAPTER NINE

Source 1: "Civil Disobedience" is reprinted from *Walden and Civil Disobedience* by Henry David Thoreau, A Norton Critical Edition, Edited by Owen Thomas, by permission of W. W. Norton & Company, Inc. Copyright © 1966 by W. W. Norton & Company, Inc.

CHAPTER TEN

Sources 1, 3, 10, 28, 30–31: Excerpts from pages 33, 162, 243–244 from James McPherson, *The Negro's Civil War*, reprinted by courtesy of Pantheon Books, a Division of Random House, Inc.

Sources 4, 7, 9, 13–15: From *The Collected Works of Abraham Lincoln*, edited by Roy P. Basler. Copyright © 1953 by the Abraham Lincoln Association. Reprinted by permission of Rutgers University Press.

Source 20: Selections are reprinted from *The Sable Arm: Negro Troops in the Union Army, 1861–1865*, by Dudley Taylor Cornish, by permission of W. W. Norton & Company, Inc. Copyright © 1966 by W. W. Norton & Company, Inc. Copyright © 1956 by Dudley Taylor Cornish.

Sources 23–26, 29, 32, 34–36: From Robert F. Durden, *The Gray and the Black*. Reprinted by permission of the publisher, Louisiana State University Press.

Sources 27, 33: Letters of Warren Akin, Confederate Congressman by Bell Irwin Wiley, © 1959 by The University of Georgia Press.

CHAPTER ELEVEN

Sources 1–12: From Morton Keller, *The Art and Politics of Thomas Nast* (New York: Oxford University Press, 1968), plates 108; 55 and 56; 22; 17; 27; 32; 47; 50; 38; 196; 197; 155; 209, respectively. Courtesy of the publisher.

Source 13: From J. Chal Vinson, *Thomas Nast, Political Cartoonist* (Athens: University of Georgia Press, 1967). Courtesy of the publisher.